# OTTO'S NATURALISM AND RELIGION

# NATURALISM AND RELIGION

BY

## Dr. RUDOLF OTTO
PROFESSOR OF THEOLOGY IN THE UNIVERSITY OF GOTTINGEN

TRANSLATED BY

### J. ARTHUR THOMSON
PROFESSOR OF NATURAL HISTORY IN THE UNIVERSITY OF ABERDEEN

AND

### MARGARET R. THOMSON

EDITED WITH AN INTRODUCTION BY
Rev. W. D. MORRISON, LL.D.

WIPF & STOCK · Eugene, Oregon

Wipf and Stock Publishers
199 W 8th Ave, Suite 3
Eugene, OR 97401

Naturalism and Religion
By Otto, Rudolf and Thomson, J. Arthur
Softcover ISBN-13: 978-1-6667-3354-9
Hardcover ISBN-13: 978-1-6667-2826-2
eBook ISBN-13: 978-1-6667-2827-9
Publication date 8/5/2021
Previously published by G. P. Putnam's Sons, 1907

This edition is a scanned facsimile of
the original edition published in 1907.

# PREFACE

It is a remarkable and in some respects a disquieting fact that whilst rival ecclesiastical parties are engaged in a furious and embittered debate as to the precise shade of religious instruction to be given in public elementary schools, the thinking classes in modern Europe are becoming more and more stirred by the really vital question whether there is room in the educated mind for a religious conception of the world at all. The slow silent uninterrupted advance of research of all kinds into nature, life, and history, has imperceptibly but irrevocably, revolutionised our traditional outlook upon the world, and one of the supreme questions before the contemporary mind is the probable issue of the great struggle now taking place between the religious and the non-religious conception of human life and destiny. When we look at the development of this great fundamental conflict we feel that disputes between rival ecclesiastical systems are of trifling moment; the real task at the present time before every form of religion is the task of vindicating itself before a hostile view of life and things.

It is the consciousness of this fact which has led to the translation and publication in English of Professor Otto's volume. Professor Otto is well known on the

## PREFACE

Continent as a thinker who possesses the rare merit of combining a high philosophic discipline with an accurate and comprehensive knowledge of the science of organic nature. It is this combination of aptitudes which has attracted so much attention to his work on Naturalism and Religion, and which gives it a value peculiar to itself. At a time when so much loose and incoherent thinking exists about fundamental problems, and when so many irrelevant claims are made, sometimes on behalf of religion and sometimes on behalf of hypotheses said to be resting upon science, it is a real satisfaction to meet with such a competent guide as Dr. Otto. Although his book is written for the general reader, it is in reality a solid scientific contribution to the great debate at present in progress between two different conceptions of the ultimate nature and meaning of things. As such it is to be hoped that it will receive the favourable consideration which it deserves at the hands of the English-speaking world.

W. D. M.

# CONTENTS

## CHAPTER I

|  | PAGE |
|---|---|
| THE RELIGIOUS INTERPRETATION OF THE WORLD . | 1 |
| What is distinctive in the Religious Outlook | 6 |

## CHAPTER II

| NATURALISM | 17 |
|---|---|
| What is distinctive in the Naturalistic Outlook | 18 |
| The true Naturalism | 22 |
| Goethe's Attitude to Naturalism | 24 |
| The two kinds of Naturalism | 28 |
| Aim and Method of Naturalism | 30 |

## CHAPTER III

| FUNDAMENTAL PRINCIPLES | 34 |
|---|---|
| How the Religious and the Naturalistic Outlooks Conflict | 36 |
| Mystery . Dependence : Purpose | 41 |
| The Mystery of Existence remains unexplained | 43 |

## CONTENTS

|   | PAGE |
|---|---|
| Evolution and New Beginnings | 51 |
| The Dependence of the Order of Nature | 54 |
| The "Contingency" of the World | 61 |
| The Real World | 65 |
| The Antinomy of our Conception of Time | 69 |
| The Antinomy of the Conditioned and the Unconditioned | 71 |
| The Antinomy of Our Conception of Space | 72 |
| Intuitions of Reality | 74 |
| The Recognition of Purpose | 77 |
| Teleological and Scientific Interpretations are Alike Necessary | 82 |

### CHAPTER IV

| DARWINISM IN GENERAL | 85 |
|---|---|
| The Development of Darwinism | 86 |
| Darwinism and Teleology | 89 |
| The Characteristic Features of Darwinism | 91 |
| Various Forms of Darwinism | 94 |
| The Theory of Descent | 97 |
| Haeckel's Evolutionist Position | 101 |
| Weismann's Evolutionist Position | 103 |
| Virchow's Position | 106 |
| Other Instances of Dissatisfaction with the Theory of Descent | 111 |

### CHAPTER V

| RELIGION AND THE THEORY OF DESCENT | 128 |
|---|---|
| The Problema Continui | 134 |

# CONTENTS

## CHAPTER VI

|  | PAGE |
|---|---|
| DARWINISM IN THE STRICT SENSE | 139 |
| Differences of Opinion as to the Factors in Evolution | 142 |
| Weismannism | 145 |
| Natural Selection | 154 |

## CHAPTER VII

| CRITICS OF DARWINISM | 160 |
|---|---|
| Lamarck and Neo-Lamarckism | 164 |
| Theory of Definite Variation | 170 |
| De Vries's Mutation Theory | 172 |
| Eimer's Orthogenesis | 174 |
| The Spontaneous Activity of the Organism | 177 |
| Contrast between Darwinian and post-Darwinian Views | 182 |

## CHAPTER VIII

| THE MECHANICAL THEORY OF LIFE | 187 |
|---|---|
| The Conservation of Matter and Energy | 194 |
| The Organic and the Inorganic | 196 |
| Irritability | 201 |
| Spontaneous Generation | 205 |
| The Mechanics of Development | 209 |
| Heredity | 211 |

*b*

## CHAPTER IX

| | PAGE |
|---|---|
| CRITICISM OF MECHANICAL THEORIES | 220 |
| The Law of Conservation of Energy | 232 |
| Criticisms of the Mechanistic Theory of Life | 234 |
| Virchow's "Caution" | 237 |
| Preyer's Position | 239 |
| The Position of Bunge and other Physiologists | 242 |
| The Views of Botanists Illustrated | 248 |
| Constructive Criticism | 253 |
| The Constructive Work of Driesch | 261 |
| The Views of Albrecht and Schneider | 276 |
| How all this affects the Religious Outlook | 274 |

## CHAPTER X

| | |
|---|---|
| AUTONOMY OF SPIRIT | 278 |
| Naturalistic Attacks on the Autonomy of the Spiritual | 283 |
| The Fundamental Answer | 295 |
| Individual Development | 298 |
| Underivability | 299 |
| Pre-eminence of Consciousness | 302 |
| Creative Power of Consciousness | 304 |
| Activity of Consciousness | 311 |
| The Ego | 313 |
| Self-Consciousness | 313 |
| The Unity of Consciousness | 314 |
| Consciousness of the Ego | 315 |

## CHAPTER XI

|  | PAGE |
|---|---|
| FREEDOM OF SPIRIT | 317 |
| Feeling | 326 |
| Individuality | 326 |
| Genius | 329 |
| Mysticism | 329 |
| Mind and Spirit. The Human and the Animal Soul | 330 |
| Personality | 336 |
| Parallelism | 337 |
| No Parallelism | 342 |
| The Supremacy of Mind | 350 |
| "The Unconscious" | 352 |
| Is there Ageing of the Mind? | 353 |
| Immortality | 356 |

## CHAPTER XII

THE WORLD AND GOD . . . . . 360

# CHAPTER I

THE RELIGIOUS INTERPRETATION OF THE WORLD

THE title of this book, contrasting as it does the naturalistic and the religious interpretation of the world, indicates that the intention of the following pages is, in the first place, to define the relation, or rather the antithesis, between the two; and, secondly, to endeavour to reconcile the contradictions, and to vindicate against the counter-claims of naturalism, the validity and freedom of the religious outlook. In doing this it is assumed that there is some sort of relation between the two conceptions, and that there is a possibility of harmonising them.

Will this be admitted? Is it not possible that the two views are incommensurable, and would it not be most desirable for both sides if this were so, for if there is no logical antithesis then there can be no real antagonism? And is not this actually the case? Surely we have now left far behind us the primitive expressions of the religious outlook which were concerned with the creation of the world in six days, the making of Eve out of Adam's rib, the story of Paradise and the angelic and demoniacal forces, and the accessory miracles and accompanying signs by means of which the Divine control of the world was supposed to manifest itself. We have surely learnt by this time to distinguish between the simple mythical or legendary forms of expression in the religious archives, and their spiritual value and ethical content. We can give to natural science and to religious feeling what is due to each, and thus have done for ever with tedious apologetic discussion.

It were well indeed if we had really attained to this! But the relations, and therefore the possibilities of conflict between religion and world-science, are by no means so easily disposed of. No actually existing form of religion is so entirely made up of "feeling," "subjectivity," or "mood," that it can dispense with all assumptions or convictions regarding the nature and import of the world. In fact, every form, on closer examination, reveals a more or less fixed framework of convictions, theoretical assumptions, and presuppositions in regard to man, the world, and existence: that is to say, a theory, however simple, of the universe. And this theory must be harmonised with the conceptions of things as they are presented to us in general world-lore, in natural and historical science, in particular sciences, in theories of knowledge, and perhaps in metaphysics; it must measure itself by and with these, and draw from them support and corroboration, and possibly also submit to contradiction and correction.

There is no form of religion, not even the most rare-

## THE RELIGIOUS INTERPRETATION 3

fied (which makes least claim because it has least content), that does not include in itself some minute Credo, some faith, implying attachment to a set of doctrines and conclusions however few. And it is always necessary to show that these conclusions are worthy of adherence, and that they are not at variance with conclusions and truths in regard to nature and the world drawn from other sources. And if we consider, not the efflorescences and artificial products of religion, but religion itself, it is certain that there is, and always must be, around it a borderland and fringe of religious world-theory, with which it is not indeed identical, but without which it is inconceivable; that is, a series of definite and characteristic convictions relating to the world and its existence, its meaning, its " whence " and " whither"; to man and his intelligence, his place and function in the world, his peculiar dignity, and his destiny; to time and space, to infinity and eternity, and to the depth and mystery of Being in general.

These convictions and their fundamental implications can be defined quite clearly, both singly and as a whole, and later we shall attempt so to define them. And it is of the greatest importance to religion that these presuppositions and postulates should have their legitimacy and validity vindicated. For they are at once the fundamental and the minimal postulates which religion must make in its outlook on the world, which it must make if it is to exist at all. And they are so constituted that, even when they are released from their primitive and naive form and association, and permitted speculative development and freedom, they must, nevertheless, just because they contain a theory of the world, be brought into comparison, contact, or relation of some kind, whether hostile or friendly, with other world-conceptions of different origin. This relation will be hostile or friendly according to the form these other conceptions have taken. It is impossible to imagine any religious view of the world whose network of conceptions can have meshes so wide, or constituents so elastic and easily adjustable, that it will allow every theoretical conception of nature and the world to pass through it without violence or friction, offering to none either let or hindrance.

It has indeed often been affirmed that religion may, without anxiety about itself, leave scientific knowledge of the world to go its own way. The secret reservation in this position is always the belief that scientific knowledge will never in any case reach the real depth and meaning of things. Perhaps this is true. But the assumption itself would remain, and would have to be justified. And if religion had no other interest in general world-theory, it would still have this pre-eminent one, that, by defining the limitations of scientific theory, and showing that they can never be transcended, it thus indicates for itself a position beyond them in which it can dwell securely. In reality religion has never ceased to turn its never-resting, often anxious gaze towards the progress, the changes, the secure results

## THE RELIGIOUS INTERPRETATION 5

and tentative theories in the domain of general world-science, and again and again it has been forced to come to a new adjustment with them.

One great centre of interest, though by no means the only or even the chief one, lies in the special field of world-lore and theoretical interpretation comprised in the natural sciences. And in the following pages we shall make this our special interest, and shall endeavour to inquire whether our modern natural science consists with the "minimal requirements" of the religious point of view, with which we shall make closer acquaintance later; or whether it is at all capable of being brought into friendly relations with that point of view.

Such a study need not necessarily be "apologetic," that is to say, defensive, but may be simply an examination. For in truth the real results of investigation are not now and never were "aggressive," but are in themselves neutral towards not only religious but all idealistic conceptions, and leave it, so to speak, to the higher methods of study to decide how the material supplied is to be taken up into their different departments, and brought under their particular points of view. Our undertaking only becomes defensive and critical because, not from caprice or godlessness, but, as we shall see, from an inherent necessity, the natural sciences, in association with other convictions and aims, tend readily to unite into a distinctive and independent system of world-interpretation, which, if it were valid and sufficient, would drive the religious view into difficulties, or make it impossible. This independent system is Naturalism, and against its attacks the religious conception of the world has to stand on the defensive.

### What is Distinctive in the Religious Outlook

At the very beginning and throughout we must keep the following points clearly before us, otherwise all our endeavours will only lead us astray, and be directed towards an altogether false issue.

Firstly, everything depends and must depend upon vindicating the validity and freedom of the religious view of the world as contrasted with world-science in general; but we must not attempt to derive it directly from the latter. If religion is to live, it must be able to demonstrate—and it can be demonstrated—that its convictions in regard to the world and human existence are not contradicted from any other quarter, that they are possible and may be believed to be true. It can, perhaps, also be shown that a calm and unprejudiced study of nature, both physical and metaphysical reflection on things, will supplement the interpretations of religion, and will lend confirmation and corroboration to many of the articles of faith already assured to it. But it would be quite erroneous to maintain that we must be able to read the religious conception of the world out of nature, and that it must be, in the first instance, derivable from nature, or that we can, not to say

## THE RELIGIOUS INTERPRETATION 7

must, regard natural knowledge as the source and basis of the religious interpretation of the world. An apologetic based on such an idea as this would greatly overestimate its own strength, and not only venture too high a stake, but would damage the cause of religion and alter the whole position of the question. This mistake has often been made. The old practice of finding " evidences of the existence of God " had exactly this tendency. It was seriously believed that one could thereby do more than vindicate for religious conviction a right of way in the system of knowledge. It was seriously believed that knowledge of God could be gained from and read out of nature, the world, and earthly existence, and thus that the propositions of the religious view of the world could not only gain freedom and security, but could be fundamentally proved, and even directly inferred from Nature in the first instance. The strength of these evidences was greatly overestimated, and Nature was too much studied with reference to her harmony, her marvellous wealth and purposeful wisdom, her significant arrangements and endless adaptations; and too little attention was paid to the multitudinous enigmas, to the many instances of what seems unmeaning and purposeless, confused and dark. People were far too ready to reason from finite things to infinite causes, and the validity or logical necessity of the inferences drawn was far too rarely scrutinised. And, above all, the main point was overlooked. For even if these " evidences " had succeeded better, if they had been as sufficient as they were insufficient, it is certain that religion and the religious conception of the world could never have arisen from them, but were in existence long before any such considerations had been taken into account.

Long before these were studied, religion had arisen from quite other sources. These sources lie deep in the human spirit, and have had a long history. To trace them back in detail is a special task belonging to the domain of religious psychology, history, and philosophy, and we cannot attempt it here, but must take it for granted. Having arisen from these sources, religion has long lived a life of its own, forming its own convictions in regard to the world and existence, possessing these as its faith and truth, basing their credibility, and gaining for them the adherence of its followers, on quite other grounds than those used in " proving the existence of God." Ideas and conclusions which have not arisen in this way can hardly be said to be religious, though they may resemble religious ideas. But having thus arisen, the religious view comes into contact with knowledge in general, and then a need for justification, or even a state of antagonism, may arise. It may then be asked whether convictions and ideas which, so far, have come solely from within, and have been affirmed and recognised as truths only by heart and conscience, can possibly be adhered to in the face of the insight afforded by an investigation and scientific knowledge of nature.

Let us take an example, and at once the highest that can be found. The religious recognition of the sway of an eternal Providence cannot possibly be directly derived from, or proved by, any consideration of nature and history. If we had not had it already, no apologetic and no evidences of the existence of God would have given it to us. The task of an apologetic which knows its limitations and its true aims can only be to inquire whether there is scope and freedom left for these religious ideas alongside of our natural knowledge of the world; to show that the latter, because of its proper limitations, has no power to make a pronouncement in regard to the highest meaning of the world; and to point to certain indications in nature and history that justify us in interpreting the whole in terms of purpose and ultimate import. This is the case with all the conceptions and conclusions of the religious view of the world. No single one of them can be really proved from a study of nature, because they are much too deep to be reached by ordinary reasoning, and much too peculiar in their character and content to be discovered by any scientific consideration of nature or interpretation of the world. It is, however, at the same time obvious that all apologetic must follow religion, and can never precede it. Religion can only be awakened, never coerced. Once awakened, it can reflect on its validity and freedom; but it alone can really understand both. And apart from religion, or without its presence, all apologetic endeavours are gratuitous, and are, moreover, expressly forbidden by its own highest authorities (Matt. xxiii. 15).

The second point is even more important. Religion does not hold its theory of the world and its interpretations of the nature and meaning of things in the same way as poetry does its fine-spun, airy dreams, whose chief value lies in the fact that they call up moods and arouse a play of feeling, and which may be grave or gay, elegiac or idyllic, charming or sublime, but may be true or false indifferently.

For there is this outstanding difference between religion and all " moods "—all poetic or fanciful views of nature—that it lives by the certainty of its ideas, suffers if they be uncertain, and dies if they be shown to be untenable, however charming or consoling, sublime or simple they may be. Its theories of the world are not poems; they are convictions, and these require to be first of all not pleasing but true. (Hence it is that criticism may arise out of religion itself, since religion seeks for its own sake to find secure foundations.) And in this respect the religious conception of the world is quite in line with world-theory in general. Both desire to express reality. They do not wish to lay gaily-coloured wreaths and garlands about reality that they may enjoy it, plunged in their respective moods; they desire to understand it and give an account of it.

But there is at once apparent a characteristic difference between the propositions and conclusions of the religious view and those of the secular, a difference not

## THE RELIGIOUS INTERPRETATION 11

so much of content, which goes without saying, but in the whole form, manner and method, and tone. As Schleiermacher put it: "You can never say that it advances with the sure tread" of which science in general is capable, and by which it is recognisable. The web of religious certainty is much more finely and delicately woven, and more susceptible of injury than the more robust one of ordinary knowledge. Moreover, where religious certainty has attained its highest point in a believing mind, and is greater rather than less than the certainty of what is apprehended by the senses or experienced day by day, this characteristic difference is most easily discerned. The believer is probably much more confident about "the care of his Heavenly Father," or "the life eternal," than he is about this life with its varying and insignificant experiences and content. For he knows about the life beyond in quite a different way. The truths of the religious outlook cannot be put on the same level as those of ordinary and everyday life. And when the mind passes from one to the other it does so with the consciousness that the difference is in kind. The knowledge of God and eternity, and the real value, transcending space and time, of our own inner being, cannot even in form be mixed up with the trivial truths of the normal human understanding or the conclusions of science. In fact, the truths of religion exhibit, in quite a special way, the character of all ideal truths, which are not really true for every day at all, but are altogether bound up with exalted states of feeling. This is expressed in the old phrase, "Deus non scitur sed creditur" [God is not known but believed in]. For the Sorbonne was quite right and protected one of the essential interests of religion, when it rejected as heresy the contrary position, that it was possible to "know" God. Thus, in the way in which I "know" that I am sitting at this writing-table, or that it rained yesterday, or that the sum of the angles in a triangle are equal to two right angles, I can know nothing of God. But I can know of Him something in the way in which I know that to tell the truth is right, that to keep faith is duty, propositions which are certain and which state something real and valid, but which I could not have arrived at without conscious consent, and a certain exaltation of spirit on my own part. This, and especially the second part of it, holds true in an increased degree of all religious conceptions. They weave themselves together out of the most inward and subtle experiences, out of impressions which are coarsened in the very act of expressing them. Their import and value must be judged entirely by the standards of conscience and feeling, by their own self-sufficiency and validity. The best part of them lies in the intensity and vitality of their experience, and in the spontaneous acceptance and recognition which they receive. They cannot be apprehended by the prosaic, secular mind; whatever is thus apprehended is at most an indifferent analogue of religious experience, if it is not self-deception.

It is only in exaltation, in quiet enthusiasm, that religious feelings can come to life and become pervasive, and religious truth can only become a possession available for everyday use in proportion as it is possible to make this non-secular and exalted state of mind permanent, and to maintain enthusiasm as the enduring mood of life and conduct. And as this is capable of all degrees of intensity from overpowering outbursts and isolated raptures to a gentle but permanent tension and elevation of spirit, so also is the certainty and actuality of our knowledge, whether of the sway of the divine power, or of our own higher nature and destiny, or of any religious truth whatever. This is what is meant by St. Paul's "Praying without ceasing" and his "Being in the Spirit" as a permanent mood; and herein lies the justification of the statement of enthusiasm that truth is only found in moments of ecstasy. In fact, religion and religious interpretations are nothing if not "enthusiasms," that is to say, expressions of the art of sustaining a permanent exaltation of spirit. And any one who is not capable of this inward exaltation, or is too little capable of it, is badly qualified for either religion or religious outlook. The "enthusiasts" will undoubtedly make a better figure in the "kingdom of God," as well as find an easier entrance therein, than the prosaic matter-of-fact people.

This is really the source of much that is vexatious in all apologetic efforts, and indeed in all theorising about religion, as soon as we attempt to get beyond the periphery into the heart of the matter. For in order to understand the subject at all a certain amount of " enthusiasm " is necessary, and in most cases the disputants fail to reach common ground because this enthusiasm is lacking in one or both. If they both have it, in that case also dialectics are out of the question.

Finally, it must be remarked that, as Luther puts it, " Faith always goes against appearances." The religious conception of the world not only never grows directly out of a scientific and general study of things, but it can never be brought into absolute congruence with it. There are endless tracts and domains of the world, in nature and history, which we cannot bring under the religious consideration at all, because they admit of no interpretation from the higher or more general points of view; they lie before us as everlasting unrelated mysteries, uncomprehended as to their import and purpose. Moreover, the religious theory of the world can never tell us, or wish to tell us, what the world is as a whole, or what is the meaning of its being. It is enough for us that it throws light on our own being, and reveals to us our place and destiny, and the meaning of our existence. It is enough if, in this respect, reality adapts itself to the interpretations of religion, admits of their truth and allows them scope, and corroborates them in important ways and instances. It actually does this, and it can be demonstrated that it does. And in demonstrating this the task of an apologetic that knows its own limitations alone consists.

It must be aware that it will succeed even in this, only if it is supported by a courageous will to believe and joy in believing, that many gaps and a thousand riddles will remain, that the ultimate and highest condition of the search after a world-interpretation is personal decision and personal choice, which finally depends upon " what manner of man one is." Faith has always meant going against appearances. It has gone against them not from obstinacy or incorrigible lack of understanding, but because it has had strong reasons, impossible to set aside, for regarding appearances literally as appearances. It has suffered from the apparent, often even to the point of extinction, and has again drawn from it and from its opposition its highest strength. That they overmastered appearances made of the heroes of faith the greatest of all heroes. And thus religion lives by the very riddles which have frequently caused its death, and they are a part of its inheritance and constitution. To work continually towards their solution is a task which it will never give up. Until success has been achieved, it is of importance to show, that what comes into conflict with faith in these riddles at the present day is not something new and previously unheard of. In cases where faith has died because of them we almost invariably find the opinion that religion might have been possible in earlier and more naive times, but that it is no longer possible to us, with our deeper insight into the dark mystery of nature and destiny. This is foolishness. When faith dies thus, it dies of one of its infantile diseases. For from the tragedies of Job and of Jeremiah to the Tower of Siloam and the horror of the Mont-Pelée eruption there runs a direct lineage of the same perennial riddle. Well-developed religion has never existed without this—at once its shadow and its touchstone.

# CHAPTER II

## NATURALISM

NATURALISM is not of to-day or of yesterday, but is very ancient,— as old, indeed, as philosophy,—as old as human thought and doubt. Indeed, we may say that it almost invariably played its part whenever man began to reflect on the whence and the how of the actual world around him. In the philosophical systems of Leucippus and Democritus and Epicurus it lies fully developed before us. It persisted as a latent and silently dreaded antagonist, even in times when "orthodox" anti-naturalistic and super-naturalistic systems were the officially prevailing ones, and were to all appearance generally adhered to. So in the more modern systems of materialism and positivism, in the *Système de la nature* and in the theory of *l'homme machine*, in the materialistic reactions from the idealistic nature-speculations of Schelling and Hegel, in the discussions of materialism in the past century, in the naturalistic writings of Moleschott, Czolbe, Vogt, Buchner, and Haeckel, and in the still dominant naturalistic tendency and mood which acquired new form and deep-rooted individuality through Darwinism,— in all these we find naturalism, not indeed originating as something new, but simply blossoming afresh with increased strength. The antiquity of Naturalism is no reproach, and no reason for regarding it as a matter long since settled; it rather indicates that Naturalism is not a chance phenomenon, but an inevitable growth. The favourite method of treating it as though it were the outcome of modern scepticism, malice, or obduracy, is just as absurd as if the "naturalists" were to treat the convictions of their opponents as the result of incredible narrow-mindedness, priestly deception, senility, or calcification of the brain-cells. And as naturalism is of ancient origin so also do its different historical phases and forms resemble each other in their methods, aims, and arguments, as well as in the moods, sympathies, and antipathies which accompany them. Even in its most highly developed form we can see that it did not spring originally from a completed and unified principle, but was primarily criticism of and opposition to other views.

### What is Distinctive in the Naturalistic Outlook.

At first tentative, but becoming ever more distinctly conscious of its real motive, Naturalism has always arisen in opposition to what we may call "supernatural" propositions, whether these be the naïve mythological explanations of world-phenomena found in primitive religions, or the supernatural popular metaphysics which usually accompanies the higher forms. It is actuated at the same time by one of the

## THE NATURALISTIC OUTLOOK 19

most admirable impulses in human nature,—the impulse to explain and understand,—and to explain, if possible, through simple, familiar, and ordinary causes. The sane human understanding sees all about it the domain of everyday and familiar phenomena. It is quite at home in this domain; everything seems to it well-known, clear, transparent, and easily understood; it finds in it intelligible causes and certain laws which govern phenomena, as well as a constant association of cause and effect. Here everything can be individually controlled and examined, and everything "happens naturally." Things govern themselves. Nothing unexpected, nothing that has not its obvious causes, nothing mysterious or miraculous happens here. Sharply contrasted with this stands the region of the apparently inexplicable, the supernatural, with all its influences and operations, and results. To the religious interpretation in its naive, pious, or superstitious forms of expression, this region of the supernatural seems to encroach broadly and deeply on the domain of the everyday world. But with the awakening of criticism and reflection, and the deepening of investigation into things, it retreats farther and farther, it surrenders piece after piece to the other realm of thought, and this arises doubt and suspicion. With these there soon awakens a profound conviction that a similar mode of causal connection binds all things together, a glimmering of the uniformity and necessity embracing, comprehending, and ultimately explaining all things. And these presentiments, in themselves at first quite childishly and almost mythologically conceived, may still be, even when they first arise, and while they are still only vaguely formulated, anticipations of later more definite scientific conceptions. Such a beginning of naturalistic consciousness may remain quite naive and go no farther than a silent but persistent protest. It makes free use of such familiar expressions as "everything comes about of itself"; "everything happens by natural means"; "it is all 'nature' or 'evolution.'" But from the primitive naturalistic outlook there may arise reconstructions of nature and cosmic speculations on a large scale, expanding into naturalistic systems of the most manifold kinds, beginning with those of the Ionic philosophers and coming down to those of the most recent times. Their watchwords remain the same, though in an altered dialect: "nature and natural phenomena," the denial of "dualism," the upholding of the one principle "monism," the all-sufficiency of nature, and the absence of any intervening influences from without or beyond nature. Rapidly and of necessity this last item becomes transformed into a "denial of teleology": nature knows neither will nor purpose, it has only to do with conditions and results. With these it deals and through them it works. Even in the most elementary naturalistic idea, that "everything happens of itself," there lurks that aversion to purpose which characterises all naturalistic systems.

A naturalism which has arisen and grown in this

## THE NATURALISTIC OUTLOOK 21

manner has in itself nothing to do with concrete and exact knowledge of nature. It may comprise a large number of ideas which are sharply opposed to "science," and which may be in themselves mythological, or poetical, or even mystical. For what "nature" itself really is fundamentally, how it moves, unfolds, or impels, how things actually happen "naturally," this naturalism has never attempted to think out. Indeed, naturalism of this type, though it opposes "dualism," does not by any means usually intend to set itself against religion. On the contrary, in its later developments, it may take it up into itself in the form of an apotheosis and a worship of nature. Almost invariably naturalism which begins thus develops, not into atheism, but into pantheism. It is true that all is nature and happens naturally. But nature itself, as Thales said, is "full of gods," instinct with divine life. It is the all-living which, unwearied and inexhaustible, brings forth form after form and pours out its fulness. It is Giordano Bruno's "Cause, Principle, and Unity," in endless beauty and overpowering magnificence, and it is Goethe's "Great Goddess," herself the object of the utmost admiration, reverence, and devotion. This mood may readily pass over into a kind of worship of God and belief in Him, "God" being regarded as the soul and mind, the "Logos" of Heraclitus and the Stoics, the inner meaning and reason of this all-living nature. And thus naturalism in its last stages may sometimes be quite devout, and may assure us that it is compelled to deny only the transcendental and not the immanent God, the Divine being enthroned above the world, but not the living God dwelling within it. And ever anew Goethe's verse is quoted:

> What God would *outwardly* alone control,
> And on His finger whirl the mighty Whole?
> He loves the *inner* world to move, to view
> Nature in Him, Himself in nature too,
> So that what in Him works, and is, and lives,
> The measure of His strength, His spirit gives.

## The True Naturalism

But naturalism becomes fundamentally different when it ceases to remain at the level of naive or fancifully conceived ideas of "nature" and "natural occurrences," when, instead of poetry or religious sentiments, it incorporates something else, namely, exact natural science and the idea of a mathematical-mechanical calculability in the whole system of nature. "Nature" and "happening naturally", as used by the naive intelligence, are half animistic ideas and modes of expression, which import into nature, or leave in it, life and soul, impulse, and a kind of will. And that speculative form of naturalism which tends to become religious develops this fault to its utmost. But a "nature" like this is not at all a possible subject for natural science and exact methods, not a subject for experiment, calculation, and fixed laws, for precise interpretation, or for interpretation on simple rational

## THE TRUE NATURALISM

principles. Instead of the naive, poetical, and half mystical conceptions of nature we must have a really scientific one, so that, so to speak, the supernatural may be eliminated from nature, and the apparently irrational rationalised; that is, so that all its phenomena may be traced back to simple, unequivocal, and easily understood processes, the actual why and how of all things perceived, and thus, it may be, understood; so that, in short, everything may be seen to come about " by natural means."

There is obviously one domain and order of processes in nature which exactly fulfils those requirements, and is really in the fullest sense "natural," that is, quite easily understood, quite rational, quite amenable to computation and measurement, quite rigidly subordinate to laws which can be formulated. These are the processes of physics and chemistry, and in a still higher degree those of movement in general, the processes of mechanics in short. And to bring into this domain and subordinate to its laws everything that occurs in nature, all becoming, and passing away, and changing, all development, growth, nutrition, reproduction, the origin of the individual and of the species, of animals and of man, of the living and the not living, even of sensation and perception, impulse, desire and instinct, will and thought—this alone would really be to show that things "happen naturally," that is, to explain everything in terms of natural causes. And the conviction that this can be done is the only true naturalism.

Naturalism of this type is fundamentally different in mood and character from the naive and poetic form, and is, indeed, in sharp contrast to it. It is working against the very motives which are most vital to the latter—namely, reverence for and deification of nature. Where the two types of naturalism really understand themselves nothing but sharp antagonism can exist between them. Those on the one side must condemn this unfeeling and irreverent, cold and mathematical dissection and analysis of the "Great Goddess" as a sacrilege and outrage. And those on the other side must utterly reject as romantic the view which is summed up in the confession: "Ist nicht Kern der Natur Menschen im Herzen?" [Is not the secret of nature in the human heart?]

### Goethe's Attitude to Naturalism

The most instructive example we can take is Goethe: his veneration for nature on the one hand, and on the other his pronounced opposition to the naturalism both of the materialists and of the mathematicians. Modern naturalists are fond of seeking repose and mental refreshment in Goethe's conception of the world, under the impression that it fits in best and most closely with their own views. That they do this says much for their mood and taste, but not quite so much for their powers of discrimination or for their consistency. It is even more thoughtless than when the empiricists and sensationalists acclaim as their hero, Spinoza, the strict, pure rationalist, the despiser of empiricism and of knowledge acquired through the senses. For to Goethe nature is far from being a piece of mechanism which can be calculated on and summed up in mathematical formulæ, an everlasting " perpetuum mobile," a magnificent all-powerful machine. In fact, all this and especially the word " machine " expresses exactly what Goethe's conception was most directly opposed to. To him nature is truly the " Goddess," the great Diana of the Ephesians, the everlasting Beauty, the artist of genius, ceaselessly inventing and creating, in floods of Life, in Action's storm—an infinite ocean, a restless weaving, a glowing Life. Embracing within herself the highest and the humblest, she is in all things, throughout all change and transformation, the same, shadowing forth the most perfect in the simplest, and in the highest only unfolding what she had already shown in the lowliest. Therefore Goethe hated all divisions and rubrics, all the contrasts and boundaries which learned analysis attempts to introduce into nature. Passionately he seized on Herder's idea of evolution, and it was towards establishing it that all his endeavours, botanical, zoological, morphological and osteological, were directed. He discovered in the human skull the premaxillary bone which occurs in the upper jaw of all mammals, and this " keystone to man " gave him, as he himself said, " such joy that all his bowels moved." He interpreted the skull as developed from three modified vertebræ. He sketched a hypothesis of the primitive plant, and the theory that all the organs of the plant are modifications and developments of the leaf. He was a friend of Etienne Geoffroy St. Hilaire, who defended " l'unité de composition organique " in the forms of nature, and evolution by gradual stages, and he was the vehement opponent of Cuvier, who attempted to pick the world to pieces according to strictly defined architectural plans and rigid classes. And what the inner impulse to all this was he has summed up in the motto to his " Morphology " from the verse in Job :

> Lo, he goeth by me, and I see him not ;
> He is transformed, but I perceive him not.

He further declares it in the introductory verse to his Osteology :

> Joyfully some years ago,
> Zealously my spirit sought
> To explore it all, and know
> How all nature lived and wrought
> And 'tis ever One in all,
> Though in many ways made known ,
> Small in great, and great in small,
> Each in manner of its own.
> Ever shifting, yet fast holding ;
> Near and far, and far and near ;
> So, with moulding and remoulding,—
> To my wonder I am here.

In all this there is absolutely nothing of the characteristic mood and spirit of " exact " naturalism, with its mechanical and mathematical categories. It matters little that Goethe, when he thought of evolution, never

## GOETHE'S ATTITUDE TO NATURALISM 27

had present to his mind the idea of Descent which is characteristic of " Darwinism," but rather development in the lofty sense in which it is worked out in th nature-philosophy of Schelling and of Hegel. The chief point is, that to him nature was the all-living and ever-living, whose creating and governing cannot be reduced to prosaic numbers or mathematical formulæ, but are to be apprehended as a whole by the perceptions of genius rather than worked out by calculation or in detail. Any other way of regarding nature Goethe early and decisively rejected. And he has embodied his strong protest against it in his " Dichtung und Wahrheit " :

" How hollow and empty it seemed to us in this melancholy, atheistical twilight. . . . Matter, we learnt, has moved from all eternity, and by means of this movement to right and left and in all directions, it has been able, unaided, to call forth all the infinite phenomena of existence.

The book—the " Système de la Nature "—" seemed to us so grey, so Cimmerian, so deathlike that it was with difficulty we could endure its presence."

And in a work with remarkable title and contents, " Die Farbenlehre," Goethe has summed up his antagonism to the " Mathematicians," and to their chief, Newton, the discoverer and founder of the new mathematical-mechanical view of nature. Yet the mode of looking at things which is here combated with so much labour, wit, and, in part, injustice, is precisely that of those who, to this day, swear by the name of Goethe with so much enthusiasm and so little intelligence.

### The two Kinds of Naturalism

But let us return to the two kinds of naturalism we have already described. Much as they differ from one another in reality, they are very readily confused and mixed up with one another. And the chief peculiarity of what masquerades as naturalism among our educated or half-educated classes to-day lies in the fact that it is a mingling of the two kinds. Unwittingly, people combine the moods of the one with the reasons and methods of the other; and having done so they appear to themselves particularly consistent and harmonious in their thought, and are happy that they have been able thus to satisfy at once the needs of the intellect and those of the heart.

On the one hand they stretch the mathematical-mechanical view as far as possible from below upwards, and even attempt to explain the activities of life and consciousness as the results of complex reflex mechanisms. And on the other hand they bring down will, soul and instincts into the lowest stages of existence, and become quite animistic. They wish to be nothing if not "exact," and yet they reckon Goethe and Bruno among the greatest apostles of their faith, and set their verses and sayings as a *credo* and motto over their own opinions. In this way there arises a "world

## THE TWO KINDS OF NATURALISM 29

conception" so indiarubber-like and Protean that it is as difficult as it is unsatisfactory to attempt to come to an understanding with it. If we attempt to get hold of it by the fringe of poetry and idealism it has assumed, it promptly retires into its "exact" half. And if we try to limit ourselves to this, in order to find a basis for discussion, it spreads out before us all the splendours of a great nature pantheism, including even the ideas of the good, the true, and the beautiful. One thing only it neglects, and that is, to show where its two very different halves meet, and what inner bond unites them. Thus if we are to discuss it at all, we must first of all pick out and arrange all the foreign and mutually contradictory constituents it has incorporated, then deal with Pantheism and Animism, and with the problem of the possibility of "the true, the good, the beautiful" on the naturalistic-empiric basis, and finally there would remain a readily-grasped residue of naturalism of the second form, to come to some understanding with which is both necessary and instructive.

In the following pages we shall confine ourselves entirely to this type, and we shall not laboriously disentangle it from the bewildering medley of ideas foreign to it, or attempt to make it consistent; we shall neglect these, and have regard solely to its clear fundamental principles and aims. Thus regarded, its horizons are perfectly well-defined. It is startling in its absolute poverty of ideal content, warmth, and charm, but impressive and grand in the perseverance and tenacity with which it adheres to one main point of view throughout. In reality, it is aggressive to nothing, but cold and indifferent to everything, and for this very reason is more dangerous than all the excited protests and verdicts of the enthusiastic type of naturalism, which it is impossible to attack, because of its lack of definite principles, and which, in the pathetic stress it lays on worshipping nature, lives only by what it has previously borrowed from the religious conceptions of the world.

### Aim and Method of Naturalism

The aim and method of the strict type of naturalism may be easily defined. In its details it will become more distinct as we proceed with our analysis. Taking it as a whole, we may say that it is an endeavour on a large scale after consistent simplification and gradual reduction to lower and lower terms. Since it aims at explaining and understanding everything according to the axiom *principia non temere esse multiplicanda* [principles are not to be heedlessly multiplied], explaining, that is, with the fewest, simplest, and most obvious principles possible, it is incumbent upon it to attempt to refer all phenomena to a single, uniform mode of occurrence, which admits of nothing outside of or beyond itself, and which regulates itself according to its own system of fundamentally similar causal sequences. It is further incumbent upon it to trace back this universal

## AIM AND METHOD OF NATURALISM 31

mode of occurrence to the simplest and clearest form possible, and its uniformities to the fewest and most intelligible laws, that is, ultimately, to laws which can be determined by calculation and summed up in formulæ. This tracing back is equivalent to an elimination of all incommensurable causes, of all "final causes," that is, of ultimate causes and "purposes" which, in an unaccountable manner, work into the network of proximate causes and control them, and by thus interrupting their connectedness, make it difficult to come to a clear understanding of the "Why?" of things. And this elimination is again a "reduction to simpler terms," for it replaces the "teleological" consideration of purposes, by a purely scientific consideration of causes, which inquires only into the actual conditions antecedent to certain sequences.

But Being and Becoming include two great realms: that of "Nature" and that of "Mind," *i.e.* consciousness and the processes of consciousness. And two apparently fundamentally different branches of knowledge relate to these: the natural sciences, and the mental sciences. If a unified and "natural" explanation is really possible, the beginning and end of all this "reducing to simpler terms" must be to bridge over the gulf between these; but this, in the sense of naturalism, necessarily means that the mental sciences must in some way be reduced to terms of natural science, and that the phenomena, processes, sequences, and laws of consciousness must likewise be made "commensurable" with and be linked on to the apparently simpler and clearer knowledge of " Nature," and, if possible, be subordinated to its phenomena and laws, if not indeed derived from them. As it is impossible to regard consciousness itself as corporeal, or as a process of movement, naturalism must at least attempt to show that the phenomena of consciousness are attendant and consequent on corporeal phenomena, and that, though they themselves never become corporeal, they are strictly regulated by the laws of the corporeal and physical, and can be calculated upon and studied in the same way.

But even the domain of the natural itself, as we know it, is by no means simple and capable of a unified interpretation. Nature, especially in the realm of organic life, the animal and plant world, appears to be filled with marvels of purposefulness, with riddles of development and differentiation, in short with all the mysteries of life. Here most of all it is necessary to "reduce" the "teleological view" to terms of the purely causal, and to prove that all the results, even the evolution of the forms of life, up to their highest expressions and in the minutest details of their marvellous adaptations, came "of themselves," that is to say, are quite intelligible as the results of clearly traceable causes. It is necessary to reduce the physiological and developmental, and all the other processes of life, to terms of physical and chemical processes, and thus to reduce the living to the not living, and to derive the organic from the forces and substances of inanimate nature.

## AIM AND METHOD OF NATURALISM 33

The process of reduction does not stop even here. For physical and chemical processes are only really understood when they can be resolved into the simplest processes of movement in general, when all qualitative changes can be traced back to purely quantitative phenomena, when, finally, in the mechanics of the great masses, as well as of the infinitely small atoms, everything becomes capable of expression in mathematical terms.

But naturalism of this kind is by no means pure natural science; it consciously and deliberately oversteps in speculation the bounds of what is strictly scientific. In this respect it bears some resemblance to the nature-philosophy associated with what we called the first type of naturalism. But its very poverty enables it to have a strictly defined programme. It knows exactly what it wants, and thus it is possible to argue with it. The religious conception of the world must come to an understanding with it, for it is quite obvious that the more indifferent this naturalism is to everything outside of itself, and the less aggressive it pretends to be, the more does the picture of the world which it attempts to draw exert a cramping influence on religion. Where the two come into contact we shall endeavour to make clear in the following pages.

## CHAPTER III

### FUNDAMENTAL PRINCIPLES

THE fundamental convictions of naturalism, its general tendencies, and the points of view which determine its outlook, are primarily related to that order of facts which forms the subject of the natural sciences, to "Nature." It is only secondarily that it attempts to penetrate with the methods of the natural sciences into the region of the conscious, of the mind, into the domain that underlies the mental sciences, including history and the æsthetic, political, and religious sciences, and to show that, in this region as in the other, natural law and the same principles of interpretation obtain, that here, too, the " materialistic conception of history holds true, and that there is no autonomy of mind."

The interests of religion here go hand in hand with those of the mental sciences, in so far as these claim to be distinct and independent. For the question is altogether one of the reality, pre-eminence, and independence of the spiritual as opposed to the "natural." Occasionally it has been thought that the whole problem of the relations between religion and naturalism was concentrated on this point, and the study of nature has

## FUNDAMENTAL PRINCIPLES 35

been left to naturalism as if it were indifferent or even hopeless, thus leaving a free field for theories of all kinds, the materialistic included. It is only in regard to the Darwinian theory of evolution and the mechanical theory of the origin and nature of life, and particularly in regard to the relatively unimportant question of " spontaneous generation " that a livelier interest is usually awakened. But these isolated theories are only a part of the " reduction," which is characteristic of naturalism, and they can only be rightly estimated and understood in connection with it. We shall turn our attention to them only after we have carefully considered what is fundamental and essential. But the idea that religion may calmly neglect the study of nature as long as naturalism leaves breathing-room for the freedom and independence of mind is quite erroneous. If religion is true, nature must be of God, and it must bear tokens which allow us to interpret it as of God. And such signs are to be found. What we shall have to say in regard to them may be summed up in the following propositions —

1. Even the world, which has been brought under the reign of scientific laws, is a mystery; it has been *formulated*, but not *explained*.

2. The world governed by law is still dependent, conditioned, and " contingent."

3. The conception of Nature as obedient to law is not excluded but rather demanded by belief in God.

4, 5. We cannot comprehend the true nature and

depth of things, and the world which we do comprehend is not the true Reality of things; it is only its appearance. In feeling and intuition this appearance points beyond itself to the true nature of things.

6. Ideas and purposes, and with them Providence and the control of things, can neither be established by the natural sciences nor disputed by them.

7. The causal interpretation demanded by natural science fits in with an explanation according to purpose, and the latter presupposes the former.

## How the Religious and the Naturalistic Outlooks Conflict

Religion comes into contact with naturalism and demands to be reconciled with it, not merely at its periphery, but at its very core, namely, with its characteristic ideal of a mathematical-mechanical interpretation of the whole world. This ideal seems to be most nearly, if not indeed completely, attained in reference to the inter-relations of the great masses, in the realm of astronomy, with the calculable, inviolable, and entirely comprehensible conditions which govern the purely mechanical correlations of the heavenly bodies. To bring the same clearness and intelligibility, the same inevitableness and calculability into the world in general, and into the whole realm of nature down to the mysterious law determining the development of the daintiest insect's wing, and the stirrings of the grey matter in the cortex of the brain which reveal themselves to us as sensation, desire, and thought, this has always been the aim and secret faith of the naturalistic mode of thought. It is thus aiming at a Cosmos of all Being and Becoming, which can be explained from itself, and comprehended in itself alone, supported by its own complete and all-sufficing causality and uniformity, resting in itself, shut up within itself, complete in itself—a God sufficient unto himself and resting in himself.

We do not need to probe very deeply to find out how strongly religion resists this attempt, and we easily discover what is the disturbing element which awakens hostile feeling. It is of three kinds, and depends on three characteristic aims and requirements of religion, which are closely associated with one another, yet distinct from one another, though it is not always easy to represent them in their true proportions and relative values. The first of these interests seems to be "teleology," the search after guiding ideas and purposes, after plan and directive control in the whole machinery, that sets itself in sharp opposition to a mere inquiry into proximate causes. Little or nothing is gained by knowing how everything came about or must have come about; all interest lies in the fact that everything has come about in such a way that it reveals intention, wisdom, providence, and eternal meaning, realising itself in details and in the whole. This has always been rightly regarded as the true concern and interest of every religious conception of the world. But it has been sometimes forgotten that this is by no means the only, or even the primary interest that religion has in world-lore. We call it its highest and ultimate interest, but we find, on careful study, that two others are associated with and precede it.

For before all belief in Providence and in the divine meaning of the world, indeed before faith at all, religion is primarily feeling—a deep, humble consciousness of the entire dependence and conditionality of our existence, and of all things. The belief we have spoken of is, in relation to this feeling, merely a form—as yet not in itself religious. It is not only the question "Have the world and existence a meaning, and are phenomena governed by ideas and purposes?" that brings religion and its antagonists into contact; there is a prior and deeper question. Is there scope for this true inwardness of all religion, the power to comprehend itself and all the world in humility in the light of that which is not of the world, but is above world and existence? But this is seriously affected by that doctrine which attempts to regard the Cosmos as self-governing and self-sufficing, needing nothing, and failing in nothing. It is this and not Darwinism or the descent from a Simian stock that primarily troubles the religious spirit. It is more specially sensitive to the strange and antagonistic tendency of naturalism shown even in that marvellous and terrifying mathematical-mechanical system of the great heavenly bodies, in this clock of the universe which, in obedience to clear and inviolable laws, carries on its soundless play from everlasting to everlasting, needing no pendulum and no pedestal, without any stoppage and without room for dependence on anything outside of itself, apparently entirely godless, but absolutely reason and God enough for itself. It shrinks in terror from the thought that the same autonomy and self-regulation may be brought down from the stage of immensity into the play of everyday life and events.

But we must penetrate still deeper. Schleiermacher has directed our attention anew to the fact that the most profound element in religion is that deep-lying consciousness of all creatures, "I that am dust and ashes," that humble feeling of the absolute dependence of every being in the world on One that is above all the world. But religion does not fully express itself even in this; there is yet another note that sounds still deeper and is the keynote of the triad. "Let a man examine himself." Is it not the case that we ourselves, in as far as the delight in knowledge and the enthusiasm for solving riddles have taken hold of us, rejoice in every new piece of elucidation and interpretation that science succeeds in making, that we are in the fullest sympathy with the impulse to understand everything and bring reason and clearness into it, and that we give hearty adherence to the leading ideas which guide the investigations of natural science? Yet on the other hand, in as far as we are religious, do we not sometimes feel a sudden inward recoil from this almost profane eagerness to penetrate into the mystery of things, this desire to have everything intelligible, clear, rational and transparent ? This feeling which stirs in us has always existed in all religious minds and will only die with them  And we need not hesitate to say so plainly. For this is the most real characteristic of religion ; it seeks depth in things, reaches out towards what is concealed, uncomprehended, and mysterious. It is more than humility; it is piety. And piety is experience of mystery.

It is at this point that religion comes most violently into antagonism with the meaning and mood of naturalism. Here they first conflict in earnest. And it is here above all that scientific investigation and its materialistic complement seem to take away freedom and truth, air and light from religion. For science is seeking especially this. Deeper penetration into and illumination of the world. It presses with macroscope and microscope into its most outlying regions and most hidden corners, into its abysses and fastnesses. It explains away the old idea of two worlds, one on this side and one on that, and rejects heavenly things with the notice " No Room " of which D. Fr. Strauss speaks. It aims at discovering the mathematical world-formulæ, if not indeed one great general formula which embraces, defines unequivocally, and rationalises all the processes of and in infinity, from the movements of Sirius to those of the cilia of the infusorian in the drop of water, and which not only crowds " heaven " out of the world, but strips away from things the fringe of the mysterious and incommensurable which seemed to surround them.

MYSTERY : DEPENDENCE : PURPOSE.

There is then a threefold religious interest, and there are three corresponding points of contact between the religious and the naturalistic interpretations of the world, where, as it appears, they are necessarily antagonistic to one another. Arranging them in their proper order we find, first, the interest, never to be relinquished, of experiencing and acknowledging the world and existence to be a mystery, and regarding all that is known and manifested in things merely as the thin crust which separates us from the uncomprehended and inexpressible. Secondly, there is the desire on the part of religion to bring ourselves and all creatures into the "feeling of absolute dependence," and, as the belief in creation does, to subordinate ourselves and them to the Eternal Power that is not of the world, but is above the world. Finally, there is the interest in a teleological interpretation of the world as opposed to the purely causal interpretation of natural science; that is to say, an interpretation of the world according to eternal God-willed purposes, governing ideas, a plan and aim. In all three respects, it is important to religion that it should be able to maintain its validity and freedom as contrasted with naturalism.

But while religion must inquire of itself into the

reality of things, with special regard to its own needs, there are two possibilities which may serve to make peace between it and natural science. It may, for instance, be possible that the mathematical-mechanical interpretation of things, even if it be sufficient within its own domain, does not take away from nature the characters which religion seeks and requires in it, namely, purpose, dependence and mystery. Or it may be that nature itself does not correspond at all to this ideal of mathematical explicability, that this ideal may be well enough as a guide for investigation, but that it is not a fundamental clue really applying to nature as a whole and in its essence. It may be that nature as a whole cannot be scientifically summed up without straining the mechanical categories. And this suggests another possibility, namely, that the naturalistic method of interpretation cannot be applied throughout the whole territory of nature, that it embraces certain aspects but not others, and, finally, that it is distinctly interrupted and held in abeyance at particular points by the incommensurable which breaks forth spontaneously out of the depths of phenomena, revealing a depth which is not to be explained away.

All these possibilities occur. And though they need not necessarily be regarded as the key to our order of discussion, in what follows we shall often meet them singly or together.

## The Mystery of Existence Remains Unexplained

1. Let us begin with the problem of the mystery of all existence, and see whether it remains unaffected, or whether it disappears in face of naturalistic interpretation, with its discovery and formulation of law and order, with its methods of measuring and computing. More primary even than faith and heartfelt trust in everlasting wisdom and purposeful Providence there is piety; there is devout sense of awe before the marvellous and mysterious, before the depth and the hidden nature of all things and all being, before unspeakable mysteries over which we hover, and abysmal depths over which we are borne. In a world which had not these, and could not be first felt in this way, religion could not live at all. It could not sail on its too shallow waters, or breathe its too thin air. It is indeed a fact that what alone we can fitly speak of and love as religion—the sense of mystery and the gentle shuddering of piety before the depth of phenomena and their everlasting divine abysses,—has its true place and kingdom in the world of mind and history, with its experiences, riddles, and depths. But mystery is to be found in the world of nature as well. It is only to a very superficial study that it could appear as though nature were, or ever could become, plain and obvious, as if the veil of Isis which shrouds its depths from all investigation could ever be torn away. From this point of view it would make no

difference even though the attempt to range the whole realm of nature under the sway of inviolable laws were to be immediately successful. This is expressed in the first of our main propositions (p. 35).

In order to realise this it is necessary to reflect for a little on the relation of "explanation" and "description" to one another, and on what is meant by "establishing laws" and "understanding" in general. The aim of all investigation is to understand the world. To understand it obviously means something more than merely to know it. It is not enough for us to know things, that is, to know what, how many, and what different kinds of things there are. On the contrary, we want to understand them, to know how they came to be as they are, and why they are precisely as they are. The first step towards this understanding is merely to know, that is, we must rightly apprehend and disentangle the things and processes of the world, grouping them, and describing them adequately and exhaustively.

But what I have merely described I have not yet understood; I am only preparing to try to understand it. It stands before me enveloped in all its mystery, and I must now begin to attempt to solve it, for describing is not explaining; it is only challenging explanation. The next step is to discover and formulate the laws. For when man sifts out things and processes and follows them out into their changes and stages he discovers the iron regularity of sequences, the strictly defined lines and paths, the inviolable order and con-

## THE MYSTERY UNEXPLAINED 45

nection in things and occurrences, and he formulates these into laws, ascribing to them the idea of necessity which he finds in himself. In so doing he makes distinct progress, for he can now go beyond what is actually seen, he can draw inferences with certainty as to effects and work back to causes. And thus order, breadth of view, and uniformity are brought into his acquaintance with facts, and his science begins. For science does not merely mean acquaintance with phenomena in their contingent or isolated occurrence, manifold and varied as that may be; it is the discovery and establishment of the laws and general modes of occurrence. Without this we might collect curiosities, but we should not have science. And to discover this network of uniformities throughout all phenomena, in the movements of the heavenly bodies and in the living substance of the cell alike, is the primary aim of all investigation. We are still far away from this goal, and it is more than questionable whether we shall ever reach it.

But if the goal should ever be reached, if, in other words, we should ever be able to say with certainty what must result if occurrences $a$ and $b$ are given, or what $a$ and $b$ must have been when $c$ occurs, would explanation then have taken the place of description? Or would understanding have replaced mystery? Obviously not at all. It has indeed often been supposed that this would be the case. People have imagined they have understood, when they have seen that

"that is always so, and that it always happens in this particular way." But this is a naive idea. The region of the described has merely become larger, and the riddle has become more complex. For now we have before us not only the things themselves, but the more marvellous laws which "govern" them. But laws are not forces or impelling causes. They do not cause anything to happen, and they do not explain anything. And as in the case of things so in that of laws, we want to know how they are, whence they come, and why they are as they are and not quite different. The fact that we have described them simply excites still more strongly the desire to explain them. To explain is to be able to answer the question "Why?"

Natural science is very well aware of this. It calls its previous descriptions "merely historical," and it desires to supplement these with ætiology, causal explanation, a deeper interpretation, that in its turn will make laws superfluous, because it will penetrate so deeply into the nature of things that it will see precisely why these, and not other laws of variation, of development, of becoming, hold sway. This is just the meaning of the "reductions" of which we have already spoken. For instance, in regard to crystal formation, "explanation" will have replaced description only when, instead of demonstrating the forms and laws according to which a particular crystal always and necessarily arises out of a particular solution, we are able to show why, from a particular mixture and because

## THE MYSTERY UNEXPLAINED 47

of certain co-operating molecular forces, and of other more primary, more remote, but also intelligible conditions, these forms and processes of crystallisation should always and of necessity occur. If this explanation were possible, the "law" would also be explained, and would therefore become superfluous. From this and similar examples we can learn at what point "explanation" begins to replace description, namely, when processes resolve themselves into simpler processes from the concurrence of which they arise. This is exactly what natural science desires to bring about, and what naturalism hopes ultimately to succeed in, thereby solving the riddle of existence.

But this kind of reduction to simpler terms only becomes "explanation" when these simpler terms are themselves clear and intelligible and not merely simple; that is to say, when we can immediately see why the simpler process occurs, and by what means it is brought about, when the question as to the "why" is no longer necessary, because, on becoming aware of the process, we immediately and directly perceive that it is a matter of course, indisputable, and requiring no proof. If this is not the case, the reduction to simpler terms has been misleading. We have only replaced one unintelligibility by another, one description by another, and so simply pushed back the whole problem. Naturalism supposes that by this gradual pushing back the task will at least become more and more simple, until at last a point is reached where the riddle will solve itself, because description becomes equivalent to explanation. This final stage is supposed to be found in the forces of attraction and repulsion, with which the smallest similar particles of matter are equipped. Out of the endlessly varied correlations of these there arise all higher forms of energy and all the combinations which make up more complex phenomena.

But in reality this does not help us at all. For now we are definitely brought face to face with the quite unanswerable question, How, from all this homogeneity and unity of the ultimate particles and forces, can we account for the beginnings of the diversity which is so marked a characteristic of this world? Whence came the causes of the syntheses to higher unities, the reasons for the combination into higher resultants of energy?

But even apart from that, it is quite obvious that we have not yet reached the ultimate point. For can "attraction," influence at a distance, *vis a fronte*, be considered as a fact which is in itself clear? Is it not rather the most puzzling fundamental riddle we can be called upon to explain? Assuredly. And therefore the attempt is made to penetrate still deeper to the ultimate point, the last possible reduction to simpler terms, by referring all actual "forces" and reducing all movement, and therewith all "action," to terms of attraction and repulsion, which are free from anything mysterious, whose mode of working can be unambiguously and plainly set forth in the law of the parallelogram of forces. Law? Set forth? Therefore still

## THE MYSTERY UNEXPLAINED

only description ? Certainly only description, not explanation in the least. Even assuming that it is true, instead of a mere Utopia, that all the secrets and riddles of nature can be traced back to matter moved by attraction and repulsion according to the simplest laws of these, they would still only be summed up into a great general riddle, which is only the more colossal because it is able to embrace all others within itself. For attraction and repulsion, the transference of motion, and the combination of motion according to the law of the parallelogram of forces—all this is merely description of processes whose inner causes we do not understand, which appear simple, and are so, but are nevertheless not self-evident or to be taken as a matter of course; they are not in themselves intelligible, but form an absolute "world-riddle." From the very root of things there gazes at us the same Sphinx which we had apparently driven from the foreground.

But furthermore, this reduction to simpler terms is an impossible and never-ending task. There is fresh confusion at every step. In reducing to simpler terms, it is often forgotten that the principle of combination is not inherent in the more simple, and cannot be "reduced." Or else there is an ignoring of the fact that a transition has been made, not from resultants to components, but to quite a different kind of phenomena. Innumerable as are the possible reductions to simpler terms, and mistaken as it would be to remain prematurely at the level of description, it cannot be denied that the fundamental facts of the world are pure facts which must simply be accepted where they occur, indisputable, inexplicable, impenetrable, the "whence" and the "how" of their existence quite uncomprehended. And this is especially true of every new and peculiar expression of what we call energy and energies. Gravitation cannot be reduced to terms of attraction and repulsion, nor action at a distance to action at close quarters; it might, indeed, be shown that repulsion in its turn presupposes attraction before it can become possible; the "energies" of ponderable matter cannot be reduced to the "ether" and its processes of motion, nor the complex play of the chemical affinities to the attraction of masses in general or to gravity. And thus the series ascends throughout the spheres of nature up to the mysterious directive energies in the crystal, and to the underivable phenomena of movement in the living substance, perhaps even to the functions of will-power. All these can be discovered, but not really understood. They can be described, but not explained. And we are absolutely ignorant as to why they should have emerged from the depth of nature, what that depth really is, or what still remains hidden in her mysterious lap. Neither what nature reveals to us nor what it conceals from us is in any true sense "comprehended," and we flatter ourselves that we understand her secrets when we have only become accustomed to them. If we try to break the power of this accustomedness and to consider the actual relations of things there dawns in us a feeling already awakened by direct impressions and experience; the feeling of the mysterious and enigmatical, of the abyssmal depths beneath, and of what lies far above our comprehension, alike in regard to our own existence and every other. The world is at no point self-explanatory, but at all points marvellous. Its laws are only formulated riddles.

### Evolution and New Beginnings

All this throws an important light upon two subjects which are relevant in this connection, but which cannot here be exhaustively dealt with,—evolution and new beginnings. Let us consider, for instance, the marvellous range and diversity of the characteristic chemical properties and interrelations of substances. Each one of them, contrasted with the preceding lower forms and stages of "energy," contrasted with mere attraction, repulsion, gravitation, is something absolutely new, a new interpolation (of course not in regard to time but to grade), a phenomenon which cannot be "explained" by what has gone before. It simply occurs, and we find it in its own time and place. We may call this new emergence "evolution," and we may use this term in connection with every new stage higher than those preceding it. But it is not evolution in a crude and quantitative sense, according to which the "more highly evolved" is nothing more than an addition and combination of what was already there, it is evolution in the old sense of the word, according to which the more developed is a higher analogue of the less developed, but is in its own way as independent, as much a new beginning as each of the antecedent stages, and therefore in the strict sense neither derivable from them nor reducible to them.

It must be noted that in this sense evolution and new beginnings are already present at a very early stage in nature and are part of its essence. We must bear this in mind if we are rightly to understand the subtler processes in nature which we find emerging at a higher level. It is illusory to suppose that it is a "natural" assumption to "derive" the living from lower processes in nature. The non-living and the inorganic are also underivable as to their individual stages, and the leap from the inorganic to the organic is simply much greater than that from attraction in general to chemical affinity. As a matter of fact, the first occurrence— undoubtedly controlled and conditioned by internal necessity—of crystallisation, or of life, or of sensation has just the same marvellousness as everything individual and everything new in any ascending series in nature. In short, every new beginning has the same marvel.

Perhaps this consideration goes still deeper, throwing light upon or suggesting the proper basis for a study of the domain of mind and of history. It is immediately obvious that there, at any rate, we enter into a

## EVOLUTION AND NEW BEGINNINGS

region of phenomena which cannot be derived from anything antecedent, or reduced to anything lower. It must be one of the chief tasks of naturalism to explain away these facts, and to maintain the sway of "evolution," not in our sense but in its own, that is " to explain " everything new and individual from that which precedes it. But the assertion that this can be done is here doubly false. For, in the first place, it cannot be proved that methods of study which are relatively valid for natural phenomena are applicable also to those of the mind. And in the second place we must admit that even in nature—apart from mind—we have to do with new beginnings which are underivable from their antecedents.

All being is inscrutable mystery as a whole, and from its very foundations upwards through each successively higher stage of its evolution, in an increasing degree, until it reaches a climax in the incomprehensibility of individuality. It is a mystery that does not force itself into nature as supernatural or miraculous, but is fundamentally implicit in it, a mystery that in its unfolding assuredly follows the strictest law, the most inviolable rules, whether in the chemical affinities a higher grade of energies reveals itself, or whether—unquestionably also in obedience to everlasting law—the physical and chemical conditions admit of the occurrence of life, or whether in his own time and place a genius arises.*

* This has been urged often enough even by scientific investigators. In such cases they have frequently been reproached for dragging

## THE DEPENDENCE OF THE ORDER OF NATURE

(2 and 3). The "dependence" of all things is the second requirement of religion, without which it is altogether inconceivable. We avoid the words "creation" and "being created," because they involve anthropomorphic and altogether insufficient modes of representation. But throughout we have in mind, as suggested by Schleier-

miracles into nature when they call a halt in face of the "underivable" and the "mysterious." This is a complete misunderstanding. With miracles and with the supernatural in the historical sense of these words, this mode of regarding nature has nothing whatever to do. It would be much more reasonable to maintain the converse that there exists between supernatural ideas and the belief in the absolute explicability and rationalisation of nature a peculiar mutual relation and attraction. For, if we think out the relation clearly, we must see that all real and consistent belief in miracles demands as its most effective background the clearest possible explicability of nature. It pictures to itself two natures, so to speak nature and supernature, and the latter of these interpolates itself into the former in the form of sudden and occasional interruptions, that is to say, as miracles. The purpose of miracles is to be recognised as such, as events absolutely different from the ordinary course of happening. And they are most likely thus to be recognised when nature itself is translucent and mathematical. Thus we find that supernaturalism quite readily accepts, and even insists upon a rationalistic explanation of nature. But this is quite incorrect Nature is not so thoroughly rationalised and calculable as such a point of view would have us believe.

The really religious element in belief in miracles is that it, too, in its own way, is seeking after mystery, dependence and providence It fails because it naively seeks for these in isolated and exceptional acts, which have no analogy to other phenomena. It regards these as arbitrary acts, and does so because it overlooks or underestimates the fact that they have to be reckoned with throughout the whole of nature.

## THE DEPENDENCE OF NATURE

macher's expression already quoted, what all religion means when it declares nature and the world to be *creatures*. The inalienable content of this idea is that deep and assured feeling that our nature and all nature does not rest in its own strength and self-sufficiency, that there must be more secure reasons for nature which are absolutely outside of it, and that it is dependent upon, and conditioned through and through by something above itself, independent, and unconditioned. "I believe that God has created me together with all creatures." (Luther.)

This faith seemed easier in earlier times, when men's eyes were not yet opened to see the deep-lying connectedness of all phenomena, the inexorableness of causal sequences, when it was believed that, in the apparently numerous interruptions of the causal sequences, the frailty and dependence of this world and its need for heavenly aid could be directly observed, when, therefore, it was not difficult to believe that the world was "nothing" and perishable, that it had been called forth out of nothing, and that in its transient nature it carried for ever the traces of this origin. But to-day it is not so easy to believe in this dependence, for nature seems to show itself, in its inviolable laws and unbroken sequences, as entirely sufficient unto itself, so that for every phenomenon a sufficient cause is to be found within nature, that is, in the sum of the antecedent states and conditions which, according to inevitable laws, must result in and produce what follows.

We have already noted that this is most obviously discernible in the world of the great masses, the heavenly bodies which pursue their courses from everlasting to everlasting, mutually conditioning themselves and betraying no need for or dependence upon anything outside of themselves. Everything, even the smallest movement, is here determined strictly by the dependence of each upon all and of all upon each. There is no variation, no change of position for which an entirely satisfactory cause cannot be found in the system as a whole, which works like an immense machine. Nothing indicates dependence upon anything external. And as it is to-day so it was yesterday, and a million years ago, and innumerable millions of years ago. It seems quite gratuitous to suppose that something which does not occur to-day was necessary at an earlier period, and that everything has not been from all eternity just as it is now.

We saw that naturalism is attempting to extend this character of independence and self-sufficiency from the astronomical world to the world as a whole. Shall we attempt, then, to oppose it in this ambition, but surrender the realm of the heavenly bodies as already conquered? By no means. For religion cannot exclude the solar system from the dependence of all being upon God. And this very example is the most conspicuous one, the one in regard to which the whole problem can be most definitely formulated.

Astronomy teaches us that all cosmic processes are

## THE DEPENDENCE OF NATURE 57

governed by a marvellous far-reaching uniformity of law, which unites in strictest harmony the nearest and the most remote. Has this fact any bearing upon the problem of the dependence of the world ? No. It surely cannot be that a world without order could be brought under the religious point of view more readily than one governed by law! Let us suppose for a moment that we had to do with a world without strict nexus and definite order of sequence, without law and without order, full of capricious phenomena, unregulated associations, an inconstant play of causes. Such a world would be to us unintelligible, strange, absurd. But it would not necessarily be more "dependent," more "conditioned" than any other. Had I no other reasons for looking beyond the world, and for regarding it as dependent on something outside of itself, the absence of law and order would assuredly furnish me with none. For, assuming that it is possible at all to conceive of a world and its contents as independent, and as containing its own sufficient cause within itself, it would be quite as easily thought of as a confused lawless play of chances as a well-ordered Cosmos. Perhaps more easily ; for it goes without saying that such a conglomeration of promiscuous chances could not possibly be thought of as a world of God. Order and strict obedience to law, far from being excluded, are required by faith in God, are indeed a direct and inevitable preliminary to thinking of the world as dependent upon God Thus we may state the paradox, that only a

Cosmos which, by its strict obedience to law, gives us the impression of being sufficient unto itself, can be conceived of as actually dependent upon God, as His creation. If any man desires to stop short at the consideration of the apparent self-sufficiency of the Cosmos and its obedience to law, and refuses to recognise any reasons outside of the world for this, we should hardly be able, according to our own proposition, to require him to go farther. For we maintained that God could not be read out of nature, that the idea of God could never have been gained in the first instance from a study of nature and the world. The problem always before us is rather, whether, having gained the idea from other sources, we can include the world within it. Our present question is whether the world, as it is, and just because it is as it is, can be conceived of as dependent upon God. And this question can only be answered in the affirmative, and in the sense of Schiller's oft-quoted lines:

> The great Creator
> We see not—He conceals himself within
> His own eternal laws   The sceptic sees
> Their operation, but beholds not Him,
> "Wherefore a God!" he cries, "the world itself
> Suffices for itself!" and Christian prayer
> Ne'er praised him more, than does this blasphemy.

God's world could not possibly be a conglomeration of chances; it must be orderly, and the fact that it is so proves its dependence.

But while we thus hold fast to our canon, we shall

## THE DEPENDENCE OF NATURE 59

find that the assertion of the world's dependence receives indirect corroboration even in regard to the astronomical realm, from certain signs which it exhibits, from certain suggestions which are implied in it. We must not wholly overlook two facts which, to say the least, are difficult to fit in with the idea of the independence and self-sufficiency of the world; these are, on the one hand, the difficulties involved in the idea of an eternal machine, and on the other the difficult fact of " entropy." We have already compared the world to a mighty clock, or a machine which, as a whole, represents what can never be found in one of its parts, a *perpetuum mobile*. Let us however leave aside the idea of a *perpetuum mobile*, and dwell rather on the comparison with a machine. It seems obvious that in order to be a machine there must be a closed solidarity in the system. But how could a machine have come into existence and become functional if it is driven by wheels, which are driven by wheels, which are again driven by wheels . . . and so on unceasingly? It would not be a machine. The idea falls to pieces in our hands. Yet our world is supposed to be just such an infinitely continuous " system." How does it begin to depend upon and be sufficient unto itself? But further. It is a clock, we are told, which ever winds itself up anew, which, without fatigue and in ceaseless repetition, adjusts the universal cycles of becoming, and disappearing, and becoming again. It seems a corroboration of the old Heraclitian and Stoic conception, that the eternal primitive fire brings forth all things out of itself, and takes them back into itself to bring them forth anew  Even to-day the conception is probably general that, out of the original states of the world-matter, circling fiery nebulæ form themselves and throw off their rings, that the breaking up of these rings gives rise to planets which circle in solar systems for many æons through space, till, finally, their energy lessened by friction with the ether, they plunge into their suns again, that the increased heat restores the original state and the whole play begins anew.

All this was well enough in the days of naively vitalistic ideas of the world as having a life and soul. But not in these days of mechanics, the strict calculation of the amount of energy used, and the mechanical theory of heat. The world-clock cannot wind itself up. It, too, owes its activity to the transformation of potential energy into kinetic energy. And, since movement and work take place within it, there is in the clock as a whole just as in every one of its parts, a mighty process of relaxation of an originally tense spring, there is dissipation and transformation of the stored potential energy into work and ultimately into heat. And with every revolution of the earth and its moon the world is moving slowly but inexorably towards a final stage of complete relaxation of her powers of tension, a state in which all energy will be transformed into heat, in which there will be no different states but only the most uniform distribution, in which also all

# "CONTINGENCY" OF THE WORLD

life and all movement will cease and the world-clock itself will come to a standstill.

How does this fit in with the idea of independence and self-sufficiency? How could the world-clock ever wind itself up again to the original state of tension which was simply there as if shot from a pistol " in the beginning"? Where is the everlasting impressive uniformity and constancy of the world? How does it happen that the world-clock has not long ago come to a standstill? For even if the original sum of potential energy is postulated as infinite, the eternity that lies behind us is also infinite. And so one infinity swallows another. And innumerable questions of a similar kind are continually presenting themselves.

### THE "CONTINGENCY" OF THE WORLD.

But we need not dwell in the meantime on these and the many other difficulties and riddles presented by our cosmological hypothesis. However these may be solved, a general consideration will remain—namely, that whether the world is governed by law or not, whether it is sufficient unto itself or not, there *is* a world full of the most diverse phenomena and there *are* laws. Whence then have both these come? Is it a matter of course, is it quite obvious that they should exist at all, and that they should be exactly as they are? We do not here appeal without further ceremony to the saying "everything must have a cause, therefore the world also." It is not absolutely correct. For instance, if the world were so constituted that it would be impossible for it not to exist, that the necessity for its existence and the inconceivability of its non-existence were at once explicit and obvious, then there would be no sense in inquiring after a cause. In regard to a "necessary" thing, if there were any such, we cannot ask, "Why, and from what cause does this exist?" If it was necessary, that implies that to think of it as not existing would be ridiculous, and logically or metaphysically impossible. Unfortunately there are no "necessary" things, so that we cannot illustrate the case by examples. But there are at least necessary truths as distinguished from contingent truths. And thus some light may be brought into the matter for the inexpert. For instance, a necessary truth is contained in the sentence, "Everything is equal to itself," or, "The shortest distance between two points is a straight line." We cannot even conceive of the contrary. Therefore these axioms have no reasons, and can neither be deduced nor proved. Every question as to their reasons is quite meaningless. As examples of a "contingent" truth we may take "It rains to-day," or "The earth revolves round the sun." For neither one nor the other of these is necessarily so. It is so as a matter of fact, but under other circumstances it might have been otherwise. The contrary can be conceived of and represented, and has in itself an equal degree of possibility. Therefore such a fact requires to

## "CONTINGENCY" OF THE WORLD

be and is capable of being reasoned out. I can and must ask, "How does it happen that it rains to-day? What are the reasons for it?" But as we must seek for sufficient reasons for "contingent" truths, that is, for those of which the contrary was equally possible, so assuredly we must seek for sufficient causes for "contingent" phenomena and events, those which can be thought of as not existing, or as existing in a different form. For these we must find causes and actual reasons. Otherwise they have no foundation. The element of "contingency" must be done away with; they must be shown to result from sufficient causes. That is to say nothing less than that they must be traced back to some necessity. For it is one of the curious fundamental convictions of our reason, and one in which all scientific investigation has its ultimate roots, that what is "contingent" is only apparently so, and in reality is in some way or other based on necessity. Therefore reason seeks causes for everything.

The search for causes involves showing that a thing was necessary. And this must obviously apply to the world as a whole. If it were quite obvious that the world and its existence as it is were necessary, that is, that it would be contrary to reason to think of the world, and its phenomena, and their obedience to law as non-existent, or as different from what they are, all inquiry would be at an end. This would be *the* ultimate necessity in which all the apparent contingency of isolated phenomena and existences was firmly based.

But this is far from being the case. That anything exists, and that the world exists, is for us absolutely the greatest "contingency" of all, and in regard to it we can and must continually ask, "Why does anything exist at all, and why should it not rather be non-existent?" Indeed, all our quest for sufficient causes here reaches its climax. In more detail: that these celestial systems and bodies, the ether, attraction and gravitation should exist, and that everything should be governed by definite laws, all literally "as if shot from a pistol," there must undoubtedly be some sufficient reason, certain as it is that we shall never discover it. It is true, as some one has said, that we live not only in a very fortuitous world, but in an incredibly improbable one. And this is not affected by the fact that the world is completely governed by law. Law only confirms it. The fact that all details may be clearly and mathematically calculated in no way prevents them from being fundamentally contingent. For they are only so calculable on the basis of the given fundamental characters of the world. And that is precisely the problem: "Why do these characters exist and not quite different ones, and why should any exist at all?"

If any one should say: "Well, we must just content ourselves with recognising the essentially 'contingent' nature of existence, for we shall never be able to get beyond that," he would be right in regard to the second statement. To get beyond that and to see what it is—

THE REAL WORLD 65

eternal and in itself necessary—that lies at the basis of this world of "contingency" is indeed impossible. But he would be wrong as to the first part of the assertion. For no one *will* " content himself." For that all chance is only apparently chance, and is ultimately based in necessity, is a deeply-rooted and fundamental conviction of our reason, one which directs all scientific investigation, and which cannot be ignored. It demands ceaselessly something necessary as the permanent basis of contingent existence. And this fact is and remains the truth involved in the "cosmological proofs of the existence of God" of former days. It was certainly erroneous to suppose that "God" could be proved. For it is a long way from that "idea of necessity" to religious experience of God. And it was erroneous, too, to suppose that anything could be really "proved." What is necessary can never really be proved from what is contingent. But the recognition of the contingent nature of the world is a stimulus that stirs up within our reason the idea of the necessary, and it is a fact that reason finds rest only in this idea.

## The Real World

(4.) What was stated separately in our first and second propositions, and has hitherto been discussed, now unites and culminates in the fourth. For if we note the vital expressions of religion wherever it occurs, we find above all one thing as its most characteristic sign, indeed as its very essence, in all places and all times, often only as a scarce uttered wish or longing, but often breaking forth with impetuous might. This one thing is the impulse and desire to get beyond time and space, and beyond the oppressive narrowness and crampingness of the world surrounding us, the desire to see into the depth and "other side" of things and of existence. For it is the very essence of religion to distinguish this world from, and contrast it as insufficient with the real world which is sufficient, to regard this world which we see and know and possess as only an image, as only transiently real, in contrast with the real world of true being which is believed in. Religion has clothed this essential feature in a hundred mythologies and eschatologies, and one has always given place to another, the more sublimed to the more robust. But the fundamental feature itself cannot disappear.

In apologetics and dogmatics the interest in this matter is often concentrated more or less exclusively upon the question of "immortality." Wrongly so, however, for this quest after the real world is not a final chapter in religion, it is religion itself. And in the religious sense the question of immortality is only justifiable and significant when it is a part of the general religious conviction that this world is not the truly essential world, and that the true nature of things, and of our own being, is deeper than we can comprehend, and lies beyond this side of things, beyond

## THE REAL WORLD 67

time and space. To the religious mind it cannot be of great importance whether existence is to be continued for a little at least beyond this life. In what way would such a wish be religious? But the inward conviction that "all that is transitory is only a parable," that all here is only a veil and a curtain, and the desire to get beyond semblance to truth, beyond insufficiency to sufficiency, concentrate themselves especially in the assertion of the eternity of our true being.

It is with this characteristic of religion that the spirit and method of naturalism contrast so sharply. Naturalism points out with special satisfaction that this depth of things, this home of the soul is nowhere discoverable. The great discoveries of Copernicus, Kepler, and Newton have done away with the possibility of that. No empyrean, no corner of the world remains available. Even the attempted flight to sun, moon, or stars does not help. It is true that the newly discovered world is without end, but, beyond a doubt, in its outermost and innermost depths it is a world of space and time. Even in the stellar abysses "everything is just the same as with us."

All this is doubtless correct, and it is very wholesome for religion. For it prompts religion no longer to seek its treasure, the true nature of things, and its everlasting home in time and space, as the mythologies and eschatologies have sought them repeatedly. It throws religion back on the fundamental insight and on the convictions which it had attained long before philosophy and criticism of knowledge had arrived at similar views: namely, that time and space, and this world of time and space, do not comprise the whole of existence, nor existence as it really is, but are only a manifestation of it to our finite and limited knowledge. Before the days of modern astronomy, and without its help, religion knew that God was not confined to "heaven," or anywhere in space, and that time as it is for us was not for Him. Even in the terms "eternity" and "infinity" it shows an anticipatory knowledge of a being and reality above time and space. These ideas were not gained from a contemplation of nature, but before it and from independent sources.

But though it is by no means the task of apologetics to build up these ideas directly from a study of things, it is of no little importance to inquire whether religion possesses in these convictions only postulates of faith, for which it must laboriously and forcibly make a place in the face of knowledge, or whether a thorough and self-critical knowledge does not rather confirm them, and show us, within the world of knowledge itself, unmistakable signs that it cannot be the true, full reality, but points to something beyond itself.

To study this question thoroughly would involve setting forth a special theory of knowledge and existence. This cannot be attempted here. But Kant's great doctrine of the "Antinomy of Reason" has for all time broken up for us the narrowness of the naturalistic way of thinking. Every one who has felt cramped by

OUR CONCEPTION OF TIME 69

the narrow limits in which reality was confined by a purely mundane outlook must have experienced the liberating influence of the Kantian Antinomy if he has thought over it carefully. The thick curtain which separates being from appearance seems to be torn away, or at any rate to reveal itself as a curtain. Kant shows that, if we were to take this world as it lies before us for the true reality, we should land in inextricable contradictions. These contradictions show that the true world itself cannot coincide with our thought and comprehension, for in being itself there can be no contradictions. Otherwise it would not exist. The ancient problems of philosophy, from the time of the Eleatic school onwards, find here their adequate formulation. Kant's disciple, Fries, has carried the matter further, and has attempted to develop what for Kant still remained a sort of embarrassment of reason to more precise pronouncements as to the relation of true being to its manifestation.

THE ANTINOMY OF OUR CONCEPTION OF TIME

A few examples may serve to make the point clear. The first of the antinomies is also the most impressive. It brings before us the insufficiency of our conceptions of time, and shows the impossibility of transferring, from the world as it appears to us, to real Being any mode of conceiving time which we possess. The difficulty is, whether we are to think of our world as having had a beginning or not. The naive outlook will at once assume without further ado a beginning of all things. Everything must have had a beginning, though that may have been a very long time ago. But on more careful reflection it is found impossible to imagine this, and then the assumption that things had no beginning is made with as little scruple. Let us suppose that the beginning of things was six thousand, or, what is quite as easy, six thousand billion years ago. We are at once led to ask what there was the year before or many years before, and what there was before that again, and so on until we face the infinite and beginningless. Thus we find that we have never really thought of a beginning of things, and never could think of it, but that our thinking always carries us into the infinite. Time, at any rate, we have thought of as infinite. We may then amuse ourselves by trying to conceive of endless time as empty, but we shall hardly be able to give any reason for arriving at that idea. If time goes back to infinity, it seems difficult to see why it should not always have been filled, instead of only being so filled from some arbitrary point. And in any case the very fact of the existence of time makes the problem of beginning or not beginning insoluble. For such reasons Aristotle asserted that the world had no beginning, and rejected the contrary idea as childish.

But the idea of no beginning is also childish or rather impossible, and in reality inconceivable. For if it be assumed that the world and time have never had

## CONDITIONED AND UNCONDITIONED 71

a beginning, there stretches back from the time at which I now find myself a past eternity. It must have passed completely as a whole, for otherwise this particular point in time could never have been arrived at. So that I must think of an infinity which nevertheless comes to an end. I cannot do this. It would be like wooden iron.

The matter sounds simple but is nevertheless difficult in its consequences. It confronts us at once with the fact, confirmed by the theory of knowledge, that time as we know it is an absolutely necessary and fundamental form of our conceptions and knowledge, but is likewise the veil over what is concealed, and cannot be carried over in the same form into the true nature of things. As the limits and contradictions in the time-conception reveal themselves to us, there wakes in us the idea which we accept as the analogue of time in true being, an idea of existence under the form of " eternity," which, since we are tied down to temporal concepts, cannot be expressed or even thought of with any content.*

### THE ANTINOMY OF THE CONDITIONED AND THE UNCONDITIONED

The antinomy of the conditioned and the unconditioned leads us along similar lines. Every individual finite thing or event is dependent on its causes and

* Not even after the scholastic manner of regarding eternity as a "nunc stans," a stationary now, an everlasting present. "Present" is a moment in our own time, and an " everlasting " present is nonsense.

conditions, which precede it or co-exist in inter-relation with it. It is conditioned, and is only possible through its conditions. But that implies that it can only occur or be granted when all its conditions are first given in complete synthesis. If any one of them failed, it would not have come about. But every one of its conditioning circumstances is in its turn conditioned by innumerable others, and every one of these again by others, and so on into the infinite, backwards and on all sides, so that here again something without end and incapable of end must have come to an end, and must be thought of as having an end, before any event whatever can really come to pass. But this again is a sheer impossibility for our thinking: we require and must demand something completed, because now is really now, and something happens now, and yet in the world as it appears to us we are always forced to face what cannot have an end.

### The Antinomy of Our Conception of Space

To bring our examples to a conclusion, we find the same sort of antinomy in regard to space, and the world as it is extended in space. Here, too, it becomes apparent that space as we imagine it, and as we carry it with us as a concept for arranging our sense-impressions, cannot correspond to the true reality. As in regard to time, so also in regard to space, we can never after any distance however enormous come to a halt and say, " Here is the end of space." Whether we think of the diameter

## OUR CONCEPTION OF SPACE 73

of the earth's orbit or the distance to Sirius, and multiply them by a million we always ask, "What lies behind?" and so extend space into the infinite. And as a matter of course we people it also without end with heavenly bodies, stars, nebulæ, Milky Ways and the like. For here again there can be no obvious reason why space in our neighbourhood should be filled, while space at a greater distance should be thought of as empty. Therefore we actually think of star beyond star, and, as far as we can reckon, stars beyond that without end. For space extends not merely so far, but always farther. And the number of the stars is not so many, but always one more. This sounds quite obvious, but it has exactly the same impossibility as we found in our "past infinity." For although we are carried by our conceptions into the infinite, and to what never could have an end, it is impossible to assume the same of reality.

It is remarkable and quite characteristic that the whole difficulty and its peculiar nature become much more intelligible to us through the familiar images and expressions of religion. There we readily admit that we cannot comprehend the number of the stars and stellar spaces, because for us they never reach an end, there being always one more; but that in the eyes of God all is embraced in His universality, in a "perfect synthesis," and that to Him Being is never and in no point "always one more." God does not count.

Without the help of religious expressions we say: Being itself is always itself and never implies any more;

for if there were "always one more" it would not be Being. It can only exist "as a perfect synthesis," which does not mean an endless number, which nevertheless somewhere comes to an end—again wooden iron —but something above all reckoning and beyond all number, as it is beyond space and time. And that which we are able to weigh and measure and number is therefore not reality itself, but only its inadequate manifestation to our limited capacity for understanding.

But enough of this. The puzzles in the doctrines of the simple and the complex, of the causeless and the caused, into which this world of ours forces us, should teach us further to recognise it for what it is—insufficient and pointing beyond itself,—to its own transcendent depths. So, too, the problems that arise when we penetrate farther and farther into the ever more and more minute, and the indefiniteness of our thought-horizons in general should have the same effect.

### Intuitions of Reality

(5.) There are other evidences of this depth and hidden nature of things, towards which an examination of our knowledge points. For "in feeling and intuition appearance points beyond itself to real being." So ran our fifth proposition. This subject indeed is delicate, and can only be treated of in the hearing of willing ears. But all apologetic counts upon willing ears; it is not conversion of doubters that is aimed at, it is religion which seeks to reassure itself. Our proposition

## INTUITIONS OF REALITY

does not speak of dreams but of facts, which are not the less facts because they are more subtle than others. What we are speaking of are the deep impressions, which cannot properly be made commensurable at all, which may spring up directly out of an inward experience, an apprehension of nature, the world and history, in the depths of the spirit. They call forth in us an "anamnesis," a "reminiscence" in Plato's sense, awakening within us moods and intuitions in which something of the essence and meaning of being is directly experienced, although it remains in the form of feeling, and cannot easily, if at all, find expression in definable ideas or clear statements. Fries, in his book, "Wissen, Glaube, und Ahnung," unhappily too much forgotten, takes account of this fact, for he places this region of spiritual experience beside the certainties of faith and knowledge, and regards these as "animated" by it. He has in mind especially the impressions of the beautiful and the sublime which far transcend our knowledge of nature, and to which knowledge and its concepts can never do adequate justice, facts though they undoubtedly are. In them we experience directly, in intuitive feeling, that the reality is greater than our power of understanding, and we feel something of its true nature and meaning. The utterances of Schleiermacher[*] in regard to religion follow the same lines. For this is precisely what he means when he insists

[*] "Reden über die Religion, an die Gebildeten unter ihren Verachtern." Neu herausgegeben von R. Otto. 1906

that the universe must be experienced in intuition and feeling as well as in knowing and doing. He is less incisive in his expressions than Fries, but wider in ideas. He includes in this domain of "intuitive feeling" not only the æsthetic experiences of the beautiful and sublime, but takes the much more general and comprehensive view, that the receptive mind may gather from the finite impressions of the infinite, and may through its experiences of time gain some conception of the eternal. And he rightly emphasises, that such intuition has its true place in the sphere of mind and in face of the events of history, rather than in the outer court of nature. He, too, lays stress on the fact that doctrinal statements and ideas cannot be formulated out of such subtle material.

The experience of which we are speaking may be most directly and impressively gained from the great, the powerful, the sublime in nature. It may be gained from the contemplation of nature's harmonies and beauties, but also of her overflowing abundance and her enigmatical dæmonic strength, from the purposeful intelligibility as well as the terrifying and bewildering enigmas of nature's operations, from all the manifold ways in which the mind is affected and startled, from all the suggestive but indefinable sensations which may be roused in us by the activity of nature, and which rise through a long scale to intoxicated self-forgetfulness and wordless ecstasy before her beauty, and her half-revealed, half-concealed mystery. If any or all of these be stirred up

THE RECOGNITION OF PURPOSE 77

in a mind which is otherwise godless or undevout, it remains an indefinite, vacillating feeling, bringing with it nothing else. But in the religious mind it immediately unites with what is akin to it or of similar nature, and becomes worship. No dogmas or arguments for disputatious reasoning can be drawn from it. It can hardly even be expressed, except, perhaps, in music. And if it be expressed it tends easily to become fantastic or romantic pomposity, as is shown even by certain parts of the writings of Schleiermacher himself.

THE RECOGNITION OF PURPOSE

(6.) We must now turn to the question of "teleology." Only now, not because it is a subordinate matter, for it is in reality the main one, but because it is the culminating point, not the starting point, of our argument. If the world be from God and of God, it and all that it contains must be for some definite purpose and for special ends. It must be swayed by eternal ideas, and must be subject to divine providence and guidance. But naturalism, and even, it appears, natural science, declares: Neither purposes nor ideas are of necessity to be assumed in nature. They do not occur either in the details or in the whole. The whole is an absolutely closed continuity of causes, a causal but blind machinery, in regard to which we cannot ask, What is meant to be produced by this? but only, What causes have produced what exists? This opposition goes deep and raises difficulties. And in all vindication or defence of religion it ought rightly to be kept in the foreground of attention, although the points we have already insisted on have been wrongly overlooked. The opposition concentrates itself to-day almost entirely around two theories of naturalism, which do not, indeed, set forth the whole case, but which are certainly typical examples, so that, if we analyse them, we shall have arrived at an orientation of the fundamental points at issue. The two doctrines are Darwinism and the mechanical theory of life, and it is to these that we must now turn our attention. And since the best elucidation and criticism of both theories is to be found in their own history, and in the present state of opinion within their own school, we shall have to combine our study of their fundamental principles with that of their history.

We can here set forth, however, only the chief point of view, the gist of the matter, which will continue to exist and hold good however the analysis of details may turn out. For the kernel of the question may be discussed independently, without involving the particular interests of zoology or biology, though we shall constantly come across particular and concrete cases of the main problem in our more detailed study.

The struggle against, and the aversion to ideas and purposes on the part of the nature-interpreters is not in itself directed against religion. It does not arise from any antagonism of natural science to the religious conception of the world, but is primarily an antagonism of

## THE RECOGNITION OF PURPOSE 79

one school of science to another, the modern against the mediæval-Aristotelian. The latter, again, was not in itself a religious world-outlook, it was simply an attempt at an interpretation of the processes of nature, and especially of evolution, which might be quite neutral towards religion, or might be purely naturalistic. It was the theory of Entelechies and *formæ substaniales*. In order to explain how a thing had come to be, it taught that the idea of the finished thing, the "form," was implicit in it from the very beginning, and determined the course of its development. This "form," the end aimed at in development, was "potentially," "ideally," or "virtually" implicit in the thing from the beginning, was the *causa finalis*, the ultimate cause which determined the development. Modern natural science objects to this theory that it offers no explanation, but merely gives a name to what has to be explained. The aim of science, it tells us, is to elucidate the play of causes which brought about a particular result. The hypothetical *causa finalis* it regards as a mere *asylum ignorantiæ*, and as the problem itself not as its solution. For instance, if we inquire into the present form and aspect of the earth, nothing is advanced by stating that the "form," the primitive model of the evolving earth was implicit in it from the beginning, and that it gradually determined the phases and transition-stages of its evolution, until the ultimate state, the end aimed at, was attained. The task of science is, through geology, geognosy, mineralogy, geodesy, physical geography, meteorology, and other sciences to discover the physical, chemical, and mechanical causes of the earth's evolution and their laws, and from the co-operation of these to interpret everything in detail and as a whole.

Whether modern natural science is right in this or not, whether or not it has neglected an element of truth in the old theory of Entelechies which it cannot dispense with, especially in regard to living organisms, it is beyond dispute that, from the most general point of view, and in particular with reference to teleology, religion does not need to concern itself in the least about this opposition. " Purposes," " ideas," " guidance " in the religious sense, are quite unaffected by the manner in which the result is realised; everything depends upon the special and particular value of what has been attained or realised. If a concatenation of causes and stages of development lead to results in which we suddenly discern a special and particular value, then, and not till then, have we a reason and criterion for our assumption that it is not simply a result of a play of chances, but that it has been brought about by purposeful thought, by higher intervention and guidance of things. Certainly not before then. Thus we can only speak of purposes, aims, guidance, and creation in so far as we have within us the capacity for feeling and recognising the value, meaning and significance of things. But natural science itself cannot estimate these. It can or will only

## THE RECOGNITION OF PURPOSE 81

examine how everything has come about, but whether this result has a higher value than another, or has a lower, or none at all, it can neither assert nor deny. That lies quite outside of its province.

Let us try to make this clear by taking at once the highest example—man and his origin. Let it be assumed that natural science could discover all the causes and factors which, operating for many thousands of years, have produced man and human existence. Even if these causes and factors had actually been pure "ideas," *formæ substantiales* and the like, that would in no way determine whether the whole process was really subject to a divine idea of purpose or not. If we had not gained, from a different source, an insight into the supreme and incomparable worth of human existence, spiritual, rational, and free, with its capacity for morality, religion, art and science, we should be compelled to regard man, along with every other natural result, as the insignificant product of a blind play of nature. But, on the other hand, if we have once felt and recognised this value of human existence, its highest dignity, the knowledge that man has been produced through a play of highly complex natural processes, fulfilling themselves in absolute obedience to law, in no way prevents our regarding him as a "purpose," as the realisation of a divine idea, in accordance with which nature in its orderliness was planned. In fact, this consideration leads us to discover and admire eternal plan and divine guidance in nature.

For it does not rest with natural science either to discover or to deny "purpose" in the religious sense in nature; it belongs to quite a different order of experience, an entirely inward one. Just in proportion as I become aware of, and acknowledge in the domain of my inward experience and through my capacity of estimating values, the worth of the spiritual and moral life of man, so, with the confidence of this peculiar mode of conviction, I subordinate the concatenations of events and causes on which the possibility and the occurrence of the spiritual and moral life depend, to an eternal teleology, and see the order of the world that leads to this illuminated by everlasting meaning and by providence.

## Teleological and Scientific Interpretations are Alike Necessary

(7.) Thus religion confidently subjects the world to a teleological interpretation. And to a teleological study in this sense the strictly causal interpretations of natural science are not hostile, but indispensable. For how do things stand? Natural science endeavours by persistent labour to comprehend the whole of the facts occurring in our world, up to the existence of man, as the final outcome and result of an age-long process of evolution, attempts also to follow this process ever higher up the ladder of strictly causal and strictly law-governed sequences, and finally to connect it with the primary and simplest fundamental facts of existence, beyond which it cannot go, and which must simply be

## TELEOLOGY AND SCIENCE 83

accepted as "given." If these results of this causally interpreted evolution reveal themselves to our inward power of valuation as full of meaning and value, indeed of the deepest and most incomparable value, the causal mode of explanation is in no way affected, but its results are all at once placed in a new light and reveal a peculiarity which was previously not discoverable, yet which is their highest import. They become a strictly united system of *means*. And purposefulness as a potentiality is thus carried back to the very foundation and "beginning," to the fundamental conditions and primary factors of the cosmos itself. The strict nexus of conditions and causes is thus nothing more than the "endeavour after end and aim," the carrying through and realisation of the eternal purpose, which was implicit potentially in the fundamental nature of things. The absolute obedience to law, and the inexorableness of chains of sequence are, instead of being fatal to this position, indispensable to it. When there is a purpose in view, it is only where the system of means is perfect, unbroken, and absolute, that the purpose can be realised, and therefore that intention can be inferred. In the inexplicable datum of the fundamental factors of the world's existence, in the strict nexus of causes, in the unfailing occurrence of the results which are determined by both these, and which reveal themselves to us as of value and purpose, teleology and providence are directly realised. The only assumptions are, that it is possible to judge the results according to their value, and that both the original nature of the world and the system of its causal sequences —that is, the world as we know it—can be conceived of in accordance with the ideas of dependence and conditionedness. Both assumptions are not only possible, but necessary.

In thinking out this most general consideration, we find the real and fundamental answer to the question as to the validity and freedom of the religious conception of the world with regard to teleology in nature. And if it be held fast and associated with the insight into the autonomy of the spiritual and its underivability from the natural, we are freed at once from all the petty strife with the naturalistic doctrines of evolution, descent, and struggle for existence. We shall nevertheless be obliged to discuss these to some extent, because it is not a matter of indifference whether the detailed study of natural evolution fits in more or less easily with the conception of purpose whose validity we have demonstrated in general. If that proves to be the case, it will be an important factor in apologetics. The conclusion which we have already arrived at on abstract grounds will then be corroborated and emphasised in the concrete.

# CHAPTER IV

## DARWINISM IN GENERAL

DARWINISM, which was originally a technical theory of the biological schools, has long since become a veritable tangle of the most diverse problems and opinions, and seems to press hardly upon the religious conception of the world from many different sides. In its theory of blind "natural selection" and the fortuitous play of the factors in the struggle for existence, it appears to surrender the whole of this wonderful world of life to the rough and ready grip of a process without method or plan. In the general theory of evolution and the doctrine of the descent of even the highest from the lowest, it seems to take away all special dignity from the human mind and spirit, all the freedom and all the nobility of pure reason and free will; it seems to reduce the higher products of religion, morality, poetry, and the æsthetic sense to the level of an ignoble tumult of animal impulses, desires and sensations. Purely speculative questions relative to the evolution theory, psychological and metaphysical, logical and epistemological, ethical, æsthetic, and finally even historical and politico-economical questions have been drawn into the coil, and usually receive from the Darwinians an answer at once robust and self-assured. A zoological theory seems suddenly to have thrown light and intelligibility into the most diverse provinces of knowledge.

But in point of fact it can be shown that Darwinism has not really done this and cannot do it. It leaves unaffected the problem of the mind with its peculiar and underivable laws, from the logical to the ethical. Whether it be right or wrong in its physiological theories, its genealogical trees and fortuitous factors, preoccupation with this theory is a task of the second order. Nevertheless it is necessary to study it, because the chief objections to the religious interpretation of the world have come from it.

### The Development of Darwinism

In studying it we should like to follow a method somewhat different from that usually observed in apologetic writings. "Darwinism," even in its technical, biological form, never was quite, and is to-day not at all a unified and consistent system. It has been modified in so many ways and presented in such different colours, that we must either refrain altogether from attempting to get into close quarters with it, or we must make ourselves acquainted to some extent with the phases of the theory as it has gradually developed up to the present day. This is the more necessary and useful since it is precisely within the circle of technical experts that revolts from and criticisms of the Darwinian theory have in recent years arisen; and these are so incisive, so varied, and so instructive, that through them we can adjust our standpoint in relation to the theory better than in any other way. And in thus letting the biologists speak for themselves, we are spared the fatal task of entering into the discussion of questions belonging to a region outside our own particular studies.

We cannot, however, give more than a short sketch. But even such a sketch may do more towards giving us a general knowledge of the question and showing us a way out of the difficulties it raises than any of the current "refutations." To supplement this sketch, and facilitate a thorough understanding of the problem, we shall give somewhat fuller references than are usual to the relevant literature. And the same method will be pursued in the following chapter, which deals with the mechanical theory of life. This method throws more upon the reader, but it is probably the most satisfactory one for the serious student.

The reactions from the Darwinism of the schools which we have just referred to, and to which the second half of this chapter is devoted, are, of course, of a purely scientific kind. And while we are devoting our attention to them, we must not be unfaithful to the canon laid down in the previous chapter, namely that with reference to the question of teleology in the religious sense no real answer can be looked for from scientific study, not even if it be anti-Darwinian. In this case, too, it is impossible to read the convictions and intuitions of the religious conception of the world out of a scientific study of nature: they precede it. But here, too, we may find some accessory support and indirect corroboration more or less strong and secure. This may be illustrated by a single example. It will be shown that, on closer study, it is not impossible to subordinate even the apparently confused tangle of naturalistic factors of evolution which are summed up in the phrase "struggle for existence" to interpretation from the religious point of view. But matters will be in quite a different position if the whole theory collapses, and instead of evolution and its paths being given over to confusion and chance, it appears that from the very beginning and at every point there is a predetermination of fixed and inevitable lines along and up which it must advance. In many other connections considerations of a like nature will reveal themselves to us in the course of our study.

Darwinism, as popularly understood, is the theory that "men are descended from monkeys," and in general that the higher forms of life are descended from the lower, and it is regarded as Darwin's epoch-making work and his chief merit—or fault according to the point of view—that he established the Theory of Descent. This is only half correct, and it leaves out the real point of Darwinism altogether. The Theory of Descent had its way prepared by the evolutionist ideas and the speculative nature-philosophy of Goethe, Schelling, Hegel and Oken; by the suggestions and glimmerings of the nature-mysticism of the romanticists; by the results of comparative anatomy and physiology; was already hinted at, at least as far as derivation of species was concerned, in the works of Linné himself; was worked out in the "zoological philosophies," by the elder Darwin, by Lamarck, Etienne Geoffroy St. Hilaire and Buffon; was in the field long before Charles Darwin's time; was already in active conflict with the antagonistic theory of the "constancy of species," and had its more or less decided adherents. Yet undoubtedly it was through and after Darwin that the theory grew so much more powerful and gained general acceptance.

### DARWINISM AND TELEOLOGY

But the essential and most characteristic importance of Darwin and his work, the reason for which he was called the Newton of biology, and which makes Darwinism at once interesting and dangerous to the religious conception of the world, is something quite special and new. It is its radical opposition to teleology. Du Bois-Reymond, in his witty lecture "Darwin versus Galiani,"* explains the gist of the matter. "Les dés de la nature sont pipés" (nature's dice are loaded). Nature is almost always throwing aces. She brings forth not what is meaningless and purposeless, but in great preponderance what is full of meaning and purpose. What "loaded" her dice like this? Even if the theory of descent be true, in what way does it directly

* Kgl. Preuss. Akademie der Wissenschaften, 1876.

help the purely scientific interpretation of the world? Would not this evolution from the lowest to the highest simply be a series of the most astonishing lucky throws of the dice by which in perplexing "endeavour after an aim," the increasingly perfect, and ultimately the most perfect is produced? And, on the other hand, every individual organism, from the Amœba up to the most complex vertebrate, is, in its structure, its form, its functions, a stupendous marvel of adaptation to its end and of co-ordination of the parts to the whole, and of the whole and its parts to the functions of the organism, the functions of nutrition, self-maintenance, reproduction, maintenance of the species, and so on. How account for the adaptiveness, both general and special, without *causæ finales*, without intention and purposes, without guidance towards a conscious aim? How can it be explained as the necessary result solely of *causæ efficientes*, of blindly working causes without a definite aim? Darwinism attempts to answer this question. And its answer is: "What appears to us 'purposeful' and 'perfect' is in truth only the manifold adaptation of the forms of life to the conditions of their existence. And this adaptation is brought about solely by means of these conditions themselves. Without choice, without aim, without conscious purpose nature offers a wealth of possibilities. The conditions of existence act as a sieve. What chances to correspond to them maintains itself, gliding through the meshes of the sieve, what does not perishes." It is an old idea of the

## CHARACTERISTICS OF DARWINISM

naturalistic philosophies, dating from Empedocles, which Darwin worked up into the theory of "natural selection" through "the survival of the fittest" "in the struggle for existence." Of course the assumption necessary to his idea is that the forms of life are capable of variation, and of continually offering in ceaseless flux new properties and characters to the sieve of selection, and of being raised thereby from the originally homogeneous to the heterogeneous, from the simple to the complex, from the lower to the higher. This is the theory of descent, and it is, of course, an essential part and the very foundation of Darwin's theory. But it is *the doctrine of descent based upon natural selection* that is Darwinism itself.

### THE CHARACTERISTIC FEATURES OF DARWINISM

We do not propose to expound the Darwinian theory for the hundredth time; a knowledge of it must be taken for granted. We need only briefly call to mind the characteristic features and catchwords of the theory as Darwin founded it, which have also been the starting points of subsequent modifications and controversies.

All living creatures are bound together in genetic solidarity. Everything has evolved through endless deviations, gradations, and differentiations, but at the same time by a perfectly continuous process. Variation continually produced a crop of heterogeneous novelties. The struggle for existence sifted these out. Heredity fixed and established them. Without method or plan variations continue to occur (indefinite variations). They manifest themselves in all manner of minute changes ("fluctuating" variations). Every part, every function of an organism may be subject individually to variation and selection. The world is strictly governed by what is useful. The whole organisation as well as the individual organs and functions bear the stamp of utility, at least, they must bear it if the theory is correct. In the general continuity the transitions are always easy; there are no fundamentally distinct "types," architectural plans, or groups of forms. Where gaps yawn the intermediate links have gone amissing. There is no fundamental difference between *genus*, *species*, and *variety*. Even the most complicated organ such as the eye, the most puzzling function such as the instinct of the bee, may be explained as the outcome of many more primitive stages.

The chief evidences of the theory of descent are to be found in homologies, in the correspondences of organs and functions, as revealed by comparative anatomy and physiology, in the recapitulation revealed by embryology, in the structure of parasites, in rudimentary organs and reversions to earlier stages, in the distribution of animals and plants, and in the possibility of still transforming, at least to a slight extent, one species into another, by experimental breeding.

Transformation and differentiation go on in nature as a vast, ceaseless, but blind process of selection. In

## CHARACTERISTICS OF DARWINISM

artificial selection evolution is secured by choosing the most fit for breeding purposes; so it is secured in natural selection by the favouring and survival of those forms which are the most fit among the many unfit or less fit, which happened to be exposed to the struggle for existence, that is, to the competition for the means of subsistence, to the struggle with enemies, to hostile environment, and to dangers of every kind. The adaptation thus brought about is of a purely "passive" kind. The variations arise fortuitously out of the organism, and present themselves for selection in the struggle for existence; they are not actively acquired by means of the struggle. The secondary factors of evolution recognised are: correlation in the growth and in the development of parts, the origin of new characters through use, their disappearance through disuse (Lamarck), the transmission of characters thus acquired, the influence of environment and sexual selection.*

The Darwinian theory, the interpretation of the teleological in the animate world by means of the theory of descent based upon natural selection, entered like a ferment into the scientific thought-movement, and in a space of forty years it has itself passed through a series of stages, differentiations, and transformations which have in part resulted in the present state of the theory, and have in part anticipated it. These are represented

* Some of these subsidiary factors are difficult to harmonise with the main principle of selection; they endanger it or it endangers them, as we shall see when we consider the controversies within the Darwinian camp.

by the names of workers belonging to a generation which has for the most part already passed away: Darwin's collaborateurs, such as Alfred Russel Wallace, who independently and simultaneously expounded the theory of natural selection, Haeckel and Fritz Muller, Nägeli and Askenasy, von Kolliker, Mivart, Romanes and others. The differentiation and elaboration of Darwin's theories has gone ever farther and farther; the grades and shades of doctrine held by his disciples are now almost beyond reckoning.

### Various Forms of Darwinism

The great majority of these express what may be called popular Darwinism ["Darwinismus vulgaris"], theoretically worthless, but practically possessed of great powers of attraction and propagandism. It expresses in the main a conviction, usually left unexplained, that everything "happens naturally," that man is really descended from monkeys, and that life has "evolved from lower stages" of itself, that dualism is wrong, and that monism is the truth. It is exactly the standpoint of the popular naturalism we have already described, which here mingles unsuspectingly and without scruple Lamarckian and other principles with the Darwinian, which is enthusiastic on the one hand over the "purely mechanical" interpretation of nature, and on the other drags in directly psychical motives, unconscious consciousness, impulses, spontaneous self-differentiation of organisms, which nevertheless adheres to "monism"

## VARIOUS FORMS OF DARWINISM 95

and possibly even professes to share Goethe's conception of nature!

Above this stratum we come to that of the real experts, the only one which concerns us in the least. Here too we find an ever-growing distance between divergent views, the most manifold differences amounting sometimes to mutual exclusion. These differences occur even with reference to the fundamental doctrine generally adhered to, the doctrine of descent. To one party it is a proved fact, to another a probable, scientific working hypothesis, to a third a "rescuing plank." One party is always finding fresh corroborations, another new difficulties. And within the same group we find the contrasts of believers in monophyletic and believers in polyphyletic evolution, the mechanists and the half-confessed or thoroughgoing vitalists, the preformationists and the believers in epigenesis. Opinions differ even more widely in regard to the *rôle* of the "struggle for existence" in the production of species. On the one hand we have the Darwinism of Darwin freed from inconsequent additions and formulated as orthodox "neo-Darwinism"; on the other hand we have heterodox Lamarckism. The "all-sufficiency" of natural selection is proclaimed by some, its impotence by others. Indefinite variation is opposed by orthogenesis, fluctuating variation by saltatory mutation (Halmatogenesis in "Greek"), passive adaptation by the spontaneous activity and self-regulation of the living organism. The struggle for existence is variously regarded as the chief factor, or as a co-operating factor, or as an indifferent, or even an inimical factor in the origination of new species.

And among the representatives of these different standpoints there are most interesting personal differences : in some, like Weismann, we find a great loyalty to, and persistence in the position once arrived at, in others the most surprising transitions and changes of opinion. Thus Fleischmann, a pupil of Selenka's, after illustrating during many years of personal research the orthodox Darwinian standpoint, finally developed into an outspoken opponent not only of the theory of selection but of the doctrine of descent. So also Friedmann.[*] Driesch started from the mechanical theory of life and advanced through the connected series of his own biological essays to vitalism. Romanes, a prominent disciple of Darwin, ended in Christian theism, and Wallace, the discoverer of " the struggle for existence," landed in spiritualism.

Nothing like an exhaustive view of the present state of Darwinism and its many champions can here be attempted. But it will be necessary to get to know what we may call its possibilities by a study of typical and leading examples. In the course of our study many of the problems to which the theory gives rise will reveal themselves, and their orientation will be possible.

This task falls naturally into two subdivisions : (1) the

[*] H. Friedmann, "Die Konvergenz der Organismen," Berlin, 1904.

## THE THEORY OF DESCENT

present state of the theory of Evolution and Descent, and how far the religious conception of the world is or is not affected by it, (2) the truth as to the originative and directive factors of Evolution, especially as to "natural selection in the struggle for existence," whether they are tenable and sufficient, and what attitude religion must take towards them. These two problems must be kept distinct throughout, and must be discussed in order. For the validity of what is characteristically *Darwinism* is in no way decided by proving descent and evolution, although it appears so in most popular expositions.*

### THE THEORY OF DESCENT

Again and again we hear and read, even in scientific circles and journals, that Darwinism breaks down at many points, that it is insufficient, and even that it has quite collapsed. Even the assurances of its most convinced champions are rather forced, and are somewhat suggestive of bills payable in the future.† But here again it is obvious that we must distinguish clearly between the Theory of Descent and Darwinism. Of the Theory of Descent it is by no means true that it has "broken down." With a slight exaggeration, but on the whole with justice, Weismann has asserted that the

* It is somewhat confusing that even Weismann in his most recent work professes to give "Lectures on the Theory of Descent," and in reality only assumes it, concerning himself with the Darwinian theory in the strict sense. The English translation is more correctly entitled "The Evolution Theory."

† *Cf.* Wagner, "Zur gegenwartigen Lage des Darwinismus." "Die Umschau," January, 1900.

Theory of Descent is to-day a "generally accepted truth." Even Weismann's most pronounced opponents, such as Eimer, Wolff, Reinke, and others, are at one with him in this, that there has been evolution in some form; that there has been a progressive transformation of species; that there is real (not merely ideal) relationship or affiliation connecting our modern forms of life, up to and including man, with the lower and lowest forms of bygone æons.

The evidences are the same as those adduced by Darwin and before his time, but they have been multiplied and more sharply defined:—namely, that the forms of life can be arranged in an ascending scale of evolution, both in their morphological and their physiological aspects, both as regards the general type and the differentiation of individual organs and particular characters, bodily and mental. All the rubrics used by Darwin in this connection, from comparative anatomy, from the palæontological record itself, and so on, have been filled out with ever-increasing detail. Palæontology, in particular, is continually furnishing new illustrations of descent and new evidence of its probability, more telling perhaps in respect of general features and particular groups than in regard to the historical process in detail. For certain species and genera palæontology discloses the primitive forms, discovers "synthetic types" which were the starting-point for diverging branches of evolution, bridges over or narrows the yawning gulfs in evolution by the discovery of

THE THEORY OF DESCENT 99

"intermediate forms"; and, in the case of certain species, furnishes complete genealogical trees. The same holds true of the facts of comparative anatomy, embryology, and so on. In all detailed investigations into an animal type, in the study of the structure, functions, or the instincts of an ant, or of a whale or of a tape-worm, the standpoint of the theory of descent is assumed, and it proves a useful clue for further investigation.

In regard to man—so we are assured—the theory finds confirmation through the discovery of the Neanderthal, Spy, Schipka, La Naulette skulls and bones—the remains of a prehistoric human race, with " pithecoid " (ape-like) characters. And the theory reaches its climax in Dubois' discovery of the remains of " Pithecanthropus," the upright ape-man, in Java, 1891-92, the long sought-for Missing Link between animals and man;* and in the still more recent proofs of " affinity of blood" between man and ape, furnished by experiments in transfusion. Friedenthal has revived the older experiments of transfusing the blood of one animal into another, the blood of an animal of one species into that of another, of related species into related species, more remote into more remote, and finally even from animals into man. The further apart the two species are, the more different are the physiological

* Eugen Dubois (Military Surgeon of the Dutch Army), "Pithecanthropus erectus, a man-like transition-form from Java." Batavia 1904.

characters of the blood, and the more difficult does a mingling of the two become. Blood of a too distantly related form does not unite with that of the animal into which it is transfused, but the red corpuscles of the former are destroyed by the serum of the latter, break up and are eliminated. In nearly related species or races, however, the two kinds of blood unite, as in the case of horse and ass, or of hare and rabbit. Human blood serum behaves in a hostile fashion to the blood of eel, pigeon, horse, dog, cat, and even to that of Lemuroids, or that of the more remotely related " non-anthropoid" monkey; human blood transfused from a negro into a white unites readily, as does also that of orang-utan transfused into a gibbon. But human blood also unites without any breaking-up or disturbance with the blood of a chimpanzee; from which the inference is that man is not to be placed in a separate sub-order beside the other sub-orders of the Primates, the platyrrhine and catarrhine monkeys, not even in a distinct sub order beside the catarrhines; but is to be included with them in one zoological sub-order. This classification was previously suggested by Selenka on other grounds, namely, because of the points in common in the embryonic development of the catarrhine monkeys and of man, and their common distinctiveness as contrasted with the platyrrhines.†

† H. Friedenthal. "Ueber einen experimentellen Nachweis von Blutsverwandtschaft." Archiv. f. Anatomie und Physiologie, 1900, p. 494.

## Haeckel's Evolutionist Position

The average type of the Theory of Descent of the older or orthodox school, which still lingers in the background with its Darwinism unshaken, is that set forth by Haeckel, scientifically in his "Generelle Morphologie der Organismen" (1866), and "Systematische Phylogenie" (1896), and popularly in his "Natural History of Creation" and "Riddles of the Universe," with their many editions. We may assume that it is well known, and need only briefly recall its chief characteristics. The "inestimable value," the "incomparable significance," the "immeasurable importance" of the Theory of Descent lies, according to Haeckel, in the fact that by means of it we can explain the origin of the forms of life "in a mechanical manner." The theory, especially in regard to the descent of man from the apes, is to him not a working hypothesis or tentative mode of representation; it is a result comparable to Newton's law of gravitation or the Kant-Laplace cosmogony. It is "a certain historical fact." The proofs of it are those already mentioned.

What is especially Haeckelian is the "fundamental biogenetic law," "ontogeny resembles phylogeny," that is to say, in development, especially in embryonic development, the individual recapitulates the history of the race. Through "palingenesis," man, for instance, recapitulates his ancestral stages (protist, gastræad, vermine, piscine, and simian). This recapitulation is condensed, disarranged, or obscured in detail by "cenogenesis" or "cænogenesis." The groups and types of organisms exhibit the closest genetic solidarity. The genealogical tree of man in particular runs directly through a whole series. From the realm of the protists it leads to that of the gastræadæ (nowadays represented by the Cœlentera), thence into the domain of the worms, touches the hypothetical "primitive chordates" (for the necessary existence of which "certain proofs" can be given), the class of tunicates, ascends through the fishes, amphibians and reptiles to forms parallel to the modern monotremes, then directly through the marsupials to the placentals, through lemuroids and baboons to the anthropoid apes, from them to the "famous Pithecanthropus" discovered in Java, out of which *homo sapiens* arose. (The easy transition from one group of forms to another is to be noted. For it is against this point that most of the opposition has been directed, whether from "grumbling" critics, or thoroughgoing opponents of the Theory of Descent.)

Haeckel's facile method of constructing genealogical trees, which ignores difficulties and discrepant facts, has met with much criticism and ridicule even among Darwinians. The "orator of Berlin," Du Bois-Reymond, declared that if he must read romances he would prefer to read them in some other form than that of genealogical trees. But they have at least the merit that they give a vivid impression of what is most plausible and attractive in the idea of descent, and moreover

## WEISMANN'S EVOLUTIONIST POSITION

they have helped towards orientation in the discussion. Nor can we ignore the very marked taxonomic and architectonic talent which their construction displays.

### WEISMANN'S EVOLUTIONIST POSITION

The most characteristic representative, however, of the modern school of unified and purified Darwinism is not Haeckel, but the Freiburg zoologist, Weismann. Through a long series of writings he has carried on the conflict against heterodox, and especially Lamarckian theories of evolution, and has developed his theories of heredity and the causes of variation, of the non-transmissibility of acquired characters, and the all-sufficiency of natural selection. In his latest great work, in two volumes, "Lectures on the Theory of Descent,"* he has definitely summed up and systematised his views. These will interest us when we come to inquire into the problem of the factors operative in evolution. For the moment we are only concerned with his attitude to the Theory of Descent as such. It is precisely the same as Haeckel's, although he is opposed to Haeckel in regard to the strictly Darwinian standpoint. The Theory of Descent has conquered, and it may be said with assurance, for ever. That is the firm conviction on which the whole work is based, and it is really rather treated as a self-evident axiom than as a statement to be proved. Weismann takes little trouble to

* Jena, 1904. Trans. "The Evolution Theory," Arnold. London, 1904.

prove it. All the well-known, usually very clear proofs from palæontology, comparative anatomy, &c., which we are accustomed to meet with in evolutionist books are wanting here, the genealogical trees of the Equidæ, with the gradually diminishing number of toes and the varying teeth, of *Planorbis multiformis*, of the ammonites, the graduated series of stages exhibited by individual organs, for instance, from the ganglion merely sensitive to light up to the intricate eye, or from the rayed skeleton of the paired fins in fishes up to the five-fingered hands and feet of the higher vertebrates, &c. These are only briefly touched upon in the terse "Introduction," and the whole of the comprehensive work is then directed to showing what factors can have been operative, and to proving that they must have been "Darwinian" (selection in the struggle for existence), and not Lamarckian or any other. This is shown in regard to the coloration of animals, the phenomena of mimicry, the protective arrangements of plants, the development of instinct in animals, and the origin of flowers.

In reality Weismann only adduces *one* strict proof, and even that is only laying special stress on what is well known in comparative embryology; namely, the possibility of "predicting" on the basis of the theory of descent, as Leverrier "predicted" Neptune. For instance, in the lower vertebrates from amphibians upwards there is an *os centrale* in the skeleton of wrist, but there is none in man. Now if man be descended

## WEISMANN'S EVOLUTIONIST POSITION

from lower vertebrates, and if the fundamental biogenetic law be true (that every form of life recapitulates in its own development, especially in its embryonic development, the evolution of its race, though with abbreviations and condensations), it may be predicted that the *os centrale* is to be found in the early embryonic stages of man. And Rosenberg found it. In the same way the "gill-clefts" of the fish-like ancestors have long since been discovered in the embryo of the higher vertebrates and of man. Weismann himself "predicted" that the markings of the youngest stage of the caterpillars of the Sphingidæ (hawk-moths) would be found to be not oblique but longitudinal stripes, and ten years later a fortunate observation verified the prediction. Because of the abundance of evidential facts Weismann does not go into any detailed proof of evolution. "One can hardly take up any work, large or small, on the finer or more general structural relations, or on the development of any animal, without finding in it proofs for the evolution theory."

But assured as the doctrine of descent appears,* and certain as it is that it has not only maintained its hold since Darwin's day, but has strengthened it and has gained adherents, this foundation of Darwinism is

* A defence of this very confident Darwinian point of view, for the benefit of non-scientific readers, will be found in the recent "Gemeinverstandlichen darwinistischen Vortragen und Abhandlungen," by Plate, Simroth, Schmidt, and others. See also Ziegler's "Ueber den derzeitigen Stand der Descendenzlehre in der Zoologie."

nevertheless not the unanimous and inevitable conclusion of all scientific men in the sense and to the extent that the utterances of Weismann and others would lead us to suppose. Apart from all apologetic attempts either in religious, ethical, or æsthetic interests, apart, too, from the superior standpoint of the philosophers, who have not, so to speak, taken the theory very seriously, but regard it as a provisional theory, as a more or less necessary and useful method of grouping our ideas in regard to the organic world, there are even among the biologists themselves some who, indifferent towards religious or philosophical or naturalistic dogma, hold strictly to fact, and renounce with nonchalance any pretensions at completeness of knowledge if the data do not admit of it, and on these grounds hold themselves aloof from evolutionist generalisation. From among these come the counsels of "caution," admissions that the theory is a scientific hypothesis and a guide to research, but not knowledge, and confessions that the Theory of Descent as a whole is verifiable rather as a general impression than in detail.

### Virchow's Position

Warnings of this kind have come occasionally from Du Bois-Reymond, but the true type of this group, and its mode of thought, is Virchow. It will repay us and suffice us to make acquaintance with it through him. His opposition to Darwinism and the theory of descent was directed at its most salient point: the

## VIRCHOW'S POSITION 107

descent of man from the apes. In lectures and treatises, at zoological and anthropological congresses, especially at the meetings of his own Anthropological-Ethnological Society in Berlin, from his " Vortrage uber Menschen-und Affen-Schadel " (Lectures on the Skulls of Man and Apes, 1869), to the disputes over Dubois' *Pithecanthropus erectus* in the middle of the nineties, he threw the whole weight of his immense learning— ethnological and anthropological, osteological, and above all " craniological "—into the scale against the Theory of Descent and its supporters. Virchow has therefore been reckoned often enough among the anti-Darwinians, and has been quoted by apologists and others as against Darwinism, and he has given reason for this, since he has often taken the field against " the Darwinists " or has scoffed at their " longing for a pro-anthropos." * Sometimes even it has been suggested that he was actuated by religious motives, as when he occasionally championed not only freedom for science, but, incidentally, the right of existence for "the churches," leaving, for instance, in his theory of psychical life, gaps in knowledge which faith might occupy in moderation and modesty. But this last proves nothing. With Virchow's altogether unemotional nature it is unlikely that religious or spiritual motives had any rôle in the establishment of his convictions, and in Haeckel's naive blustering at religion, there is, so to speak, more

* " Rassenbildung und Erblichkeit," Festschrift fur Bastian, p. 9

religion than in the cold-blooded connivance with which Virchow leaves a few openings in otherwise frozen ponds for the ducks of faith to swim in! And he has nothing of the pathos of Du Bois-Reymond's "ignorabimus." He is the neutral, prosaic scientist, who will let nothing "tempt him to a transcendental consideration,"* either theological or naturalistic, who holds tenaciously to matters of fact, who, without absolutely rejecting a general theory, will not concern himself about it, except to point out every difficulty in the way of it; in short, he is the representative of a mood that is the ideal of every investigator and the despair of every theoriser.

His lecture of 1869 already indicates his subsequent attitude. "Considered logically and speculatively" the Theory of Descent seems to him "excellent,"† indeed a logical moral (!) hypothesis, but unproved in itself, and erroneous in many of its particular propositions. As far back as 1858, before the publication of Darwin's great work, he stated at the Naturalists' Congress in Carlsruhe, that the origin of one species out of another appeared to him a necessary scientific inference, but—— And throughout the whole lecture he alternates between favourable recognition of the theory in general, and emphasis of the difficulties which confront it in detail. The skull, which, according to Goethe's theory, has

* "Rassenbildung und Erblichkeit," Festschrift fur Bastian, p 6.
† "Sammlung gemeinverstandl. Vortrage, hrsg. v. Virchow und Holtzendorf," Heft 96. "Menschen- und Affenschadel," Berlin, 1870

## VIRCHOW'S POSITION 109

evolved from three modified vertebræ, is fundamentally different in man and monkeys, both in regard to its externals, crests, ridges and shape, and especially in regard to the nature of the cavity which it forms for the brain. Specifically distinctive differences in the development and structure of the rest of the body must also be taken into account. The so-called ape-like structures in the skull and the rest of the body, which occasionally occur in man (idiots, microcephaloids, &c.) cannot be regarded as atavisms and therefore as proofs of the Theory of Descent; they are of a pathological nature, entirely facts *sui generis*, and " not to be placed in a series with the normal results of evolution." A man modified by disease " is still thoroughly a man, not a monkey."

Virchow continued to maintain this attitude and persisted in this kind of argument. He energetically rejected all attempts to find " pithecoid " characters in the prehistoric remains of man. He declared the narrow and less arched forehead, the elliptical form, and the unusually large frontal cavities of the " Neanderthal skull " found in the Wupperthal in 1856, to be simply pathological features, which occur as such in certain examples of *homo sapiens*.* He explained the abnormal appearance of the jaw from the Moravian cave of Schipka as a result of the retention of teeth,† accompanied by directly " antipithecoid " characters.

* " Zeitschrift fur Ethnologie," 1882, p 276.
† " Verh. Berlin anthropolog. Gesellschaft iv " (1872), p. 132. It

The proceedings at the meetings of the Ethnological Society in 1895, at which Dubois was present, had an almost dramatic character.* In the diverse opinions of Dubois, Virchow, Nehring, Kollmann, Krause and others, we have almost an epitome of the present state of the Darwinian question. Virchow doubted whether the parts put together by Dubois (the head of a femur, two molar teeth, and the top of a skull) belonged to the same individual at all, disputed the calculations as to the large capacity of the skull, placed against Dubois' very striking and clever drawing of the curves of the skull-outline, which illustrated, with the help of the Pithecanthropus, the gradual transition from the skull of a monkey to that of man, his own drawing, according to which the Pithecanthropus curve simply coincides with that of a gibbon (*Hylobates*), and asserted that the remains discovered were those of a species of gibbon, refusing even to admit that they represented a new genus of monkeys. He held fast to his *ceterum censeo* : " As yet no diluvial discovery has been made which can be referred to a man of a pithecoid type." Indeed, his polemic or " caution " in regard to the Theory of Descent went even further. He not only refused to admit the proof of the descent of man from monkey, he would not even allow that the descent of one race from another has been demon-

does, however, appear strange to the lay mind that it should have been only the pathological subjects of prehistoric times that had their remains preserved for our modern study

\* *Cf.* " Zeitschrift fur Ethnologie," 1895, pp. 78, 735.

## THE THEORY OF DESCENT 111

strated.* In spite of all the plausible hypotheses it remains "so far only a *pium desiderium*." The race obstinately maintains its specific distinctness, and resists variation, or gradual transformation into another. The negro remains a negro in America, and the European colonist of Australia remains a European.

Yet all Virchow's opposition may be summed up in the characteristic words, which might almost be called his motto, " I warn you of the need for caution," and it is not a seriously-meant rejection of the Theory of Descent. In reality he holds the evolution-idea as an axiom, and in the last-named treatise he shows distinctly how he conceives of the process. He starts with variation (presumably "kaleidoscopic"), which comes about as a "pathological" phenomenon, that is to say, not spontaneously, but as the result of environmental stimulus, as the organism's reaction to climatic and other conditions of life. The result is an alteration of previous characteristics, and a new stable race is established by an "acquired anomaly."†

OTHER INSTANCES OF DISSATISFACTION WITH THE
THEORY OF DESCENT.

What was with Virchow only a suggestion of the

\* *Cf.* "Rassenbildung und Erblichkeit." Festschrift fur Bastian, 1895.

† See also " Descendenz und Pathologie " Arch f. path. Anat. u. Physiol., 1886 , "Transformation und Abstammung." Berliner Klin. Wochenschrift, 1893.

need for caution, or controversial matter to be subsequently allowed for or contradicted, had more serious consequences to others, and led to still greater hesitancy as regards evolutionist generalisations and speculations, and sometimes to sharp antagonism to them.

One of the best known of the earlier examples of this mood is Kerner von Marilaun's large and beautiful work on "Plant Life."* He does, indeed, admit that our species are variations of antecedent forms, but only in a very limited sense. Within the stocks or grades of organisation which have always existed, variations have come about, through "hybridisation," through the crossing of similar, but relatively different forms; these variations alter the configuration and appearance in detail, but neither affect the general character nor cause any transition from "lower" to "higher."

Kerner disposes of the chief argument in favour of the theory of descent, the homology of individual organs, by explaining that the homology is due to the similarity of function in the different organisms. A similar argument is used in regard to "ontogeny recapitulating phylogeny." Palæontology does not disclose in the plant-world any "synthetic types," which might have been the common primitive stock from which many now divergent branches have sprung, nor does it disclose any "transition links" really inter-

* First edition, Leipzig, 1887. A second edition and an English translation have since been published. See especially the discussion of the origin and history of species in the second volume.

THE THEORY OF DESCENT 113

mediate, for instance, between cryptogams and gymnosperms, or between gymnosperms and angiosperms. That the higher races are apparently absent from the earlier strata is not a proof that they have never existed. The peat-bog flora must have involved the existence of a large companion-flora, without which the peat could not have been formed, but all trace of this is absent in the still persistent vestiges of these times.* Life, with energy and matter, has existed as a phenomenon of the universe from all eternity, and thus its chief forms and manifestations have not "arisen," but have always been. If facts such as these contradict the Kant-Laplace theory of the universe, then the latter must be corrected in the light of them, not conversely. The extreme isolation of Kerner and his theory is probably due especially to this corollary of his views.

Among the most recent examples of antagonism to the Evolution-Theory, the most interesting is a book by Fleischmann, professor of zoology in Erlangen, published in 1901, and entitled, "The Theory of Descent." It consists of "popular lectures on the rise and decline of a scientific hypothesis" (namely, the Theory of Descent), and it is a complete recantation by a quondam Darwinian of the doctrine of his school, even of its fundamental proposition, the concept of evolution itself. For Fleischmann is not guilty, like Weismann, of the inaccuracy of using "Theory of

* See English translation of Kerner's "Plant Life."

Descent" as equivalent to Darwinism; he is absolutely indifferent to the theory of natural selection. His book keeps strictly to matters of fact, and rejects as speculation everything in the least beyond these; it does not express even an opinion on the question of the origin of species, but merely criticises and analyses.

It does not bring forward any new and overwhelming arguments in refutation of the Theory of Descent, but strongly emphasises difficulties that have always beset it, and discusses these in detail. The old dispute which interested Goethe, Geoffroy St. Hilaire, and Cuvier, as to the unity or the fundamental heterogeneity of the "architectural plan" in nature is revived. Modern zoology recognises not merely the four types of Cuvier, but seventeen different styles, "phyla," or groups of forms, to derive one of which from another is hopeless. And what is true of the whole is true also of the subdivisions within each phylum; *e.g.*, within the vertebrate phylum with its fishes, amphibians, reptiles, birds and mammals. No bridge leads from one to the other. This is proved particularly by the very instance which is the favourite illustration in support of the Theory of Descent—the fin of fishes and its relation to the five-fingered hand of vertebrates. The so-called transition forms (Archæopteryx, monotremes, &c.) are discredited. So with the "stalking-horse" of evolutionists—the genealogical tree of the Equidæ, which is said to be traceable palæontologically right back, without a break, from the one-toed horses of the present day to

THE THEORY OF DESCENT 115

the normal five-toed ancestry; and so with another favourite instance of evolution, the history of the pond-snails (*Planorbis multiformis*), the numerous varieties of which occur with transitions between them in actual contiguity in the Steinheim beds, and thus seem to afford an obvious example of the transformation of species. Against these cases, and against using the palæontological archives as a basis for the construction of genealogical trees in general, the weighty and apparently decisive objection is urged, that nowhere are the soft parts of the earlier forms of life preserved, and that it is impossible to establish relationships with any certainty on the basis of hard parts only, such as bones, teeth and shells. Even Haeckel admits that snails of very different bodily structure may form very similar and even hardly distinguishable shells.

Fleischmann further asserts that Haeckel's "fundamental biogenetic law" has utterly collapsed. "Recapitulation" does not occur. Selenka's figures of ovum-segmentation show that there are specific differences in the individual groups. The origin and development of the blastoderm or germinal disc has nothing to do with recapitulation of the phylogeny. It is not the case that the embryos of higher vertebrates are indistinguishable from one another. Even the egg-cell has a specific character, and is totally different from any unicellular organism at the Protistan level. The much-cited "gill-clefts" of higher vertebrates in the embryonic stage are not persistent reminiscences of earlier lower stages; they are rudiments or primordia shared by all vertebrates, and developing differently at the different levels; (thus in fishes they become breathing organs, and in the higher vertebrates they become in part associated with the organs of hearing, or in part disappear again).

Though Fleischmann's vigorous protest against over-hastiness in construction and over-confidence on the part of the adherents of the doctrine of descent is very interesting, and may often be justified in detail, it is difficult to resist the impression that the wheat has been rejected with the chaff.*

Even a layman may raise the following objections: Admitting that the great groups of forms cannot be traced back to one another, the palæontological record still proves, though it may be only in general outline, that within each phylum there has been a gradual succession and ascent of forms. How is the origin of what is new to be accounted for? Without doing violence to our thinking, without a sort of intellectual autonomy, we cannot rest content with the mere fact that new elements occur. So, in spite of all "difficulties," the assumption of *an actual descent* quietly forces itself upon us as the only satisfactory clue. And the fact, which Fleischmann does not discuss, that even at present we may observe the establishment of what are at least new breeds, impels us to accept an analogous

* *Cf.* a criticism of the book from the Darwinian point of view by Plate in Biologisches Centralblatt, 1901.

THE THEORY OF DESCENT 117

origin of new species. Even if the biogenetic law really "finds its chief confirmation in its exceptions," even if we cannot speak of a strict recapitulation of earlier stages of evolution, there are indisputable facts which are most readily interpreted as reminiscences, as due to affiliation (ideal or hereditary), with ancestral forms. (Note, for instance, Weismann's "prediction," &c.*) Even if Archæopteryx and other intermediate forms cannot be regarded as connecting links in the strict sense, i.e., as being stages in the actual pedigree, yet the occurrence of reptilian and avian peculiarities side by side in one organism, goes far to prove the close relationship of the two classes.

Fleischmann's book strengthens the impression gained elsewhere, that a general survey of the domain of life as a whole gives force and convincingness to the Theory of Descent, while a study of details often results in breaking the threads and bringing the difficulties into prominence. But the same holds true of many other theoretical constructions, and yet we do not seriously doubt their validity. (Take, for instance, the Kant-Laplace theory, and theories of ethnology, of the history of religion, of the history of language, and so on.) And it is quite commonly to be observed that those who have an expert and specialist knowledge, who are aware of the refractoriness of detailed facts, often take up a sceptical attitude towards every comprehen-

* That this points only to the fact of evolution, and not necessarily to actual descent, will be seen later on.

sive theory, though the ultimate use of detailed investigation is to make the construction of general theories possible. Fleischmann does exactly what, say, an anthropologist would do if, under the impression of the constancy and distinctiveness of the human races, which would become stronger the more deeply he penetrated, he should resignedly renounce all possibility of affiliating them, and should rest content with the facts as he found them. Similarly, those who are most intimately acquainted with the races of domesticated animals often resist most strenuously all attempts, although these seem to others a matter of course, to derive our " tame " forms from " wild" species living in freedom.

But to return. Even where the Theory of Descent is recognised, whether fully or only half-heartedly, the recognition does not always mean the same thing. Even the adherents of the general, but in itself quite vague view that a transformation from lower forms to higher, and from similar to different forms, has taken place, may present so many points of disagreement, and may even stand in such antagonism to one another, that onlookers are apt to receive the impression that they occupy quite different standpoints, and are no longer at one even in the fundamentals of their hypotheses.

The most diverse questions and answers crop up; whether evolution has been brought about "monophyletically" or "polyphyletically," *i.e.*, through one or many genealogical trees ; whether it has taken place in

THE THEORY OF DESCENT 119

a continuous easy transition from one type to another, or by leaps and bounds; whether through a gradual transformation of all organs, each varying individually, or through correlated "kaleidoscopic" variations of many kinds throughout the whole system; whether it is essentially asymptotic, or whether organisms pass from "labile" phases of vital equilibrium by various halting-places to stable states, which are definitive, and are, so to speak, the blind alleys and terminal points of evolutionary possibilities, *e.g.*, the extinct gigantic saurians, and perhaps also man. And to these problems must be added the various answers to the question, What precedes, or may have preceded, the earliest stages of life of which we know ? Whence came the first cell ? Whence the first living protoplasm ? and How did the living arise from the inorganic ? These deeper questions will occupy us in our chapter on the theory of life. Some of the former, in certain of their aspects, will be considered in the sixth chapter, which deals with factors in evolution.

The Theory of Descent itself and the differences that obtain even among its adherents can best be studied by considering for a little the works of Reinke and of Hamann.

Reinke, Professor of Botany in Kiel, has set forth his views in his book, "Die Welt als Tat," \* and more recently in his " Einleitung in die theoretische Biologie" (1901). Both books are addressed to a wide

\* First edition, 1899, now in a second edition.

circle of readers. Reinke and Hamann both revive some of the arguments and opinions set forth in the early days of Darwinism by Wigand,* an author whose works are gradually gaining increased appreciation.

It is Reinke's " unalterable conviction " that organisms have evolved, and that they have done so after the manner of fan-shaped genealogical trees. The Theory of Descent is to him an axiom of modern biology, though as a matter of fact the circumstantial evidence in favour of it is extremely fragmentary. The main arguments in favour of it appear to him to be the general ones; the homologies and analogies revealed by comparative morphology and physiology, the ascending series in the palæontological record, vestigial organs, parasitic degeneration, the origin of those vital associations which we call consortism and symbiosis. These he illustrates mainly by examples from his own special domain and personal observation.

The simplest unicellular forms of life are to be thought of as at the beginning of evolution; and, since mechanical causes cannot explain their ascent, it must be assumed that they have an inherent "phylogenetic potential of development," which, working epigenetically, results in ascending evolution. He leaves us to choose between monophyletic and polyphyletic evolution, but himself inclines towards the latter, associating with it a

* "Genealogie der Urzellen als Lösung des Descendenzproblems" (1872), and " Der Darwinismus und die Naturforschung Newtons und Cuviers" (1874–1877).

## THE THEORY OF DESCENT 121

rehabilitation of Wigand's theory of the primitive cells. If, in the beginning, primitive forms of life arose (probably as unicellulars) from the not-living, it is not obvious why we need think of only one so arising, and, if many did so, why they should not have inherent differences which would at once result in typically different evolutionary series and groups of forms. But evolution does not go on *ad libitum* or *ad infinitum*, for the capacity for differentiation and transformation gradually diminishes. The organisation passes from a labile state of equilibrium to an increasingly stable state, and at many points it may reach a terminus where it comes to a standstill. Man, the dog, the horse, the cereals, and fruit trees appear to Reinke to have reached their goal. The preliminary stages he calls "Phylembryos," because they bear to the possible outcome of their evolution the same relation that the embryo does to the perfect individual. Thus, *Phenacodus* may be regarded as the Phylembryo of the modern horse. It is quite conceivable that each of our modern species may have had an independent series of Phylembryos reaching back to the primitive cells. But the palæontological record, and especially its synthetic types, lead Reinke rather to assume that instead of innumerable series, there have been branching genealogical trees, not one, however, but several.

These views, together or separately, which are characterised chiefly by the catch-words "polyphyletic descent," "labile and stable equilibrium," and so on, crop up together or separately in the writings of various evolutionists belonging to the opposition wing. They are usually associated with a denial of the theory of natural selection, and with theories of "Orthogenesis," "Heterogenesis," and "Epigenesis."

We shall discuss them later when we are considering the factors in evolution. But we must first take notice of a work in which the theories opposed to Darwinian orthodoxy have been most decisively and aggressively set forth. As far back as 1892 O. Hamann, then a lecturer on zoology in Gottingen, gathered these together and brought them into the field, against Haeckel in particular, in his book "Entwicklungslehre und Darwinismus." *

Hamann's main theme is that Darwinism overlooks the fact that "there cannot have been an origin of higher types from types already finished." For this "unfortunate and unsupported assumption" there are no proofs in embryology, palæontology, or anatomy. He adopts and expands the arguments and anti-Haeckelian deliverances of His in embryology, of Snell and Heer in palæontology, of Kolliker and von Baer in their special interpretation of evolution, of Snell particularly as regards the descent of man. It is impossible to derive Metazoa from Protozoa in their present finished state of evolution; even the Amoeba is so exactly adapted in organisation and functional activity

* "Eine kritische Darstellung der modernen Entwicklungslehre," Jena, 1892.

THE THEORY OF DESCENT 123

to the conditions of its existence that it is a "finished" type. It is only by a stretch of fancy that fishes can be derived from worms, or higher vertebrates from fishes. One of his favourite arguments—and it is a weighty one, though neglected by the orthodox Darwinians—is that living substance is capable, under similar stimuli, of developing spontaneously and afresh, at quite different points and in different groups, similar organs, such as spots sensitive to light, accumulations of pigment, eye-spots, lenses, complete eyes, and similarly with the notochord, the excretory organs, and the like. Therefore homology of organs is no proof of their hereditary affiliation.* They rather illustrate "iterative evolution."

Another favourite argument is the fact of "Pædogenesis." Certain animals, such as *Amphioxus lanceolatus*, *Peripatus*, and certain Medusæ, are very frequently brought forward as examples of persistent primitive stages and "transitional connecting links." But considered from the point of view of Pædogenesis, they all assume quite a different aspect, and seem rather to represent very highly evolved species, and to be, not primitive forms, but conservative and regressive forms. Pædogenesis is the phenomenon exhibited by a number of species, which may stop short at one of the stages of their embryonic or larval development, become sexually mature, and produce

* Compare Darwin's derivation of fishes from Tunicata because of the notochord which occurs in the tunicate larvæ.

offspring without having attained their own fully developed form.

Another argument is the old, suggestive, and really important one urged by Kolliker, that "inorganic nature shows a natural system among minerals (crystals) just as much as animals and plants do, yet in the former there can be no question of any genetic connection in the production of forms."

Yet another argument is found in the occurrence of "inversions" and anomalies in the palæontological succession of forms, which to some extent upsets the Darwinian-Haeckelian genealogical trees. (Thus there are forms in the Cambrian whose alleged ancestors do not appear till the Silurian. Foraminifera and other Protozoa do not appear till the Silurian.)

From embryology in particular, as elsewhere in general, we read the "fundamental biogenetic law," that evolution is from the general to the special, from the imperfect to the more perfect, from what is still indefinite and exuberant to the well-defined and precise, but never from the special to the special. According to Hamann's hypothesis we must think of evolution as going on, so to speak, not about the top but about the bottom. The phyla or groups of forms are great trunks bearing many branches and twigs, but not giving rise to one another. Still less do the little side branches of one trunk bear the whole great trunk of another animal or plant phylum. But they all grow from the same roots among the primitive forms of life. Unicellulars these must

THE THEORY OF DESCENT 125

have been, but not like our "Protists." They should be thought of as primitive forms having within themselves the potentialities of the most diverse and widely separate evolution-series to which they gave rise, as it were, along diverging fan-like rays.

It would be instructive to follow some naturalist into his own particular domain, for instance a palæontologist into the detailed facts of palæontology, or an embryologist into those of embryology, in order to learn whether these corroborate the assumptions of the Theory of Descent or not. It is just in relation to these detailed facts that criticisms or even denials of the theory have been most frequent. Koken, otherwise a convinced supporter of the theory, inquires in his "Vorwelt," *apropos* of the tortoises, what has become of the genealogical trees that were scattered abroad in the world as proved facts in the early days of Darwinism. He asserts, in regard to *Archæopteryx*, the instance which is always put forward as the intermediate link in the evolution of birds, that it does not show in any of its characters a fundamental difference from any of the birds of to-day, and further, that, through convergent development under similar influences, similar organs and structural relations result, iterative arrangements which come about quite independently of descent. He maintains, too, that the principle of the struggle for existence is rather disproved than corroborated by the palæontological record.

In embryology, so competent an authority as

O. Hertwig—himself a former pupil of Haeckel's—has reacted from the "fundamental biogenetic law." His theory of the matter is very much that of Hamann which we have already discussed; development is not so much a recapitulation of finished ancestral types as the laying down of foundations after the pattern of generalised simple forms, not yet specialised; and from these foundations the special organs rise to different levels and grades of differentiation according to the type.* But we must not lose ourselves in details.

Looking back over the whole field once more, we feel that we are justified in maintaining with some confidence that the different pronouncements in regard to the detailed application and particular features of the Theory of Descent, and the different standpoints that are occupied even by evolutionists, are at least sufficient to make it obvious that, even if evolution and descent have actually taken place, they have not run so simple and smooth a course as the over-confident would have us believe; that the Theory of Descent rather emphasises than clears away the riddles and difficulties of the case, and that with the mere corroboration of the theory we shall have gained only something relatively external, a clue to creation, which does not so much solve its problems as restate them. The whole criticism of the "right wing," from captious objections to actual denials, proves this indisputably. And it seems likely that in the course of time a sharpening of

* See Hertwig's "Biological Problem of To-day." London 1896.

## THE THEORY OF DESCENT

the critical insight and temper will give rise to further reactions from the academic theory as we have come to know it.* On the other hand, it may be assumed with even greater certainty that the general evolutionist point of view and the great arguments for descent in some form or other will ultimately be victorious if they are not so already, and that, sooner or later, we shall take the Theory of Descent in its most general form as a matter of course, just as we now do the Kant-Laplace theory.

* The justice of this prophecy has been meanwhile illustrated by the recent work of H Friedmann " Die Konvergenz der Organismen," Berlin, 1904

# CHAPTER V

### RELIGION AND THE THEORY OF DESCENT

In seeking to define our position in regard to the theory of descent it is most important that we should recognise that, when it is looked into closely, the true problem at issue is not a special zoological one, but is quite general, and also that it is not a new growth which has sprung up suddenly and found us unprepared, but that it is very ancient and has long existed in our midst. In the whole theory the question of "descent" is after all a mere accessory. Even if it fell through and were seen to be scientifically undemonstrable, "evolution in the realm of life" would remain an indisputable fact, and with it there would arise precisely the same difficulties for the religious interpretation of the world which are usually attributed to the Theory of Descent.

Evolution or development has been a prominent idea in the history of thought since the time of Aristotle, but descent is, so to speak, a modern upstart. According to long-established modes of thought, to *evolve* means to pass from δυνάμει to ἐνεργεία εἶναι, from *potentia* to *actus*, from the existence of the rudiment as in the seed to full realisation as in the tree. In the course of its

## RELIGION AND EVOLUTION

development the organism passes through many successive phases, which are related to one another like steps, each rising directly from the one beneath, and preparing for the one above. Thus all nature, and especially the realm of life, implies a ladder of " evolution." What is " potentially " inherent in the lowest form of life has in the highest, as in man, become actual or "realised" through a continuous sequence of phases, successively more and more evolved. This view in its earlier forms was very far from implying that each higher step was literally "descended" from the one below it, through the physical and mental transformation of some of its representatives. As the world, in Aristotle's view for instance, had existed from all eternity, so also had the stages and forms of life, each giving rise again to its like. Indeed, the essential idea was that each higher step is simply a development, a fuller unfolding of the lower stage, and finally that man was the complete realisation of what was potentially inherent in the lowest of all.

This doctrine of evolution was in modern times the fundamental idea of Leibnitz and Kant, of Goethe, Schelling and Hegel. It brought unity and connectedness into the system of nature, united everything by steps, denied the existence of gaping chasms, and proclaimed the solidarity of all the forms of life. But to all this the idea of actual descent was unnecessary. An actual material variation and transition from one stage to another seemed to it a wooden and gross expression of the evolution idea, an "all too childish and nebulous hypothesis" (Hegel).

All the important results of comparative morphology and physiology, which the modern supporters of the doctrine of descent so confidently utilise as arguments in its favour, would have been welcomed by those who held the original and general evolution idea, as a corroboration of their own standpoint. And as a matter of fact they all afford conclusive proofs of *evolution*, but not one of them, including even the fundamental biogenetic law and the inoculated chimpanzee, is decisive in regard to *descent*. This contention is sufficiently important to claim our attention for a little. Let us take the last example. Transfusion of blood between two species is possible, not necessarily because they are descended from one another or from a common root, but solely because of their systematic (ideal) relationship, that is to say because they are sufficiently near to one another and like one another in their physiological qualities and functions. If, assuming descent, this homology were disturbed, and the systematic relationship done away with, for instance through saltatory evolution, the mere fact of descent would not bring the two species any nearer one another. Thus the case proves only systematic relationship, and only evolution. But as to the meaning of this systematic relationship, whether it can be "explained" by descent, whether it has existed from all eternity, or how it has arisen, the experiment does not inform us.

# RELIGION AND EVOLUTION 131

The same idea may be illustrated in regard to Weismann's "predicting." This, too, is a proof of evolution, but not of descent. Exactly as Weismann predicted the striping of the hawk-moth caterpillars and the human *os centrale*, Goethe predicted the formation of the skull from modified vertebræ, and the premaxillary bone in man. In precisely the same way he "derived" the cavities in the human skull from those of the animal skull. This was quite in keeping with the manner and style of his Goddess Nature and her creative transformations, raising the type of her creations from stage to stage, developing and expanding each new type from an earlier one, yet keeping the later analogous to and recapitulative of the earlier, recording the earlier by means of vestigial and gradually dwindling parts.

But what has all this to do with descent? Even the "biogenetic law" itself, especially if it were correct, would fit admirably into the frame of the pure evolution idea. For it is quite consistent with that idea to say that the higher type in the course of its development, especially in its embryonic stages, passes through stages representative of the forms of life which are below it and precede it in the (ideal) genealogical tree. Indeed, the older doctrine of evolution took account of this long ago.

"The same step-ladder which is exhibited by the whole animal kingdom, the steps of which are the different races and classes, with at the one extreme the lowliest animals and at the other the highest, is exhibited also by every higher animal in its development, since from the moment of its origin until it has reached its full development it passes through—both as regards internal and external organisation—the essentials of all the forms which become permanent for a lifetime in the animals lower than itself. The more perfect the animal is, the longer is the series of forms it passes through."

So J. Fr. Meckel wrote in 1812 in his "Handbook of Pathological Anatomy," *with no thought of descent*. And the facts which led to the construction of the biogenetic law were discovered in no small measure by Agassiz, who was an opponent of the doctrine of descent.\*

But the advance from the doctrine of evolution to that of descent was imperatively prompted by a recognition of

---

\* If we wish to, we can even read the " biogenetic law " in Dante. See "Purgatory," p. 25, where the embryo attains successively to the plant, animal and human stages :

"Anima fatta la virtute attiva,
   Qual d'una *pianta*. . .
   . . . . . .
   Come fungo marino . . .
   . . . . . .
   Ma come *d'animal* divenga *fante* "

This is, of course, nothing else than Aristotle's theory of evolution, done into terzarima, and corrected by St. Thomas.

For the latest application of these views, even in relation to the "biogenetic fundamental law," see the finely finished "Morphogenetic Studies" of T. Garbowski (Jena, 1903) : "The greater part of what is usually referred to the so-called fundamental biogenetic law depends on illusion, since all things undeveloped or imperfect must bear a greater or less resemblance one to another."

## RELIGION AND EVOLUTION 133

the fact that the earth is not from everlasting, and that the forms of life upon it are likewise not from everlasting, that, in fact, their several grades appear in an orderly ascending series. It is therefore simpler and more plausible to suppose that each higher step has arisen from the one before it, than to suppose that each has, so to speak, begun an evolution on its own account. A series of corroborative arguments might be adduced, and there is no doubt, as we have said before, that the transition from the general idea of evolution to that of descent will be fully accomplished. But it is plain that the special idea of descent contributes nothing essentially new on the subject.

It is an oft-repeated and self-evident statement, that it is in reality a matter of entire indifference whether man arose from the dust of the earth or from living matter already formed, or, let us say, from one of the higher vertebrates. The question still would be, how much or how little of any of them does he still retain, and how far does he differ from all? Even if there be really descent, the difference may quite as well be so great —for instance, through saltatory development—that man, in spite of physical relationship, might belong to quite a new category far transcending all his ancestors in his intellectual characteristics, in his emotional and moral qualities. There is nothing against the assumption, and there is much to be said in its favour, that the last step from animal to man was such an immense one that it brought with it a freedom and richness of psychical life incomparable with anything that had gone before—as if life here realised itself for the first time in very truth, and made everything that previously had been a mere preliminary play.

On the other hand, even were there no descent but separate individual creation, man might, in virtue of his ideal relationship and evolution, appear nothing more than a stage relatively separate from those beneath him in evolution. It was not the doctrine of descent, it was the doctrine of evolution that first ranked man in a series with the rest of creation, and regarded him as the development of what is beneath him and leads up to him through a gradual sequence of stages. And his nearness, analogy, or relationship to what is beneath him is in no way increased by descent, or rendered a whit more intimate or more disturbing.

### The Problema Continui.

The problem of descent thus shows itself to be one which has neither isolated character nor special value. It is an accessory accompaniment of all the questions and problems which have been raised by, or are associated with, the doctrine of evolution, which would have been in our midst without Darwin, which are made neither easier nor more difficult by zoological knowledge, and the difficulties of which, if solved, would solve at the same time any difficulties presented by descent. The following considerations will serve to make this clear. The most oppressive corollary of the doctrine of descent is undoubtedly that through it the human race seems to become lost in the infra-human, from which it cannot be separated by any hard and fast boundaries, or absolute lines of demarcation. But it is easy to see that this problem is in fact only a part of a larger problem, and that it can really be solved only through the larger one. Even if it were possible to do away with this unpleasing inference as regards the whole human race, so that it could be in some way separated off securely from the animal kingdom, the same fatality would remain in regard to each individual human being. For we have here to face the problem of individual development by easy transitions, the ascent from the animal to the human state, and the question : When is there really soul and spirit, when man and ego, when freedom and responsibility? But this is the same problem again, only written with smaller letters, the general *problema continui* in the domain of life and mind. And the problem is very far-reaching. In all questions concerning mental health and disease, abnormalities or cases of arrest at an early stage of mental development, concerning the greater or less degree of endowment for intellectual, moral, and religious life, down to utter absence of capacity, and this in relation to individuals as well as races and peoples, and times ; and again, concerning the gradual development of the ethical and religious consciousness in the long course of history, in its continuity and gradual transition from lower to higher forms: everywhere we meet this same *problema continui*. And our oppressive difficulty is bound up with this problem, and can be dispelled only by its solution, for the gist of the difficulty is nothing else than the *gradualness of human becoming*.

This is not the place for a thoroughgoing discussion of this *problema continui*. We can only call to mind here that the "evolution idea" has been the doctrine of the great philosophical systems from Aristotle to Leibnitz, and of the great German idealist philosophers, in whose school the religious interpretation of the world is at home. We may briefly emphasise the most important considerations to be kept in mind in forming a judgment as to gradual development.

1. To recognise anything as in course of evolving does not mean that we understand its "becoming." The true inwardness of "becoming" is hidden in the mystery of the transcendental.

2. The gradual origin of the highest and most perfect from the primitive in no way affects the specific character, the uniqueness and newness of the highest stage, when compared with its antecedents. For, close as each step is to the one below, and directly as it seems to arise out of it, each higher step has a minimum and differentia of newness (or at least an individual grouping of the elements of the old), which the preceding stage does not explain, or for which it is not

a sufficient reason, but which emerges as new from the very heart of things.

3. Evolution does not diminish the absolute value of the perfect stage, which is incomparably greater than the value of the intermediate stages, it rather accentuates it. The stages from the half-developed acorn-shoot are not equivalent in value to the perfect tree; they are to it as means to an end, and are of minimal value compared with it.

4. All "descent" and "evolution," which, even in regard to the gradual development of physical organisation and its secrets, offer not so much an explanation as a clue, are still less sufficient in regard to the origin and growth of psychical capacity in general, and in relation to the awakening and autonomy of the mind in man, because the psychical and spiritual cannot be explained in terms of physiological processes, from either the quantity or the quality of nervous structure.

This problem, and the relation of the human spirit to the animal mind, will fall to be dealt with in Chapter XI. It is neither the right nor the duty of the religious conception of the world to inquire into and choose between the different forms of the idea of descent which we have met with. If it has made itself master of the general evolution idea, then descent, even in its most gradual, continuous, monophyletic form, affects it not at all. It can then look on, perhaps not with joy, but certainly without anxiety, at Dubois' monkey-man and Friedenthal's chimpanzee. On the other hand, it is obvious that a secret bond of sympathy will always unite it with the right wing of the theory of descent, with the champions of "halmatogenesis,"* heterogenesis,† kaleidoscopic readjustment, &c., because in all these the depth and wealth and the mystery of phenomena are more obviously recognisable. For the same reasons the religious outlook must always be interested in all protests against over-hastiness, against too great confidence in hypotheses, and against too rapid simplification and formulation. And it is not going beyond our province to place some reliance on the fact that there are increasing signs of revolt from the too great confidence hitherto shown in relation to the Theory of Descent. The general frame of the theory will certainly never be broken, but the enclosed picture of natural evolution will be less plain and plausible, more complex and subtle, more full of points of interrogation and recognitions of the limits of our knowledge and the depths of things.

\* *I e*, The occurrence of saltatory, transilient, or discontinuous variations or mutations.

† *I.e*, The emergence of a distinctively new pattern of organisation.

## CHAPTER VI

### DARWINISM IN THE STRICT SENSE

It remains for us to consider what is essentially Darwinian in Darwinism, namely, the theory of natural selection as the determining factor in evolution. For, given the reality of evolution and descent, and that transformations from one form to another, from lower to higher, have really taken place, what was the guiding and impelling factor in evolution, what forced it forwards and upwards? It is here that the real problem of Darwinism begins. Only from this point onwards does the doctrine of evolution, which is not in itself necessarily committed to any theory of the factors, become definitely Darwinian or anti-Darwinian. And it is this problem that is mainly concerned in the discussions taking place to-day as to whether Darwin was right, or whether Darwinism as a hypothesis has not broken down.

The most characteristic feature of Darwin's theory was "natural teleology," that is, the explanation of what is apparently full of purpose and plan in the world, purely as the necessary consequence of very simple conditions, without purpose or any striving after an aim. He sought to show that evolution and ascent can be realised through purely "natural" causes, that this world of life, man included, must have come about, but not because it was intended so to do. In this sense, indeed, his doctrine is an attempt to do away with teleology. But in another sense it is so even more emphatically. The world, and especially the world of life, is undoubtedly full of what is *de facto* purposive. The living organism, as a whole and in every one of its parts, is marvellously adapted to the end of performing its functions, maintaining its own life and reproducing. Every single living being is a miracle of inexhaustible adaptations to an end. Whence came these? They, too, are products, unsought for, unintended, and yet necessary, and coming about "of themselves," that is without teleological or any supernatural guiding principles. To eliminate purpose and the purposive creating and guiding activity of transcendental principles from interpretations of nature, and to introduce purely naturalistic principles—" principles of chance," if we understand chance in this connection not as opposed to necessity, but to plan and purpose—this is the aim of the Darwinian theory. And it only becomes definitely anti-theological because it is antiteleological.

The conclusions which Darwin arrived at as to the factors in the transformation of species, and in the production of "adaptations," have been in part supported by the specialists he influenced, in part strengthened, but in part modified and even reversed, so that a great crisis

# DARWINISM IN STRICT SENSE 141

has come about in regard to Darwinism in the strict sense—a crisis which threatens to be fatal to it. We must here attempt to take a general survey of the state of the question and to define our own position.

Darwin's interpretation is well known. It is the theory of the natural selection of the best adapted through the struggle for existence, which is of itself a natural selection, and results in the sifting out of particular forms and of higher forms. Darwin's thinking follows the course that all anti-teleological thought has followed since the earliest times. In bringing forth the forms of life, nature offers, without choice or aim or intention, a wealth of possibilities. The forms which happen to be best adapted to the surrounding conditions of life maintain themselves, and reproduce; the others perish, and are eliminated (survival of the fittest). Thus arises adaptation at first in the rough, but gradually in more and more minute detail. This adaptation, brought about by chance, gives *the impression* of intelligent creative purpose.

In Darwin this fundamental mode of naturalistic interpretation took, under the influence of the social-economic theories of Malthus, the special form of natural selection by means of the struggle for existence, in association with the assumption of unlimited and fluctuating variability in the forms of life. All living beings have a tendency to increase in number without limit. But the means of subsistence and other conditions of existence do not increase at the same rate; they are relatively constant. Thus competition must come about. Any organism that is, by fortuitous variation, more favourably equipped than its fellows maintains itself and reproduces itself; the less favoured perish. For all things living are exposed to enemies, to untoward circumstances, and the like. Every individual favoured above its rivals persists, and can transmit to its descendants its own more favourable, more differentiated, more highly equipped character. Thus evolution is begun, and is forced on into the ever more diverse and ever "higher."

To Darwin this struggle for existence and this selection according to utility seemed, at any rate, the chief factor in progress. He did, indeed, make some concessions to the Lamarckian principle that new characters may be acquired by increased use, and to other "secondary" principles. But these are of small importance as compared with his main factor.

### Differences of Opinion as to the Factors in Evolution

The theory of natural selection in the struggle for existence rapidly gained wide acceptance, but from the first it was called in question from many sides. Bronn, who translated Darwin's works into German, was and remained loyal to the idea of a "developmental law" —that there is within the organism an innate tendency towards self-differentiation and progress, thus a purely

FACTORS IN EVOLUTION 143

teleological principle.* Similarly, von Baer emphasised the idea of an endeavour to realise an aim; von Kolliker, that of "heterogenesis"; Nageli, that of an impulse towards perfection—all three thus recognising the theory of evolution, but dissenting from the view that the struggle for existence is the impelling factor and actual guide in the process. Very soon, in another direction, antagonism became pronounced between the strictly Darwinian elements of the theory (the struggle for existence and its corollaries) and the accessory Lamarckian elements. Through these and other controversies the present state of the question has emerged.

The main antithesis at present is the following. On the one side, the "all-sufficiency of natural selection" is maintained, that is, progressive evolution is regarded as coming about without direct self-exertion on the part of the organisms themselves, simply through the fact that fortuitous variations are continually presenting themselves, and are being selected and established according to their utility in the struggle for existence. On the other side—with Lamarck—the progress is regarded as due to effort and function on the part of the organism itself. (Increased use of an organ strengthens it; a changed use transforms it; disuse causes it to degenerate. Thus new characters appear, old ones pass away, and in the course of thousands of

* See H G Bronn's Appendix to his translation of Darwin's "Origin of Species." First German edition.

years the manifold diversity of the forms of life has been brought about.)

Further, by those of the one side variation is regarded as occurring by the smallest steps that could have selective value in the struggle for existence. To the others variation seems to have taken place by leaps and bounds, with relatively sudden transformations of the functional and structural equilibrium on a large scale. In regard to these the *rôle* of the struggle for existence must be merely subsidiary. This saltatory kind of evolution-process is called "halmatogenesis," or, more neatly, "kaleidoscopic variation," because, as the pictures in a kaleidoscope change not gradually but by a sudden leap to an essentially new pattern, so also do the forms of life. Associated with this is the following contrast. One side believes in free and independent variation of any organ, any part, any function, physical or mental, any instinct, and so on, apart from change or persistence in the rest of the organism; the other side believes in the close connectedness of every part with the whole, in the strict " correlation " of all parts, in variation in one part being always simultaneously associated with variation in many other parts, all being comprised in the " whole," which is above and before all the parts and determines them. And further, to one school variation seems without plan in all directions, simply plus or minus on either side of a mean; to the other, variation seems predetermined and in a definite direction—an " orthogenesis," in fact, which is inherent in the organism, and which is indifferent to utility or disadvantage, or natural selection, or anything else, but simply follows its prescribed path in obedience to innate law. The representatives of this last position differ again among themselves. Some regard it as true in detail, in regard, for instance, to the markings of a butterfly's wing, the striping of a caterpillar, the development of spots on a lizard; while others regard it as governing the general process of evolution as a whole. Finally, there is the most important contrast of all. On the one side, subordination, passivity, complete dependence on the selective or directive factors in evolution, which alone have any power; on the other, activity, spontaneous power of adaptation and transformation, the relative freedom of all things living, and—the deepest answer to the question of the controlling force in evolution—*the secret of life*. This last contrast goes deeper even than the one we have already noted, that between the Darwinian and the Lamarckian principle of explanation; and it leads ultimately from the special Darwinian problem to quite a new one, to be solved by itself—the problem of the nature and secret of living matter.

## WEISMANNISM

In regard to almost all the points to which we have referred, the most consistent and decided champion of Darwinism in its essential principles is the zoologist of Freiburg, August Weismann.* In long chapters on

* Finally and comprehensively in the two volumes we have

the protective coloration of animals, on the phenomena of mimicry—that resemblance to foreign objects (leaves, pieces of wood, bark, and well-protected animals) by which the mimics secure their own safety from enemies— on the protective devices in plants, the selective value of "the useful" is demonstrated. In regard to the marvellous phenomena of "carnivorous" plants, the still more marvellous instincts of animals, which cannot be interpreted on Lamarckian lines as "inherited habit," but only as due to the cumulative influence of selection on inborn tendencies, as well as in regard to "symbiosis," "the origin of flowers," and so on, he attempts to show that the heterodox attempts at explanation are insufficient, and that selection alone really explains. At the same time the Darwinian principle is carried still further. It is not only among the individuals, the "persons," that the selective struggle for existence goes on. Personal selection depends upon a "germinal selection" within the germ-plasm, influencing it, and being influenced by it—for instance, restrained.

In order to explain the mystery of heredity, Weis-

---

already mentioned, "Vorträge über die Deszendenztheorie," Jena, 1902 (Eng trans., London, 1904). "Natural selection depends essentially upon the cumulative augmentation of the most minute useful variations in the direction of their utility; only the useful is developed and increased, and great effects are brought about slowly through the summing up of many very minute steps . . . But the philosophical significance of natural selection lies in the fact that it shows us how to explain the origin of useful, well-adapted structures purely by mechanical factors, and without having to fall back upon a directive principle."

mann long ago elaborated, in his germ-plasm theory, the doctrine that the developing individual is materially preformed, or rather predetermined in the "idants" and "ids" of the germ-cell. Thus every one of its physical characters (and, through these, its psychical characters), down to hairs, skin spots, and birth-marks, is represented in the "id" by "determinants" which control the "determinates" in development. In the course of their growth and development these determinants are subject to diverse influences due to the position they happen to occupy, to their quality, to changes in the nutritive conditions, and so on. Through these influences variations in the determinants may be brought about. And thus there comes about a "struggle" and a process of selection among the determinants, the result of which is expressed in changes in the determinates, in the direction of greater or less development. On this basis Weismann attempts to reach explanations of the phenomena of variation, of many apparently Lamarckian phenomena, and of recognised cases of "orthogenesis," and seeks to complete and deepen Roux's theory of the "struggle of parts," which was just another attempt to carry Darwinism within the organism.

What distinguishes Weismann, and makes him especially useful for our present purpose of coming to an understanding in regard to the theory of selection is, that his views are unified, definite and consistent. In his case we have not to clear up the ground and to follow things out to their conclusions, nor to purge his theories from irrelevant, vitalistic, or pantheistic accessory theories, as we have, for instance, in the case of Haeckel. His book, too, is kept strictly within its own limits, and does not attempt to formulate a theory of the universe in general, or even a new religion on the basis of biological theories. Let us therefore inquire what has to be said in regard to this clearest and best statement of the theory of selection when we consider it from the point of view of the religious conception of the world.

Whatever else may be said as to the all-sufficiency of natural selection there can be no doubt that it presupposes two absolute mysteries which defy naturalistic explanation and every other, and which are so important that in comparison with them the problem of the struggle for efficacy and its meaning fades into insignificance. These are the functions and capacities of living organisms in general, and in particular those of variation and inheritance, of development and self-differentiation. What is, and whence comes this mysterious power of the organism to build itself up from the smallest beginnings, from the germ? And the equally mysterious power of faithfully repeating the type of its ancestors? And, again, of varying and becoming different from its ancestors? Even the "mechanical" theory of selection is forced to presuppose the secret of life. Weismann indeed attempts to solve this riddle through his germ-plasm theory, the predisposition of the future organism in the "ids," determinants, and biophors, and through the variation of the determinants in germinal selection, amphimixis and so on. But this is after all only shifting the problem to another place, and translating the mystery into algebraical terms, so to speak, into symbols with which one can calculate and work for a little, which formulate a definite series of observations, an orderly sequence of phenomena, which are, however, after all, " unknown quantities" that explain nothing.

In order to explain the developing organism Weismann assumes that each of its organs or parts, or " independent regions," is represented in the germ-plasm by a determinant, upon the fate of which the development of the future determinate depends. It is thought of as a very minute corpuscle of living matter. Thus there are determinants of hairs and scales, pieces of skin, pits, marks, &c. But every determined organ, or part, or "independent region," is itself in its turn an "organism," is indeed a system of an infinite number of interrelated component parts, and each of these again is another, down to the individual cells. And each cell is an " organism " in itself, and so on into infinity. Is all this represented in the determinants ? And how ?

Further, the individual determinate, for instance of a piece of skin, is not something isolated, but passes over without definite boundary into others. Therefore the determinants also cannot be isolated, but must be systems within systems, dependent upon and merging into one another. How, at the building up of the organism, do the determinants find their direction and their localisation? And, especially, how do they set to work to build up their organ? Here the whole riddle of the theory of epigenesis, which Weismann wished to do away with as a mystery, is repeated a thousand times and made more difficult. In order to explain puzzling processes on a large scale, others have been constructed, which on close investigation prove to be just the same mysterious and unexplained processes, only made infinitely smaller.

Moreover, even if the whole of "Weismannism," including germinal selection, could be accepted, and if it were as sufficient as it is insufficient, what we advanced at the end of Chapter III. as a standpoint of general validity in relation to teleology and theology would still hold good. Even an entirely naive, anthropomorphic, "supernatural" theology is ready to see, in the natural course of things, in the "*causæ secundariæ*," the realisation of Divine purpose, teleology, and does not fail to recognise that the Divine purpose may fulfil itself not only in an extraordinary manner, through "miracles" and "unconditioned" events, but also in ordinary ways, "through means" and the universal causal nexus. Thus it is quite consistent even with a theology of this kind to regard the whole system of causes and effects, which, according to the Darwin-Weismann doctrine, have gradually brought forth the whole diversity of the world of life, with man at its head, in a purely causal way without teleological intervention, as an immense system of means marvellous in its intricacy, in the inevitable necessity of its inter-relations, and in the exactness of its work, the ultimate result of which *must* have come about, but perhaps at the same time was *intended* to come about. Whether I regard this ultimate result as the mere consequence of blind happenings, or as an intended purpose, does not depend, as we have seen, upon the knowledge gained by natural science, but depends above all on whether this ultimate result seems to me of sufficient *value* to be thought of as the purpose of a world-governing intelligence, and thus depends upon my personal attitude to human nature, reason, mind, and the spiritual, religious, and moral life. If I venture to attribute worth, and absolute worth, to these things, nothing, not even the fact of the " struggle for existence " in its thousand forms, in its gradually transforming effects, in the almost endless nexus of its causes and results, germinal selection included, can take away my right (and eventually my duty) to regard the ultimate result *as an end*, and the nexus of causes as a system of means. To enable me to do this, it is only requisite that internal necessity should govern the system, and that the result should not be a chance one, so that it might even have been suppressed, have failed, or have turned out quite differently. Necessity and predetermination are characteristic of the relation between means and purpose. But this requisite is precisely that which natural science does afford us,—namely, the proof that all phenomena are strictly governed by law, and are absolutely predetermined by their antecedents. At this point the religious and the scientific consideration coincide exactly. The hairs of our head, and the hairs in the fur of a polar bear, which is varying towards white, and is therefore selected in the struggle for existence,* even the fluctuating variations of a determinant in the germ, are "numbered" according to both conceptions. Every variation that cropped up, every factor that "selected" the fit, and eliminated the unfit, was strictly predestined, and must of necessity have appeared as, and when, and where it did appear.†

The whole nexus of conditions and results, the inclined plane of evolution and the power of Being to move up it, has its sufficient reason in the nature and original state of the cosmos, in the constitution of its "matter," its "energy," its laws, its sequences and the grouping of its phenomena. Only from beginnings so constituted could our present world have come to be as it is, and

* If it were not white it would be observed by the seals, which would thus avoid being devoured by it. See Weismann, I., p 70. (English edition, p. 65.)

† It is almost comical when Weismann, the champion of the purely naturalistic outlook, occasionally forgets his rôle altogether, and puts in a word for "chance," or attempts to soften absolute predetermination. For if even a single wolf should destroy a stag "by chance," or if a single "id" should "chance" to grow in a manner slightly different from that laid down for it by the compelling force of preceding and accompanying circumstances, the whole Darwinian edifice would be labour lost.

# WEISMANNISM

that necessarily. Only because the primary possibility and fitness for life—vegetable, animal and human—was in it from the beginning, could all these have come to be. This primary possibility did not "come into being," it was à *priori* immanent in it. Whence came this? There is no logical, comprehensible, or any other necessity why there should be a world at all, or why it should be such that life and evolution must become part of it. Where then lies the reason why it is, rather than is not, and why it is as it is?

To this must be added what Weismann himself readily admits and expressly emphasises. The whole theory treats, and must treat plant, animal, and man as only ingenious machines, mere systems of physical processes. This is the ideal aimed at—to interpret all the phenomena of life, growth, and reproduction thus. Even instincts and mental endowments are so interpreted, since there must be corresponding morphological variations of the fine structure of the nervous organ, and instinctive actions are then "explained" as the functions of these. But how "mechanical happening" comes to have this marvellous inwardness, which we call sensation, feeling, perception, thought and will, which is neither mechanical nor derivable from anything mechanical; and, further, how physical and psychical can condition one another without doing violence to the law of the conservation of the sum of energy, is an absolute riddle. But this whole psychical world exists, with graduated stages perhaps as close to each other as in the physical world, but even less capable than these of being explained as having arisen out of their antecedent lower stages. And this psychical world, which is, indeed, related to and dependent upon the corporeal life, as also conversely, has its own quite peculiar laws: thought does not follow natural laws, but those of logic, which is entirely indifferent to exciting stimuli, for instance of the brain, which conform to natural laws. But this world, its riddles and mysteries, its great content and its history, beyond the reach of mechanical theories, is so absolutely the main thing (especially in regard to the question of the possibility of religion), that the question of bodily structure and evolution becomes beside it a mere accessory problem, and even the last is only a relatively unimportant roundabout way of coming at the gist of the business. How completely the evolution of the higher mental faculties transcends such narrow and meagre formulæ as the struggle for existence and the like, Weismann himself indicates in connection with man's musical sense, and its relation to the "musical" instinct in animals. The same and much more might be alleged in regard to the whole world of mind, of the æsthetic, ethical and religious, of the kingdom of thought, of science, and of poetry.

### Natural Selection.

We have for the moment provisionally admitted the theory of natural selection, in order to see

## NATURAL SELECTION 155

whether it could be included in a religious interpretation of things. But in reality such an admission is not to be thought of, in face of what is at present so apparent—the breaking down of this hypothesis, which has been upheld with so much persistence. We shall have to occupy ourselves with this later on. In the meantime a few more remarks must be added to what has been already said.

It might be said, paradoxically, that the worst fate that could befall this hypothesis would be to be proved, for then it would be most certainly refuted. What we mean is this: If it is really " utility " that rules the world and things, there can be no certainty and objectivity of knowledge, no guarantee of truth. The " struggle for existence " is not concerned with selecting beings who see the world as it is. It selects only the interpretation and conception of the environment that is most serviceable for the existence and maintenance of the species. But there is nothing to guarantee that the " true " knowledge will also be the most useful. It might quite well be that an entirely subjective and in itself wholly false interpretation would be the most serviceable. And if, by some extraordinary chance, the selected interpretation should be also the true one, there would be no means of establishing the fact. And what is true of this interpretation is true also of all theories that are derived from it, for example of the theory of selection itself.

Furthermore, a great part, perhaps the greatest part

of the confidence placed in the theory of selection is due to an involuntary, but entirely fallacious habit of crediting it with the probabilities in favour of the doctrine of descent. The main arguments in favour of evolution and descent are very often, though unwittingly, adduced in support of Darwinism in particular. This is a great mistake. Take, for instance, the evidence of the "palæontological" record. It affords hundreds of proofs of evolution, but not a single proof of selection. Its "intermediate" and "connecting links" do possibly prove the affiliation of species and the validity of genealogical trees. But precisely the "intermediate links" which *selection* requires—the myriads of forms of life which were not successfully adapted, the unfit competitors in the struggle for existence which must have accompanied the favourably adapted variants from step to step, from generation to generation—these are altogether awanting.

Another circumstance seems to us to have been entirely overlooked, and it is one which gives the theory of selection an inevitable appearance of truth, even if it is essentially false, and thus makes it very difficult to refute. Assuming that the recognition of teleological factors is valid, that there is an inward law of development, that "Moses" or whoever one will was undoubtedly right, it is self-evident that, because of the indubitable over-production of organisms, there would even then be a struggle for existence on an immense scale, and that it would have a far-reaching "selective" influence, because of the relative plasticity of many forms of life. Beyond doubt it would, in the course of æons, have applied its shears to many forms of life, and probably there would be no organisms, organs, or associations in the evolution of the ultimate form of which it had not energetically co-operated. Its influence would, perhaps, be omnipresent, yet it might be far from being the all-sufficient factor in evolution; indeed, as far as the actual impulse of evolution is concerned, it might be a mere accessory. Unless we are to think of the forms of life as wholly passive and wooden, the struggle for existence must necessarily be operative, and the magnitude of its results, and their striking and often bizarre outcome, will tend ever anew to conceal the fact that the struggle is after all only an inevitable accompaniment of evolution. And thus we understand how it is that interpretations from the point of view of an inward law of development, of orthogenesis, or of teleology, notwithstanding their inherent validity, have *a priori* always had a relatively difficult position as compared with the Darwinian view.

It is usual to speak of the "all-sufficiency of natural selection," yet the champion of the selection-theory admits, as he needs must, that the struggle for existence and selection can of themselves create absolutely nothing, no new character, no new or higher combination of the vital elements; they can only take what is already given; they can only select and eliminate among the wealth of what is offered.* And the offerer is Life itself by virtue of its mysterious capacity for boundless and inexhaustible variability, self-enrichment and increase. The "struggle for existence" only digs the bed through which life's stream flows, draws the guiding-line, and continually stimulates it to some fresh revelation of its wealth. But this wealth was there from the beginning; it was, to use the old word, "potential" in the living, and included with it in the universal being from which life was called forth. The struggle for existence is only the steel which strikes the spark from the flint; is, with its infinite forms and components, only the incredibly complex channel through which life forces its way upwards. If we keep this clearly in mind, the alarming and ominous element in the theory shrinks to half its dimensions.

And, finally, if we can rid ourselves of the peculiar fascination which this theory exercises, we soon begin to discover what extraordinary improbability and fundamental artificiality it implies. "Utility" is maintained to be that which absolutely, almost tyrannically, determines form and development in the realm of the living. Is this an idea that finds any analogy elsewhere in nature? Those who uphold the theory most strongly are wont to compare the development of organisms to crystal-formation in order in some way to tack on the living to the not-living. Crystal-formation,

* See Darwin, ". . . chance variations. Unless such occur, natural selection can do nothing"

# NATURAL SELECTION

with its processes of movement and form-development, is, they say, a kind of connecting link between the living and the not-living. And in truth we find here, as in the realm of life, species-formation, development into individuals, stages and systems. But all this takes place without any hint of "struggle for existence," of laboriously "selective" processes, or of ingenious accumulation of "variations." The "species" of crystals are formed not according to utility, but according to inherent, determining laws of development, to which the diversity of their individual appearances is due. If "Life" were only a higher potential of what is already stirring in crystallisation, as this view suggests, then we should expect to find fixed tendencies, determined from within, in accordance with which life would pass through the cycle of its forms and possibilities, and rise spontaneously through gradual stages.

## CHAPTER VII

### CRITICS OF DARWINISM

LET us turn now to the other side. What is opposed to Darwinism in the biological investigations of the experts of to-day is in part simple criticism of the Darwinian position as a whole or in some of its details, and in part constructive individual theories and interpretations of the evolution of organisms.

A. Fleischmann's book, "Die Darwinsche Theorie,"\* is professedly only critical. He suggests no theory of his own as to the evolution of life in contrast to Darwin's; for, as we have already seen in connection with his earlier book, "Die Deszendenztheorie," he denies evolution altogether. His agnostic position is maintained, if possible, more resolutely than before. Natural science, according to him, must keep to facts. Drawing conclusions and spinning theories is inexact, and distracts from objective study. The Darwinian theory of selection seems to him a particularly good example of this, for it is built up *a priori* on theories

\* " Die Darwinsche Theorie. Gemeinverstandliche Vorlesungen uber die Naturphilosophie der Gegenwart gehalten vor Studierenden aller Fakultaten," Leipzig, 1903. This book is the continuation of the author's " Deszendenztheorie "

CRITICS OF DARWINISM 161

and hypotheses, it stands apart from experimentation, and it twists facts forcibly to its own ends. It has, however, to be acknowledged that Fleischmann's book is without any "apologetic" intentions. It holds equally aloof from teleology. To seek for purposes and aims in nature he holds to be outside the business of science, as Kant's " Critique of Judgment " suffices to show. After having been more than a decade under the charm of the theory of selection, Fleischmann knows its fascination well, but he now regards it as so erroneous that no one who wishes to do serious work should concern himself about it at all. Point by point he follows all the details of Darwin's work, and seeks to analyse the separate views and theories which go to make up Darwinism as a whole. Darwin's main example of the evolution of the modern races of pigeons from one ancestral form, *Columba livia*, is, according to Fleischmann, not only unproved but unprovable.* For this itself is not a unified type. The process of "unconscious selection" by man is obscure, and it is not demonstrable, especially in regard to pigeon-breeding. It is a hazy idea which cannot be transferred to the realm of nature. The Malthusian assumption of the necessity of the struggle for existence is erroneous. Malthus was wrong in his law of population as applied

* Fleischmann's book compares favourably with those of other naturalists, in that he does not contrast "Moses" and natural science, as is customary, but has a deeper knowledge of the modern view of Genesis I. than is usually found among naturalists, whether of the "positive" or "negative" standpoint.

L

to human life, and Darwin was still more mistaken when he transferred it to the organic world in general. It was mere theory. Statistics should have been collected, and observations instead of theories should have been sought for. The alleged superabundance of organisms is not a fact. The marvellously intertwined conditions in the economy of nature make the proportion of supply and demand relatively constant. And even when there is actual struggle for existence, advantages of situation,* which are quite indifferent as far as selection is concerned, are much more decisive than any variational differences. The theory does not explain the first origin of new characters, which can only become advantageous when they have attained to a certain degree of development. As to the illustrations of the influence of selection given by Darwin, from the much discussed fictitious cases, in which the fleet stags select the lithe wolf, to the marvellous mutual adaptations of insects and flowers, Fleischmann objects that there is not even theoretical justification for any one of them. The spade-like foot of the mole is not " more useful " than the form of foot which probably preceded it (*cf.* Goette), it is merely " different." For when the mole took to burrowing in the earth and adapting itself to that mode of life, it *ipso facto* forfeited all the advantages of living above ground. The postulated myriads of less well-adapted forms of life are no more to be found to-day than they are in the fauna and flora of

* See also Wolff.

CRITICS OF DARWINISM 163

palæontological times. The famous giraffe story has already been disposed of by Mivart's objections. As to the whales, it is objected that the earliest stages of their whalebone and their exaggerated nakedness can have been of no use, and a series of other alleged selective effects of "utility" are critically analysed. The refutation of the most brilliant chapter in the Darwinian theory, that on protective coloration and mimicry, is very insufficient. A long concluding chapter sums up the fundamental defects of the Darwinian theory.

For the most part, Fleischmann simply brings forward objections which have been urged against the theory of selection from the first, either by naturalists or from other quarters. The chief and the most fatal of these which are still current are the following: The theory of selection does not explain the actually existing discontinuity of species. The real characteristics which distinguish species from species are in innumerable cases quite indifferent from the point of view of "utility" (Nageli, Bateson). "Selection preserves the good and weeds out the bad." But where does the good come from? (De Vries). The first beginnings of what may later be useful are almost always useless. The theory of selection might perhaps explain the useful qualities, but not the superfluous, useless, or directly injurious characters which actually exist. Confirmation of the theory of descent may be found in the palæontological record, but it affords none of the theory of selection. Natural selection is continually being neutralised by subsequent inter-crossing and reversion. Natural selection may indeed prevent degeneration within the limits of the species by weeding out what is weak and bad, but it is powerless beyond these limits, and so forth.*

These ever-repeated and ever-increasing objections are purely critical. As this is true of Fleischmann's whole book, it is therefore unsatisfactory. It leaves everything in the mist, and puts nothing in place of what it attempts to demolish. But attempts are being made in other quarters, especially among the Lamarckians, to build up an opposition theory.

### Lamarckism and Neo-Lamarckism

The " Lamarckian " view as opposed to the Darwinian continues to hold its own, and indeed is more ardently supported than ever. On this view, evolution has been accomplished not by a laborious selection of the best which chanced to present itself—a selection in relation to which organisms remained passive, but rather through the exertions of the organisms themselves. It has been especially through the use and exercise of the various

---

* See C. C. Coe, "Nature versus Natural Selection," London, 1895 Perhaps the most comprehensive, many-sided, critical analysis of the theory of natural selection See also Herbert Spencer, "The Inadequacy of Natural Selection," 1893.

## LAMARCKISM AND NEO-LAMARCKISM 165

organs in response to the requirements of life, through the increased exercise of physical and mental functions, that the organism has adapted itself more diversely and more fully to the conditions of its life. What one generation acquired in differentiation of structure, in capacities and habits, through its own exertions, it handed on to the next. By cumulative inheritance there ultimately arose the fixed specific characters, and the diversity and progressive gradations of organisms have gone hand in hand with an ever increasing activity. And as with the physical so it has been with the mental. Through continual use and exercise of the functions their capacity has been increased and modified. Through the frequent repetition of voluntary actions necessary to life the habitual use of them has come about. Habits that have become fixed are correlated with habitual psychical predispositions. These, gradually handed on by inheritance to the descendants, have resulted in the marvellous instincts of animals. Instinct is inherited habit that has become fixed. Corresponding to this there is on the other hand the recognition—in theory at least — that the disuse of an organ, the non-exercising of a function leads to degeneration of structure and so co-operates in bringing about a gradual but persistent modification of the features and constitution of organisms.

These views, which have grown out of Lamarck's fundamental ideas ("Philosophie zoologique," 1809) are now usually associated with the theory advanced chiefly by Etienne Geoffroy St. Hilaire ("Philosophie zoologique," 1830), the opponent of Cuvier, and the ally of Goethe, of the direct influence of the *monde ambiant*. The "surrounding world," the influences of climate, of locality, of the weather, of nutrition, of temperature, of the salinity of the water, of the moisture in the air, and all other conditions of existence, influence the living organism. And they do so not indirectly, as is implied in the process of selection, simply playing the part of a sieve, and not themselves moulding and transforming, but *directly* by necessitating the production of new developments in the living substance, new chemical and physiological activities, new groupings and changes of form, and new organs.

Darwin himself did not regard these two theories as opposed to the theory of selection, but utilised them as subsidiary interpretations. It is obvious, however, that at bottom they conceal an essentially different fundamental idea, which, if followed out to its logical consequences, reduces the "struggle for existence" to at most a wholly indifferent accessory circumstance. Weismann felt this, and hence his entirely consistent endeavours to show by great examples, such as the origin of flowers, the mutual adaptations of flowers and insects, the phenomena of mimicry, and many other cases, that neither the Lamarckian nor any other factor in evolution, except only natural, passive selection, suffices as an interpretation. From the Darwinian standpoint he is absolutely right, and must needs speak

## LAMARCKISM AND NEO-LAMARCKISM 167

of the "omnipotence of natural selection," for it must either be omnipotent, or it must give place to the other two factors, and retain only the significance we attributed to it in another connection (p. 157), which amounts to saying none at all. It is obvious enough why the discussion as to these factors should centre round the question of the "inheritance of acquired characters," " acquired" either through the use or disuse of organs, the exercise or non-exercise of functions, or through the stimuli of the external world.

The neo-Lamarckian conflict with Darwinism has become more and more acute in recent times, and the neo-Lamarckians have sometimes passed from contrasting rival interpretations to excluding the Darwinian factor altogether. As the particular champion of the neo-Lamarckian view, we must name Th. Eimer, the recently deceased Tubingen zoologist. His chief work is in three volumes, entitled " Die Entstehung der Arten auf Grund von Vererbung erworbener Eigenschaften, nach Gesetzen organischen Wachsens."\* It is a polemic against Weismannism in all details, even to the theory of " germinal selection." Eimer follows in the footsteps of St. Hilaire, and shows what a relatively plastic and sensitive creature the organism is to the surrounding world, the conditions of nutrition and other such influences. There is in this connection a particularly

\* Leipzig, 1888, 1897, 1901. In part translated as " Organic Evolution " We are here mainly concerned with Vols. I. and III. Later on we shall have to discuss Vol. II.

instructive chapter on the physiological and other variations brought about by external influences which act as "stimuli of the nervous system." The whole theory of Lamarck and St. Hilaire transcends—notwithstanding the protests of Eimer to the contrary—the categories of the mechanical theory of life, and this chapter does so in particular. The array of facts here marshalled as to the spontaneous self-adaptation of organisms to their environment—in relation to colour mainly—forms the most thoroughgoing refutation of Darwinism that it is possible to imagine. It is shown, too, by a wealth of examples from osteology, how use (and the necessities of the case—a consideration which again goes beyond the bounds of mere Lamarckism) may modify, increase or diminish vertebræ, ribs, skull and limbs, in short, the whole skeleton.

Kassowitz is equally keen and convinced in his opposition to natural selection, and in his comprehensive "Allgemeine Biologie"\* he attacks orthodox Darwinism from the neo-Lamarckian standpoint. The whole of the first volume is almost chapter for chapter a critical analysis, and the polemical element rather outweighs his positive personal contribution. He criticises very severely all attempts to carry the Darwinian principle of explaining adaptations into internal and minute details, arguing against Roux's "Struggle of Parts" and Weismann's "Germinal Selection." And though he himself maintains very decidedly that the

\* Wien, 1899.

## LAMARCKISM AND NEO-LAMARCKISM 169

ultimate aim of biology is to find a mechanical solution of the problem of life, he criticises the modern hypotheses in this direction without prejudice, and declares them unsuccessful and insufficient, inclining himself towards the " neo-vitalistic reaction " in its most recent expression. Along with Eimer and Kassowitz, we may name W. Haacke, especially in relation to his views on the acquisition and transmission of functional modifications and his thoroughgoing denial of Darwinism proper. But his work must be dealt with later in a different connection.\*

These neo-Lamarckian views give us a picture of the evolution of the world that is much more convincing than the strictly Darwinian one. Instead of passive and essentially unintelligent " adaptation " through the sieve of selection, we have here direct self-adaptation of organisms to the conditions of their existence, through their own continual restless activity and exertion, an ascent of their own accord to ever greater heights and perfections. A theory of this kind might easily form part of a religious conception of the world. We might think of the world with primitive tendencies and capacities, in which the potentialities of its evolution were implied, and so ordered that it had to struggle by its own exertions to achieve the full realisation of its

---

\* See Wettstein, "Neolamarckism," Jena, 1902. See also Demoor, Massart, Vandervelde, " L'Evolution régressive en Biologie et Sociologie," Paris, 1897. Bibliothèque scientific internationale, vol lxxxv. This work is on the Lamarckian basis It is original in applying Lamarckian principles to a theory of society.

possibilities, to attain to ever higher—up to the highest—forms of Being. The process of nature would thus be the direct anticipation of what occurs in the history of man and of mind. And the task set to the freedom of individual men, and to mankind as a whole, namely, to work out their own nature through their own labour and exertion, and to ascend to perfection—this deepest meaning of all individual and collective existence—would have its exact prelude and preparation in the general nature and evolution of all living creatures. The transition from these theories of nature to a teleological outlook from the highest and most human point of view is so obvious as to be almost unavoidable. And although a natural science which keeps to its own business and within its own boundaries has certainly no right to make this transition for itself, it has still less right to prevent its being made outside of its limits.

### Theory of Definite Variation

But the question now arises, whether both Darwinism and Lamarckism must not be replaced, or at least reduced to the level of accessory theories and factors, by another theory of evolution which was in the field before Darwin, and which since his time has been advanced anew, especially by Nageli, and has now many adherents who support it in whole or in part. This view affects the very foundations of the Darwinian doctrine. The theory of "indefinite" variation, bringing about easy transitions and affecting every part of

## THEORY OF DEFINITE VARIATION 171

the organism separately, which is the necessary correlate of the "struggle for existence," is rejected altogether. Evolution takes place only along a few definite lines, predetermined through the internal organisation and the laws of growth. It is wholly indifferent to "utility," and brings forth only what it must according to its own inner laws, not seldom even the monstrous. According to this view, new species arise, not in easy transition, but with a visible leap, by a considerable and far-reaching displacement of the organic equilibrium. What Darwin calls the correlation of parts, and in no way denies, is here maintained in strong opposition to his doctrine of the isolated variation of individual parts; every member or character of the organism depends upon others, and variation of one affects many, and in some way all of the rest.

This theory is for the most part intended by its champions to be purely naturalistic. But every one of its points yields support to teleological considerations, most obviously so the concrete instances of correlation. If any one were to attempt to make a theory of evolution from a decidedly teleological standpoint, he would probably construct one very similar to the one we are now considering.

It is noteworthy that it has generally been the botanists who have especially supported these views of saltatory evolution in a definite direction and according to internal law, who have therefore tended to react most strongly from Darwinism. We find examples in Nageli's large and comprehensive work, "Mechanisch-physikalische Theorie der Abstammungslehre"; and, before him, in Wigand's "Darwinismus und die Naturforschung Newton's und Cuvier's"; in von Kolliker's "Heterogenesis"; in von Baer's "Endeavour after an End"; in the chapter added by the translator, Bronn, to the first German edition of the "Origin of Species," where he urges weighty objections against the theory of selection, and refers to the "innate impulse to development, persistently varying in a definite direction"; in Askenasy's oft-quoted "Beitrage zur Kritik der Darwinschen Lehre," also referring to "variation in a definite direction," for instance, in flowers; in Delpino's views, and in the works of many other older writers. But we must leave all these out of account here, since we are concerned only with the present state of the question.

### DE VRIES'S MUTATION-THEORY

The work that has probably excited most interest in this connection is De Vries' "Die Mutationstheorie: Versuche und Beobachtungen uber die Entstehung von Arten im Pflanzenleben."* In a short preliminary paper he had previously given some account of his leading experiments on a species of evening primrose (*Œnothera lamarckiana*), and the outlines of his theory. In the work itself he extends this, adding much concrete material, and comparing his views in detail with other

* Two vols , Leipsig, 1901 and 1902

## DE VRIES'S MUTATION-THEORY 173

theories. Darwin, he says, had already distinguished between variability and mutability, the former manifesting itself in gradual and isolated changes, the latter in saltatory changes on a larger scale. The mistake made by Wallace and by the later Darwinians has been that they regarded this latter form ("single variation") as unimportant and not affecting evolution, and the former as the real method of evolutionary process. That fluctuating individual variations do occur De Vries admits, but only within narrow limits, never overstepping the type of the species. Here De Vries utilises the recent statistical investigations into the phenomena of individual variation and their laws, as formulated chiefly by Quetelet and Bateson, which were unknown to Darwin and the earlier Darwinians. The actual transition from "species to species" is made suddenly, by mutation, not through variation. And the state of equilibrium thus reached is such a relatively stable one that individual variations can only take place within its limits, but can in no way disturb it.

De Vries marshals a series of facts which present insurmountable difficulties to the Darwinian theory, but afford corroboration of the Mutation theory. In particular, he brings forward, from his years of experiment and horticultural observation, comprehensive evidence of the mutational origin of new species from old ones by leaps, and this not in long-past geological times, but in the course of a human life and before our very eyes. The main importance of the book lies in the record of these experiments and observations, rather than in the theory as such, for the way had been paved for it by other workers.

In contrast to Darwinism, De Vries states the case for "Halmatogenesis" (saltatory evolution) and "Heterogenesis" (the production of forms unlike the parents), taking his examples from the plant world, but his attitude to Darwinism is conciliatory throughout. Eimer, on the other hand, is sharply antagonistic, especially to Weismann; he takes his proofs from the animal kingdom, and in the second volume of his large work already mentioned, which deals with the "orthogenesis of butterflies," he attempts to set against the Darwinism "chance theory," a proof of "definitely directed evolution," and therefore of the "insufficiency of natural selection in the formation of species."

### Eimer's Orthogenesis

Organisation is due to internal causes. Structural characters crystallise out, as it were. "Orthogenesis," or the definitely determined tendency of evolution to advance in a few directions, is a law for the whole of the animate world. In active response to the stimuli and influences of the environment the organism expresses itself in "organic growth" without any relation to utility. Butterflies in particular, and especially their markings and coloration, are taken as illustrations. In the Darwinian theory of "mimicry" these played a brilliant part. The great resemblance

## EIMER'S ORTHOGENESIS 175

to leaves, to dried twigs, or to well-protected species which are secure from enemies. was regarded as the most convincing proof of the operation of natural selection. But Eimer shows that markings, striping, spots, the development of pattern, and the alleged or real resemblances to leaves, are really subject to definite laws of growth, in obedience to which they gradually appear, developing according to their own internal laws, varying and progressing altogether by internal necessity, and without any reference to advantage or disadvantage, In association with this orthogenesis, Eimer recognises halmatogenesis, correlation and " genepistasis " (coming to a standstill at a fixed and definite stage), and these seem to him to make the Darwinian theory utterly impossible. The text and the illustrations of the book show how, in the sequence of evolution (according to Eimer's laws of transformation), the groupings of stripes, bands, and eye-spots must have appeared on the butterfly's wing, how convex or concave curvings of the contour must have come about at certain points, so that the form of a " leaf " and the lines of its venation resulted, how the eye-spots must have been moulded and shunted, so that they produced the effect of rust or other spots on withered leaves. Particular interest attaches to the detailed arguments against the idea that the butterfly must receive some advantage from its " mimicry." Even the Darwinians have to admit that in a whole series of cases the advantage is not obvious. They talk with some embarrassment of " pseudo-mimicry." Some butterflies that are supposed to be protected have the protective markings on the underside, so that these are actually hidden when the insects are flying from pursuing birds. Many of the leaf-like butterflies are not wood-butterflies at all, but meadow species,* and so Eimer's arguments continue.

A specially energetic fellow-worker on Eimer's line is W. Haacke, a zoologist of Jena, author of "Gestaltung und Vererbung," and "Die Schopfung des Menschen und seiner Ideale." † In the first of these works Haacke combats, energetically and with much detail, Weismann's "pieformation theory," and defends "epigenesis," for which he endeavours to construct graphic diagrams, his aim being to make a foundation for the inheritance of acquired characters, definitely directed evolution, saltatory, symmetrical, and correlated variation.

The principles of the new school are very widespread to-day, but we cannot here follow their development in the works of individual investigators, such as Reinke, R. Hertwig, O. Hertwig, Wiesner, Hamann, Dreyer, Wolff, Goette, Kassowitz, v. Wettstein, Korschinsky, and others.‡

* It remains open to question whether Eimer's explanation is sufficient in all cases, even those of the exaggeratedly deceptive copies of leaves or bark, or the colour of the environment. It is certainly not the sorry explanation in terms of "Variation and Selection," but that of a spontaneous imitation of the surroundings, that forces itself irresistibly upon us in this connection.

† Jena, 1892 and 1895.

‡ See Reinke, "Einleitung in die theoretische Biologie," 1901,

THE SPONTANEOUS ACTIVITY OF THE ORGANISM

What is particularly luminous in all the theories that express the most recent anti-Darwinian tendency is that they tend to bring into prominence the mysterious powers of living organisms, by means of which, instead of passively waiting for natural selection and the continual accumulation of unceasing variations, they are able spontaneously and of themselves to bring forth what is necessary for self-maintenance, often what is new and different, of course not unlimitedly, but with considerable freedom and often with a surprising range of possibilities. It is, perhaps, partly the fault of the one-sidedness of strict Darwinism that this consideration has been so slowly brought into prominence and subjected to investigation and experiment. It is bound up with the capacity that all forms of life have of reacting spontaneously to "stimuli" and, to a certain extent, of helping themselves if the conditions of existence be unfavourable. They are able, for instance, to produce protective adaptations

especially pp. 463 onwards on "Phylogenetisches Bildungspotential." von Wettstein (On direct adaptation)," Neolamaikismus," Jena, 1902. *Cf* " Wissensch-Beitrage zum 15 Jahresberichte (1902) der Philos. Gesellschaft an der Universitat zu Wien Vorträge und Besprechungen über die Krisis der Darwinismus." M. Kassowitz, " Allgemeine Biologie," I. and II., 1899 O Hertwig, " Entwicklung der Biologie im 19. Jahrhundert." Wiesner, " Elemente der wissenschaftlichen Botanik." (*cf*. especially III. " Biologie der Pflanzen "), and on p. 288 the summary of propositions which are very similar to those formulated later by Korschinsky. (" Auf Grund des den Organismen innewohnenden Vervollkommnungstriebes.")

against cold or heat, to "regenerate" lost parts, often to replace entire organs that have been lost, and, under certain circumstances, to produce new organs altogether. If all this be true, it seems almost like caprice to follow only the roundabout theory of the struggle for existence, and not to take account of these spontaneous capacities of the living organism directly and before all other factors in the attempt to explain evolution. There is no end to the illustrations that are being adduced, that must force investigation to pass from merely superficial considerations of the struggle for existence type to the deeper and more real problems themselves.

An effectively modified and adapted type of Alpine flora has not been evolved by a laborious process of selection lasting for many thousand years; the organism may quickly and immediately produce the new characters by its own reaction. Crustaceans gradually transferred from a salt-water to a fresh-water habitat, or conversely, produce in a few generations the type of a new "species" with correlated variations (Schmankewitsch). Birds weaned by careful experiment from a diet of seeds to one of flesh, or conversely, produce changes of effective correlation and adaptation in the characters of their alimentary system. Plants that have been deprived of their normal organs for absorbing water and prevented from growing new ones produce entirely new and effective "hydatodes." *

* See the particularly beautiful and suggestive experiments of

ACTIVITY OF THE ORGANISM 179

It is instructive to notice that Darwinism seems likely to be robbed of its stock illustration, namely, "protective coloration." By its own internal power of reaction, and sometimes within one generation, and even in the lifetime of an individual, an organism may assume the colour of the substratum beneath it (soles, grasshoppers), of its surroundings (Eimer's tree frogs), the colour and spottiness of the granite rock on which it hangs, the colour of the leaves and twigs among which it lives (Poulton's butterfly pupæ), and even that of the brightly coloured sheets of paper amidst which it is kept imprisoned. Certain spiders assume a white, pink, or greenish "protective coloration" corresponding to the tinted blossom of the plants which they frequent, and so on.* Eimer alleged that direct psychical factors co-operated in bringing about these changes. In any case, all this carries us far beyond the domain of mere naturalistic factors into the mystery of life itself. Even what is called the "influence of the external world," and the "active acquirement of new characters," have their basis and the reason of their possibility in this domain. And the whole domain is saturated through and through with "teleology."

A recognition of the impressive secret of the organism led Gustav Wolff to become a very pronounced critic of Darwinism, especially in the form of Weismannism.

Haberlandt "Experimentelle Hervorrufung eines neuen Organs" In "Festschrift fur Schwendener," Berlin (Borntraeger), 1899.
* See "Nature," 1891, p. 441.

As far back as 1896, in a lecture "On the present position of Darwinism," in which he dealt only with Weismann, he criticised and analysed that author's last attempt to uphold Darwinism by the construction of his theory of "germinal selection." He concluded with the wish:

"That a spirit of earnestness would once more enter into biological investigation, which would no longer attempt to find in nature just what it wanted to find, but would be ready to follow truth at all costs, and to approach the riddle of life with an open mind."

His "Beitrage zur Kritik der Darwinischen Lehre," which appeared first as papers in the "Biologisches Centralblatt," did not see the light in book form until 1898. The doctrine of selection was regarded as so unassailable that no publisher would take the risk of the book. Its appearance is a sure indication of the general modification of opinions that had taken place in the interval. The first and second essays are merely critical objections to the theory of selection, very similar to those frequently urged before, but more precisely stated.* The third is intended to show that there is in the forms of life themselves, as a faculty of adaptation peculiar to them, a primary purposiveness, which is unquestionably active throughout the lifetime and development of every individual, but which is also the deepest cause of "phylogenesis," or the formation

* See "Nature," 1891, p. 441.

## ACTIVITY OF THE ORGANISM 181

of a race. This doctrine makes both the Darwinian and Lamarckian theories merely secondary. For the phenomena which suggest the Lamarckian interpretation presuppose this most essential factor—the primary adaptiveness. Wolff concludes with a very striking instance—discovered by himself—of this primary adaptiveness of the organism—the regeneration of the lens in the newt's eye.

More comprehensively, but from a precisely similar standpoint, Driesch has followed up the discussion of this problem.† He is, of all modern investigators, perhaps the one who has most persistently and thoroughly

† The variation-increment of the selection theory ought to be a differential. But in many cases it is not so. As for instance in symmetrical correlated variation, &c In the struggle for existence it is usually not advantages of organisation which are decisive, but the chance advantages of situation, though these have no "selective" influence. The case of the tapeworm is illustrative

His work, "Die organischen Regulationen, Vorbereitungen zu einer Theorie des Lebens," 1901, is a systematic survey of illustrations of the "autonomy" of vital processes. In his "Analytischen Theorie der organischen Entwicklung," Leipzig, 1894, his special biological ("ontogenetic") views are still in process of development. But even here his sharp rejection of Darwinism is complete (see VI., Par. 3, on "the absurd assumption of a contingent character of morphogenesis") It is not for nothing that the book is dedicated to Wigand and C F. von Baer. He says that in regard to development we must "picture to ourselves external agents acting as stimuli and achieving transformations which have the character, not analysable as to its causes, of being adapted to their end, that is, capable of life" Incomplete, but very instructive too, are his discussions on the causal and the teleological outlook, the necessity for both, and the impossibility of eliminating the latter from the study of nature. In a series of subsequent works, Driesch has defined and strengthened this position, finally reaching the worked out the problem of causal and teleological interpretation, and he has also thrown much light on the scientific and epistemological aspects of the problem. That he could, in a recent volume of the "Biologisches Zentralblatt," write a respectful and sympathetic exposition of the Hegelian nature-philosophy—as regards its aims, though not its methods—is as remarkable a symptom as we can instance of the modern trend of views and opinions.*

### Contrast Between Darwinian and Post-Darwinian Views

The new views that have thus arisen have been definitely summarised and clearly contrasted with Darwinism by the botanist Korschinsky. He died before completing his general work, "Heterogenesis und Evolution," but he has elsewhere † given an excellent summary of his results, which we append in abstract.

| Darwin | Korschinsky and the Moderns |
|---|---|
| (1) Everything organic is capable of variation. Variations | (1) Everything organic is capable of variation. This |

declaration · "Darwin belongs to history, just like that other curiosity of our century, the Hegelian philosophy. Both are variations on the theme, ' How to lead a whole generation by the nose ! ' " ("Biolog. Zentralbl." 1896, p 16) We are concerned with Driesch more particularly in Chapter IX.

* See Driesch "Kritisches und Polemisches," Biol. Zentrabl., 1902, p. 187, Note 2

† "Naturwissenschaftliche Wochenschrift," xiv, p 273.

# POST-DARWINIAN THEORIES 183

arise in part from internal, in part from external causes They are slight, inconspicuous, individual differences.

capability is a fundamental, inherent character of living forms in general, and is independent of external conditions It is usually kept latent by "heredity," but occasionally breaks forth in sudden variations

(2) The struggle for existence This combines, increases, fixes useful variations, and eliminates the useless. All the characters and peculiarities of a finished species are the results of long-continued selection , they must therefore be adapted to the external conditions.

(2) Saltatory variations — These are, under favourable circumstances, the starting-point of new and constant races The characters may sometimes be useful, sometimes quite indifferent, neither advantageous nor disadvantageous. Sometimes they are not in harmony with external circumstances.

(3) The species is subject to constant variation. It is continually subject to selection and augmentation of its characters Hence again the origin of new species.

(3) All fully developed species persist, but through heterogenesis a splitting up into new forms may take place, and this is accompanied by a disturbance of the vital equilibrium. The new state is at first insecure and fluctuating, and only gradually becomes stable. Thus new forms and races arise with gradual consolidation of their constitution.

(4) The sharper and more acute the effect of the environment, the keener is the struggle for existence, and the more rapidly and certainly do new forms arise

(4) Only in specially favourable conditions, only when the struggle for existence is weak, or when there is none, can new forms arise and become fixed. When the conditions are severe no new forms arise, or if they do they are speedily eliminated.

(5) The chief condition of evolution is therefore the struggle

(5) The struggle for existence simply decimates the overwhelm-

| | |
|---|---|
| for existence and the selection which this involves. | ing abundance of possible forms. Where it occurs it prevents the establishment of new variations, and in reality stands in the way of new developments. It is rather an unfavourable than an advantageous factor |
| (6) If there were no struggle for existence there would be no adaptation, no perfecting | (6) Were there no struggle for existence, there would be no destruction of new forms, or of forms in process of arising. The world of organisms would then be a colossal genealogical tree of enormous luxuriance, and with an incalculable wealth of forms. |
| (7) Progress in nature, the "perfecting" of organisms, is only an increasingly complex and ever more perfect adaptation to the external circumstances It is attained by purely mechanical methods, by an accumulation of the variations most useful at the time | (7) The adaptation which the struggle for existence brings about has nothing to do with perfecting, for the organisms which are physiologically and morphologically higher are by no means always better adapted to external circumstances than those lower in the scale. Evolution cannot be explained mechanically. The origin of higher forms from lower is only possible if there is a tendency to progress innate in the organism itself. This tendency is nearly related to or identical with the tendency to variation It compels the organism to perfect itself as far as external circumstances will permit. |

All this implies an admission of evolution and of descent, but a setting aside of Darwinism proper as an unsuccessful hypothesis, and a positive recognition of

## POST-DARWINIAN THEORIES 185

an endeavour after an aim, internal causes, and teleology in nature, as against fortuitous and superficial factors. This opens up a vista into the background of things, and thereby yields to the religious conception all that a study of nature can yield—namely, an acknowledgment of the possibility and legitimacy of interpreting the world in a religious sense, and assistance in so doing.

The most important point has already been emphasised. Even if the theory of the struggle for existence were correct, it would be possible to subject the world as a whole to a teleological interpretation. But these anti-Darwinian theories now emerging, though they do not directly induce teleological interpretation, suggest it much more strongly than orthodox Darwinism does. A world which in its evolution is not exposed, for good or ill, to the action of chance factors—playing with it and forcing it hither and thither—but which, exposed indeed to the most diverse conditions of existence and their influences, and harmonising with them, nevertheless carries implicitly and infallibly within itself the laws of its own expression, and especially the necessity to develop upwards into higher and higher forms, is expressly suited for teleological consideration, and we can understand how it is that the old physico-teleological evidences of the existence of God are beginning to hold up their heads again. They are wrong when they try to demonstrate God, but quite right when they simply seek to show that nature does not contradict—in fact that it allows room and validity to—belief in the Highest Wisdom as the cause and guide of all things natural.

As far as the question of the right to interpret nature teleologically is concerned, it would be entirely indifferent whether what Korschinsky calls "the tendency to progress," and the system of laws in obedience to which evolution brings forth its forms, can be interpreted "mechanically" or not, that is to say, whether or not evolution depends on conditions and potentialities of living matter, which can be demonstrated and made mechanically commensurable or not. It may be that they can neither be demonstrated nor made mechanically commensurable, but lie in the impenetrable mystery inherent in all life. Whether this mystery really exists, and whether religion has any particular interest in it if it does, must be considered in the following chapter.

## CHAPTER VIII

### THE MECHANICAL THEORY OF LIFE

WHAT is life—not in the spiritual and transcendental sense, but in its physical and physiological aspects? What is this mysterious complex of processes and phenomena, common to everything animate, from the seaweed to the rose, and from the human body to the bacterium, this ability to "move" of itself, to change and yet to remain like itself, to take up dead substances into itself, to assimilate and to excrete, to initiate and sustain, in respiration, in nutrition, in external and internal movements, the most complex chemical and physical processes, to develop and build up through a long series of stages a complete whole from the primitive beginnings in the germ, to grow, to become mature, and gradually to break up again, and with all this to repeat in itself the type of its parent, and to bring forth others like itself, thus perpetuating its own species, to react effectively to stimuli, to produce protective devices against injury, and to regenerate lost parts? All this is done by living organisms, all this is the expression in them of "Life." What is it? Whence comes it? And how can it be explained?

The problem of the nature of life, of the principle of vitality, is almost as old as philosophy itself, and from the earliest times in which men began to ponder over the problem, the same antitheses have been apparent which we find to-day. Disguised under various catchwords and with the greatest diversities of expression, the antitheses remain essentially the same through the centuries, competing with one another, often mingling curiously, so that from time to time one or other almost disappears, but always crops up again, so that it seems as if the conflict would be a never-ending one—the antitheses between the mechanical and the " vitalistic " view of life. On the one side there is the conviction that the processes of life may be interpreted in terms of natural processes of a simple and obvious kind, indeed directly in terms of those which are most general and most intelligible—namely, the simplest movements of the smallest particles of matter, which are governed by the same laws as movement in general. And associated with this is the attempt to take away any special halo from around the processes of life, to admit even here no other processes but the mechanical ones, and to explain everything as the effect of material causes. On the opposite side is the conviction that vital phenomena occupy a special and peculiar sphere in the world of natural phenomena, a higher platform ; that they cannot be explained by merely physical or chemical or mechanical factors, and that, if "explaining" means reducing to terms of such factors,

## MECHANICAL THEORY OF LIFE 189

they do in truth include something inexplicable. These opposing conceptions of the living and the organic have been contrasted with one another, in most precise form and exact expression, by Kant in certain chapters of the Kritik der Urteilskraft, which must be regarded as a classic for our subject.* But as far as their general tendency is concerned, they were already represented in the nature-philosophies of Democritus on the one hand, and of Aristotle on the other.

All the essential constituents of the modern mechanical theories are really to be found in Democritus, the causal interpretation, the denial of any operative purposes or formative principles, the admission and assertion of quantitative explanations alone, the denial of qualities, the reduction of all cosmic developments to the "mechanics of the atom" (even to attractions and repulsions, thus setting aside the "energies"), the inevitable necessity of these mechanical sequences, indeed at bottom even the conviction of the "constancy of the sum of matter and energy." (For, as he says, "nothing comes out of nothing.") And although he makes the "soul" the principle of the phenomena of life, that is in no way contradictory to his general mechanical theory, but is quite congruent with it. For the "soul" is to him only an aggregation of thinner, smoother, and

* See § 70 and subsequent sections Take, for instance, the sentences —"Every production of material things and of their forms must be interpreted as possible in terms of purely mechanical laws," and the contrast "Some products of material nature cannot be interpreted as possible in terms of purely mechanical laws "

rounder atoms, which as such are more mobile, and can, as it were, quarter themselves in the body, but nevertheless stand in a purely mechanical relation to it.

Aristotle, who was well aware of the diametrical opposition, represents, as compared with Democritus, the Socratic-Platonic teleological interpretation of nature, and in regard to the question of living organisms his point of view may quite well be designated by the modern name of " vitalism." Especially in his theory of the vegetable soul, the essence of vitalism is already contained. It is the λόγος ἔνυλος (logos enhylos), the idea immanent in the matter, the conceptual essence of the organism, or its ideal whole, which is inherent in it from its beginnings in the germ, and determines, like a directing law, all its vegetative processes, and so raises it from a state of " possibility " to one of " reality." All that we meet with later as " nisus formativus," as " life-force " (vis vitalis), as " endeavour after an end " (Zielstrebigkeit), is included in the scope of Aristotelian thought. And he has the advantage over many of his successors of being very much clearer.*

\* To Aristotle the "Soul" (ψυχὴ ρυτική Psyche, phytike) was in the first place a purely biological principle. But by means of his elastic formula of Potentiality and Actuality he was able to make the transition to the psychological with apparent ease. The biological is to him in "potentiality" what sensation, impulse, imagination are in "realisation." But the biological and the psychological are not related to one another as stages. Growth, form, development, &c., cannot be carried over through any "actualisatio" into sensation, consciousness and the like.

An essentially different question is, whether the biological may not be not indeed derivable from the psychological—that would be the

## MECHANICAL THEORY OF LIFE 191

The present state of the problem of life may be regarded as due to a reaction of biological investigation and opinion from the "vitalistic" theories which prevailed in the first half of last century, and which were in turn at once the root and the fruit of the German Nature-philosophy of that time.

Lotze in his oft-quoted article, "Leben, Lebenskraft" (Life, Vital Force), in Wagner's "Hand-Wörterbuch der Physiologie," 1842, gave the signal for this reaction. The change, however, did not take place suddenly. The most important investigators in their special domain, the physiologist Johannes Muller, the chemist Julius Liebig, remained faithful to a modified vitalistic standpoint. But in the following generation the revolution was complete and energetic. With Du Bois-Reymond, Virchow, Haeckel, the anti-vitalistic trend became more definite and more widespread. It had a powerful ally in the Darwinian theory, which had been promulgated meanwhile, and at the same time in the increasingly materialistic tendency of thought, which afforded support to the mechanical system and also sought foundations in it.

The naturalistic, "mechanical" interpretation of life was so much in the tenor of Darwin's doctrine that it would have arisen out of it if it had not existed before. It is so generally regarded as a self-evident and necessary

same mistake—but dependent on, and conditioned by it, just as we regard the voluntary moving and directing of the body as dependent on it. An imaginative interpretation of the world will always take this course.

corollary of the strictly Darwinian doctrine, that it is often included with it under the name of Darwinism, although Darwin personally did not devote any attention to the problem of the mechanical interpretation of life. Any estimate of the value of one must be associated with an estimate of the other also.

It goes without saying that the theory of life is dependent upon, and in a large measure consists of physico-chemical interpretations, investigations, and methods. For ever since the attention of investigators was directed to the problems of growth, of nutrition, of development and so on, and particularly as knowledge has passed from primitive and unmethodical forms to real science, it has been taken as a matter of course that chemical and physical processes play a large part in life, and indeed that everything demonstrable, visible, or analysable, does come about "naturally," as it is said. And from the vitalistic standpoint it has to be asked whether detailed biological investigation and analysis can ever accomplish more than the observation and tracing out of these chemical and physical processes. Anything beyond this will probably be only the defining and formulating of the limits of its own proper sphere of inquiry, and a recognition, though no knowledge, of what lies beyond and of the co-operative factors. The difference between vitalism and the mechanical theory of life is not, that the one regards the processes in the organism as opposed to those in the inorganic world while the other identifies them, but that vitalism regards

## MECHANICAL THEORY OF LIFE 193

life as a combination of chemical and physical processes, with the co-operation and under the regulation of other principles, while the mechanical theory leaves these other principles out.

Notwithstanding the many noteworthy reactions, we are bound to regard the present state of the theory of life as on the whole mechanical. The majority of experts—not to speak of the popular materialists, and especially those who, sailing under the flag of materialistic interpretation, have their ships full of vitalistic contraband—regard as the ideal of their science an ultimate analysis of the phenomena of life into mechanical processes, into "mechanics of the atom." They believe in this ideal, and without concealing that it is still very far off, do not doubt its ultimate attainability, and regard vitalistic assumptions as obstacles to the progress of investigation. Moreover, this aspect of the problem seems likely enough to be permanent with the majority, or, at any rate, with many naturalists, though it is obviously one-sided. For it has always been the task of this line of investigation to extend the sphere within which physical and chemical laws can be validly applied in interpreting vital processes, and the results reached along this line will always be so numerous and important that even on psychological grounds the mechanical point of view has the best chance for the future. Furthermore, the maxim that all the phenomena of nature must be explained by means of the simplest factors and according to the smallest possible number of laws, is usually regarded as one of the most legitimate maxims of science in general, so that the resolute pertinacity with which many investigators maintain the entire sufficiency of the mechanical interpretation, far from being condemned as materialistic fanaticism, must be respected as the expression of scientific conscience. Even when confidence in the one-sided mechanical interpretation of vital processes sometimes fails in face of the great and striking riddles of life, it is to be expected that it will revive again with each new success, great or small.*

The mechanical conception of life which now prevails is made up of the following characteristics and component elements. These also indicate the lines along which the arguments are worked out—lines which glimmered faintly through the mechanical theories of ancient times, but which have now been definitely formulated and supported by evidence.

### The Conservation of Matter and Energy

1. The whole mechanical theory is based upon a law which is not strictly biological but belongs to science in

---

\* Of course all this still gives us no ground for drawing conclusions as to the correctness of the mechanistic theory, but only affords a reason for its power of persistence. Indeed, the very fact that, in investigating the problem of life, instinct directs us towards mechanical interpretations, should give added weight to the other fact, that among the ranks of naturalists themselves there constantly arise doubts and criticisms of the adequacy of this mode of interpretation, and that many of them go over more or less completely to the vitalistic point of view.

## CONSERVATION OF ENERGY 195

general—the law of the conservation of matter and energy. This was first recognised by Kant as a general rational concept in his "Critique" and in the "Grundlegung der Metaphysik der Naturwissenschaft," and was transferred by Robert Mayer and Helmholtz * to the domain of natural science. Just as no particle of matter can come from nothing or become nothing, so no quantum of energy can come from nothing or become nothing. It must come from somewhere and must remain somewhere. The form of energy is continually changing, but the sum of energy in the universe remains invariable and constant. Therefore, it seems to follow, there can be no specific vital phenomena. The energies concerned in the up-building, growth, and decay of the organism, and the sum of the functions performed by it, must be the exact resultant and equivalent of the potential energies stored in its material substance and the co-operative energies of its environment. The particular course of transformations they follow must have its sufficient reason in the configuration of the parts of the organism, in its relations to the environment, and the like. An intervention of "vitalistic" principles, directions and so forth, would, we are told, involve a sudden obtrusion and disappearance again of energy-effects which had no efficient cause in the previous phenomena. From any point of view it would be a miracle, and in particular it would

* H. Helmholtz, " Ueber die Erhaltung der Kraft, eine physikalische Abhandlung," Berlin, 1847.

be doing violence to the law of the constancy of the sum of energy.

Apart from the inherent general "instinct"—*sit venia verbo*, for no more definite word is available—which is the quiet Socius, the concealed but powerful spring of the mechanistic convictions, as of most others, this law of the conservation of energy is probably the really central argument, and it meets us again more or less disguised in what follows.

## The Organic and the Inorganic

2. What is on *à priori* grounds demanded as a necessity, or set aside as impossible, on the strength of the axiom of the conservation of energy, must be proved *à posteriori* by investigation. It must be shown in detail that the difference between the organic and the inorganic is only apparent. And it is here that the mechanical view of life celebrates its greatest triumph.

For a long time it seemed as though there were an absolute difference between "inorganic" and "organic" chemistry, between the chemical processes and products found in free nature, and those within the "living" body. The same elements were indeed found in both, but it seemed as if they were subject in the living body to other and higher laws than those observed in inanimate nature. Out of these elements the organism builds up, by unexplained processes, peculiar chemical individualities, highly organised and complex combinations which are never attained in inorganic nature. This

## THE ORGANIC AND THE INORGANIC 197

seems to afford indubitable evidence of a vital force with mysterious super-chemical capacities.

But modern chemical science has succeeded in doing away with this absolute difference between the two departments of chemistry, for it has achieved, in retorts, in the laboratory, and with "natural" chemical means, what had hitherto only been accomplished by "organic" chemistry. Since Wöhler's discovery that urea could be built up by artificial combination, more and more of the carbon-compounds which were previously regarded as specialities of the vital force have been produced by artificial syntheses. The highest synthesis, that of proteids, has not yet been discovered, but perhaps that, too, may yet be achieved.

And further : intensive observation through the microscope and in the laboratory increases the knowledge of processes which can be analysed into simple chemical processes, both in the plant and the animal body. These are astonishing in their diversity and complexity, but nevertheless they fulfil themselves according to known chemical laws, and they can be imitated apart from the living substance. The "breaking up" of the molecules of nutritive material,—that is to say, the preparation of them as building material for the body,—does not take place magically and automatically, but is associated with definitely demonstrable chemical stuffs, which produce their effect even outside of the organism. The fundamental function of living matter—" metabolism,"—that is, the constant disruption and reconstruction of its own substance, has, it seems, been brought at least nearer to a possible future explanation by the recognition of a series of phenomena of a purely chemical nature, the catalytic phenomena (the effects of ferments or "enzymes"). Ingenious hypotheses are already being constructed, if not to explain, at least to give a general formulation of these facts, which will serve as a framework and guiding clue, as a "working hypothesis" for the further progress of investigation.

The most recent of these hypotheses is that set forth by Verworn in his book "Die Biogenhypothese."* He assumes, as the central vehicle of the vital functions, a unified living substance, the "biogen," nearly related to the proteids which form the fundamental substance of protoplasm and of the cell-nucleus, and in contrast to which the other substances found in the living body are in part raw materials and reserves, and in part of a derivative nature, or the results of disruptive metabolism. Very complex chemically, "biogen" is able to operate upon the circulating or reserve "nutritive" materials in a way comparable, for instance, to the action of "nitric acid in the production of English sulphuric acid." That is to say, it is able to set up processes of disruption and of recombination, apparently by its mere presence, but, in reality, by its own continual breaking down and building up again. At the same time it has the power,

* Max Verworn, "Die Biogenhypothese," Jena, 1903. *Cf.* criticisms by Czapek in the "Botanische Zeitung," No. 2, 1903, and by Loeb in the "Biologisches Zentralblatt," 1902.

## THE ORGANIC AND THE INORGANIC 199

analogous to that of polymerisation in molecules, of increasing, of "growing."

The case is the same in regard to physical laws. They are identical in the living and the non-living. And many of the processes of life have already been analysed into a complex of simpler physical processes. The circulation of the blood is subject to the same laws of hydrostatics as are illustrated in all other fluids. Mechanical, static, and osmotic processes occur in the organism and constitute its vital phenomena. The eye is a *camera obscura*, an optical apparatus; the ear an acoustic instrument; the skeleton an ingenious system of levers, which obey the same laws as all other levers. E. du Bois-Reymond, in his lectures on " The Physics of Organic Metabolism " (" Physik des organischen Stoffwechsels "),* compiles a long and detailed list of the physical factors associated and intertwined in the most diverse ways with the fundamental phenomenon of life, namely, metabolism :—the capacities and effects of solution, diffusion of liquids, capillarity, surface tension, coagulation, transfusion with filtration, the capacities and effects of gases, aero-diffusion through porous walls, the absorption of gases through solid bodies and through fluids, and so on.

Very impressive, too, are the manifold " mechanical " interpretations of intimate vital characteristics, such as the infinitely fine structure of protoplasm. For protoplasm does not fill the cell as a compact

* Berlin, 1900. Edited by R. du Bois-Reymond.

mass, but spreads itself out and builds itself up in the most delicate network or meshwork, of which it forms the threads and walls, enclosing innumerable vacuoles and alveoli, and Bütschli succeeded in making a surprisingly good imitation of this "structure" by mechanical means. Drops of oil intimately mixed with potash and placed between glass plates formed a very similar emulsion-like or foam-like structure with a visible network and with enclosed alveoli.*

Rhumbler, too, succeeded in explaining by "developmental mechanics" some of the apparently extremely subtle processes at the beginning of embryonic development (the invagination of the blastula to form the gastrula); by imitating the sphere of cells which compose the blastula with elastic steel bands he deduced the invagination mechanically from the model.†

Here, too, must be mentioned Verworn's attempts to explain "the movements of the living substance."‡ "Kinesis," the power to move, has since the time of Aristotle been regarded as one of the peculiar characteristics of life. From the gliding "amœboid" movements of the moneron, with its mysterious power of shifting its position, spreading itself out, and spinning out long threads ("pseudopodia"), up to the contrac-

* Bütschli, "Untersuchungen uber microscopische Schaume und das Protoplasma," Leipzig, 1892. *Cf.* Berthold, "Studien zur Protoplasmamechanik."

† Rhumbler, "Zur Mechanik des Gastrulationvorganges . ." in "Archiv. f Entwicklungsmechanik," Bd. 14.

‡ "Bewegung der lebendigen Substanz," Jena, 1892.

## IRRITABILITY

tility of the muscle-fibre, the same riddle reappears in many different forms. Verworn attacks it at the lowest level, and attempts to solve it by reference to the surface tension to which all fluid bodies are subject, and to the partial relaxation of this, which forces the mass to give off radiating processes or "pseudopodia." The mechanical causes of the suspension of the surface tension are inquired into, and striking examples of pseudopod-like rays are found in the inorganic world, for instance, in a drop of oil. Thus a starting-point is discovered for mechanical interpretations at a higher level.*

### IRRITABILITY

3. A property which seems to be quite peculiar to living matter is iritability, or the power of responding to "stimuli," that is to say, of reacting to some influence from without in such a manner that *the reaction* is not the mere equivalent of the action, but that the stimulus is to the organism as a contingent cause or impulse setting up a new process or a new series of processes, which seem as though they occurred spon-

* A short, very attractive description of these mechanical methods, and one which appeals particularly to us laymen because of its excellent illustrations, is Dreyer's "Ziele und Wege biologischer Forschung" (Jena, 1892), especially the first part, "Die Flussigkeitsmechanik als eine Grundlage der organischen Form- und Gerust-Bildung." The astonishing and fascinating forms of Radiolarian frameworks and "skeletons" (the artistic appreciation of which was made possible to a wider public by Haeckel's "Kunstformen der Natur") are here made the subject of mechanical explanations, which are certainly in a high degree plausible.

taneously and freely. Thus the sensitive plant *Mimosa pudica* droops its feathery leaves when touched. Here, too, must be classed also all the innumerable phenomena of Heliotropism, Geotropism, Rheotropism, Chemotropism, and other tropisms, in which the sun, or the earth, or currents, or chemical stimuli so affect a form of life— plant, alga, or spore—that it disposes its own movements or the arrangements of its parts accordingly, turning towards, or away from, or in an oblique direction to the source of stimulus, or otherwise behaving in some definite manner which could not have been deduced or predicted from the direct effects of the stimulating factors. The upholders of the mechanical theory have attempted to conquer this vast and mysterious domain of facts by seeking to do away with the appearance of spontaneity and freedom, by demonstrating in suitable cases that these phenomena of spontaneity and the like would be impossible were it not that the potential energies previously stored up within the organism are liberated by the stimulus. Thus the effect caused is not equivalent to the stimulus alone, but is rather the resultant of the conditions given in the chemo-physical predispositions of the organism itself, and in the architecture of its parts, *plus* the stimulus.

Directly associated with this property of irritability is another form of spontaneity and freedom in living beings—the power of adapting themselves to changed conditions of existence. Some do not show this at all, while others show it in an astonishing degree,

# IRRITABILITY

helping themselves out by new contrivances, so to speak. Thus the organism may protect itself against temperature and other influences, against injury, making damages good again by self-repairing processes, " regenerating " lost organs, and sometimes even building up the whole organism anew from amputated parts. The mechanical interpretation must here proceed in the same way as in dealing with the question of stimuli, applying to the development of form the same explanations as are there employed. And just because this domain does not lend itself readily to mechanical explanation, we can understand that confidence in the sufficiency of this mode of interpretation grows rapidly with each fresh conquest, when this or that particular process is shown to be actually explicable on mechanical principles. Processes of development or morphogenesis —which are among the most intricate and difficult—are attacked in various ways. The processes of regeneration, for instance, are compared with the similar tendencies observed in crystals, which when they are injured have the capacity of restoring their normal form. This capacity therefore obtains in the realm of the inorganic as well as among organisms, and is referred to the tendency of all substances to maintain a definite state of equilibrium, conditioned by their form, and, if that is disturbed, to return to a similar or a new state of equilibrium. Or, the procedure may be to reduce the processes of a developmental or morphogenetic category to processes of stimulation in general, and then it is believed, or even demonstrated, that chemo-physical analogies or explanations can be found for them.

Thus, for instance, it is shown that the egg of the sea-urchin may be "stimulated" to development, not exclusively by the fertilising sperm, but even by a simple chemical agent, or that spermatozoids which are seeking the ovum to be fertilised may be attracted by malic acid. These are "reductions" of the higher phenomena of life to the terms of a lower and simpler process of "stimulus," that is to say, to chemotropism in the second case and something analogous in the first. A further reduction would be to show that the movement of the spermatozoids towards the malic acid is not a "vitalistic" act, much less a psychically conditioned one, (that is, conditioned by "taste," "sensation," and the voluntary or instinctive impulse liberated thereby), but is a chemo-physical process, although perhaps an exceedingly complex one. It would be another "reduction" of this second kind, if, for instance, the well-known effect of light on plants, which makes them turn their leaves towards it (heliotropism), could be shown to be due to more rapid growth of the leaf on the shaded side, which would lift up the leaf and cause it to turn, or to an increase of turgescence on the shaded side, and if it could be shown that the increase in either case was a simple and obvious physical process, the necessary consequence of the decreased amount of light.

It is obvious, and it is also thoroughly justifiable, that all attempts along these lines of interpretation should

## SPONTANEOUS GENERATION

be undertaken in the first place in connection with the simplest and lowest forms of life. It is in the investigation of the "Protists," the study of the vital phenomena of the microscropically minute unicellular organisms, that attempts of this kind have been most frequently made. And they follow the course we have just indicated; the "apparently" vitalistic and psychical behaviour of unicellulars (impulse, will, spontaneous movement, selecting and experimenting) is interpreted in terms of reflex processes and the "irritability" of the cell, and these again are traced back, like all stimulus-processes, to the subtle mechanics of the atoms.

### SPONTANEOUS GENERATION

4 This reduction of known biological phenomena to simpler terms, the lessening of the gap between inorganic and organic chemistry, and the formulation of the doctrine of the conservation of energy, have all prepared the way for a fourth step, the establishment of the inevitable theory of *generatio spontanea sive equivoca*, the spontaneous generation of the living, that is to say, the gradual evolution of the living from the not living. Since the earth, and with it the conditions under which alone life is possible, have had a beginning in time, life upon the earth must also have had a beginning. The assumption that the first living organisms may have come to the earth on meteorites simply shifts the problem a step farther back, for according to all current

theories of the universe, if there are in any of the heavenly bodies conditions admitting of the presence of life, these conditions have arisen from others in which life was impossible. Therefore, since this suggestion is on the face of it a mere evasion of the difficulty, the theory of spontaneous generation naturally arose. There is something almost comical in the change in the attitude of the natural sciences to this theory. For centuries it was one of the beliefs of popular superstition, with its naïve way of regarding nature, that earthworms " developed " from damp soil, and vermin from shavings, and in general that the living arose from the non-living. On the other hand it was one of the characteristics and axioms of scientific thought to reject this naïve *generatio equivoca*, and to hold fast to the proposition, *omne vivum ex ovo*, or, at least, *omne vivum ex vivo*. And it was regarded as one of the triumphs of modern science when, about the middle of the last century, Pasteur gave definiteness to this doctrine, and when through him, through Virchow, and indeed the whole younger generation of naturalists, the proposition was modified, on the basis of the newly discovered cell-theory, to *omnis cellula ex cellula*. But a short time after Pasteur's discoveries, the ideas of Darwinism and the theory of evolution gained widespread acceptance. And now it appeared that, in rejecting the theory of *generatio equivoca*, naturalists had, so to speak, sawn off the branch on which they desired to sit, and thus many, like Haeckel, became enthusiastic converts to

## SPONTANEOUS GENERATION 207

the theory which natural science had previously rejected.

Constructing theories and speculations as to the possibilities of spontaneous generation is regarded by some naturalists as somewhat gratuitous (*cf.* Du Bois-Reymond). In general, it is regarded as sufficient to point out that the reduction of the phenomena of life as we know them to those of a simpler order, and the unification of organic and inorganic chemistry, have made the problem of the first origin of life essentially simpler, and that the law of the constancy and identity of energy throughout the universe permits no other theory. But others go more determinedly to work, and attempt to give concrete illustrations of the problem. The most elementary form of life known to us is the cell. From cells and their combinations, their products and secretions, all organisms, plant and animal alike, are built up. If we succeed in deriving the cell, the derivation of the whole world of life seems, with the help of the doctrine of descent, a comparatively simple matter. The cell itself seems to stand nearer to the inorganic, and to be less absolutely apart from the inanimate world than a highly organised body, differentiated as to its functions and organs, such as a mammal. It almost seems as if we might regard the lowest forms of life known to us, which seem little more than aggregated homogeneous masses of flowing rather than creeping protoplasm, as an intermediate link between the higher forms of life and the non-living. But the theory does not begin with the cell; it assumes a series of connecting-links (which may of course be as long and as complicated as the series from the cell upwards to man) between the cell and matter which is still quite "inorganic" and which is capable only of the everyday chemical and physical phenomena, and not of the higher syntheses of these, which in their increasing complexity and diversity ultimately come to represent "life" in its most primitive forms. As proteid is the chief constituent of protoplasm, it is regarded as the specific physical basis of life, and life is looked upon as the sum of its functions. And it is not doubted that, if the conditions of the universe brought about a natural combination of carbon, hydrogen, nitrogen and oxygen in certain proportions, so that proteid resulted, the transition to proteid which forms itself and renews itself from the surrounding elements, to assimilating, growing, dividing proteid, and ultimately to the most primitive plasmic structure, to non-nucleated, nucleated, and finally fully formed cells, could also come about.

Haeckel's demonstration of the possibility of spontaneous generation is along these lines. He refers to the cytodes, the blood corpuscles, to alleged or actual non-nucleated cells, to bacteria, to the simplest forms of cell-structure, as proofs of the possibility of a descending series of connecting-links. He (and with him Nageli) calls these links, below the level of the cell, Probia or Probions, and for a time he believed that he

# MECHANICS OF DEVELOPMENT 209

had discovered in *Bathybius Haeckeli* presently existing homogeneous living masses, without cell division, nucleus or structure, the "primitive slime" which apparently existed in the abysmal depths of the ocean to this day. Unfortunately, this primitive slime soon proved itself an illusion.

Opinions differ as to whether spontaneous generation took place only in the beginning of evolution, or whether it occurred repeatedly and is still going on. Most naturalists incline to the former idea; Nageli champions the latter. There are also differences of opinion as to whether the origin of life from the non-living was manifold, and took place at many different places on the earth, or whether all the forms of life now in existence have arisen from a common source (monophyletic and polyphyletic theories).

### THE MECHANICS OF DEVELOPMENT

5. The minds of the supporters of the mechanical theory had still to move along a fifth line in order to solve the riddle of the development of the living individual from the egg, or of the germ to its finished form, the riddle of morphogenesis. They cannot assume the existence of "the whole" before the part, or equip it with the idea of the thing as a *spiritus rector*, playing the part of a metaphysical controlling agency. Here as elsewhere they must demonstrate the existence of purely mechanical principles. It is simply from the potential energies inherent in its constituent

parts that the supply of energy must flow, by means of which the germ is able to make use of inorganic material from without, to assimilate it and increase its own substance, and, by using it up, to maintain and increase its power of work, to break up the carbonic acid of the atmosphere and to gain the carbon which is so important for its vital functions, to institute and organise the innumerable chemico-physical processes by means of which its form is built up. Purely as a consequence of the chemico-physical nature of the germ, of the properties of the substances included in it on the one hand, and of the implicit structure and configuration of its parts, down to the intrinsic specific undulatory rhythm of its molecules, it must follow that its mass grows exactly as it does, and not otherwise, that it behaves as it does and not otherwise, duplicating itself by division after division, and by intricate changes arranging and rearranging the results of division until the embryo or larva, and finally the complete organism, is formed.

An extraordinary amount of ingenuity has been expended in this connection, in order to avoid here, where perhaps it is most difficult of all, the use of "teleological" principles, and to remain faithful to the orthodox, exclusively mechanical mode of interpretation. To this category belong Darwin's gemmules, Haeckel's plastidules, Nageli's micellæ, Weismann's labyrinth of ids, determinants, and biophors within the germ-plasm, and Roux's ingenious hypothesis of the struggle of parts,

# HEREDITY

which is an attempt to apply the Darwinian principle within the organism in order here also to rebut the teleological interpretation by giving a scientific one.*

## Heredity

6. With this fifth line of thought a sixth is associated and intertwined. The problem of development is closely bound up with that of "heredity." A developing organism follows the parental type. The acorn in its growth follows the type of the parent oak, repeating all its morphological and physiological characters down to the most intimate detail. And the animal organism adds to this also the whole psychical equipment, the instincts, the capacities of will and consciousness which distinguish its parents. The problems of the fifth and sixth order are closely inter-related, the sixth problem being in reality the same as the fifth, only in greater complexity.

A step towards the mechanical solution of this problem was indicated in the "preformation theory" advanced by Leibnitz, and elaborated by Bonnet. According to this theory the developing organism is enclosed in the minutest possible form within the egg, and is thus included in the parental organism, in miniature indeed, but quite complete. Thus the problem of the "development of form" or of "heredity"

* *Cf.* Roux, "Archiv. fur Entwicklungsmechanik." The name sufficiently indicates the scope,

was, so to speak, ruled out of court; all that was assumed was continuous growth and self-unfolding.

Opposed to this theory was one of later growth, the theory of epigenesis, which maintained that the organism developed without preformation from the still undifferentiated and homogeneous substance of the egg. The supporters of the first theory considered themselves much more scientific and exact than those of the second. And not without reason. For the theory of epigenesis obviously required mysterious formative principles, and equally mysterious powers of recollection and recapitulation, which impelled the undifferentiated ovum substance into the final form, precisely like that of its ancestors. Nor need the preformationists have greatly feared the reproach, that the parental organism must have been included within the grandparental, and so on backwards to the first parents in Paradise. For this "Chinese box" encapsulement theory only requires that we should grant the idea of the infinitely little, and that idea is already an integral part of our thinking.

Modern biologists ridicule the preformation hypothesis as altogether too artificial. And undoubtedly it founders on the facts of embryology, which disclose nothing to suggest the unfolding of a pre-existent miniature model, but show us how the egg-cell divides into two, into four, and so on, with continued multiplication followed by varied arrangements and rearrangements of cells—in short, all the complex changes which

# HEREDITY

constitute development. But a preformation in some sense or other there must be;—some peculiar material predisposition of the germ, which, as such, supplies the directing principle for the development, and the sufficient reason for the repetition of the parental form. This is of such obvious importance from the mechanical point of view that the speculations of to-day tend to move along the old preformationist lines. To these modern preformationists are opposed the modern upholders of epigenesis or gradual differentiation, who attempt to elaborate a mechanical theory of development. And with the contrast between these two schools there is necessarily associated the discussion as to the inheritance or non-inheritance of acquired characters.

Darwin's contribution to the problem of the sixth order was his rather vague theory of "Pangenesis." The living organism, according to him, forms in its various organs, parts, and cells exceedingly minute particles of living matter (gemmules), which, "in some way or other," bear within them the special characteristics of the part in which they are produced. These may wander through the organism and meet in the germ-plasm, and then, when a child-organism is produced, they "swarm," so to speak, in it again "in some way or other," and in some fashion control the development. This gemmule-theory was too obviously a *quid pro quo* to hold its ground for long. Various theories were elaborated, and the world of the invisibly minute was flooded with speculations.

The most subtle of these, on the side of consistent Darwinism, is that of Weismann, a pronounced preformation theory which has been increasingly refined and elaborated in the course of years of reflection. According to Weismann, the individual parts and characteristics of the organism are represented in the germ-plasm, not in finished form, but as "determinants" in a definite system which is itself the directing principle in the building up of the bodily system, and with definite characteristics, which determine the peculiarities of the individual organs and parts, down to scales, hairs, skin-spots, and birth-marks. As the germ-cells have the power of growth, and can increase endlessly by dividing and re-dividing, and as each process of division takes place in such a way that each half (each product of division) maintains the previous system, there arise innumerable germ-cells corresponding to one another, from which, therefore, corresponding bodies must arise (inheritance). It is not in reality the newly developed bodies which give rise to new germ-cells and transfer to them something of their own characters; the germ-cells of the child-organism develop from that of the parent ("immortality" of the germ-cells). Therefore there can be no inheritance of acquired characters, and no modifications of type through external causes; and all variations which appear in a series of generations are due solely to internal variations in the germ-cells, whether brought about by the complication of their system through the fusion of the male and

# HEREDITY 215

female germ-cells, or through differences in the growth of the individual determinants themselves. The numerous subsidiary theses interwoven in Weismann's theory are entirely coherent, and have been thought out to their conclusions with praiseworthy determination.* To the theory as a whole, because of its fundamental conception of preformation, and to its subsidiary hypotheses, piece by piece, there has been energetic opposition on the part of the upholders of the modern mechanical theory of epigenesis. This opposition is most concretely and comprehensively expressed in Haacke's "Gestaltung und Vererbung." The infinitely complex intricacy of Weismann's minute microcosm within the germ-cell, indeed within every id in it, is justly described as a mere duplication, a repetition in the infinitely little of the essential difficulties to be explained. The complicated processes of developing in the growing and inheriting organism cannot be explained, they say, in terms of processes of the equally complex and likewise developing germ-plasm. The complex, if it is to be explained at all, must be explained by the simple—in this case by the functions of a homogeneous uniform plasm.

At an earlier date Haeckel had made an attempt in this direction in his theory of the "perigenesis of the plastidules." Peculiar states of oscillation and rhythm in the molecules of the germ-substance, handed on to it from the parent organism and transferable to all the

* For a discussion of the difficulties and impossibilities of this theory see page 148 above

assimilated matter of the offspring, represent, according to this theory, the principle which impels development to follow a particular course corresponding to the type of the parents. This was a *physical* way of interpreting the matter. Other investigators have given a *chemical* expression to their theoretical schemes for explaining heredity.

Haacke declares both these to be unsatisfactory, and replaces them by morphological formative principles. It is the *structure* of the otherwise homogeneous living matter that explains morphogenesis and inheritance. Minute " gemmæ," homogeneous fundamental particles of living substance, not to be compared to or confused with Darwin's "gemmules," are aggregated in "Gemmaria," whose configuration, stability, symmetrical or asymmetrical structure, and so on, are determined by the relative positions of the gemmæ to each other, and these in their turn control the organism and give it a corresponding symmetrical or asymmetrical, a firmly or loosely aggregated structure. The completed organism then forms a system in organic equilibrium, which is constantly exposed to variations and influences due to external causes (St. Hilaire), and to use and disuse of organs (Lamarck). These influences affect the structure of the gemmaria, and as the germ-cells consist of gemmaria, like those of the rest of the organism, the possibility of the transmission of acquired new characters is self-evident. The importance of correlated growth and orthogenesis is explained on a similar

# HEREDITY

basis, and the Darwinian conceptions of the independent variation of individual parts, of the exclusive dominance of utility, of the influence of the struggle for existence in regard to individual selection, and of the omnipotence of natural selection, are energetically denied.

Oscar Hertwig,* de Vries, Driesch † and others attempt to reconcile the preformationist and the epigenetic standpoints, and "to extract what is good and usable out of both." Hertwig and Driesch, however, can only be mentioned with reservations in this connection.

We cannot better sum up the whole tendency of the construction of mechanical theories on these last lines than in the words of Schwann: "There is within the organism no fundamental force working according to a definite idea ; it arises in obedience to the blind laws of necessity."

So much for the different lines followed by the mechanical theories of to-day. An idea of their general tenor can be gained from a series of much quoted general treatises, of which we must mention at least the "classics." In Wagner's "Handwörterbuch der Physiologie," 1842, Vol. I., Lotze wrote a long introductory article to the whole work, on " Life and Vital

* "Preformation oder Epigenesis?" Outlines of a theory of the development of organisms. Jena, 1894. (Part I. of "Zeit- und Streitfragen der Biologie.") Translated by P. Chalmers Mitchell, "The Biological Problem of To-day"

† In his earlier period Later he rejects both preformation and epigenesis, as mechanical distortions of vital processes.

Force." It was the challenge of the newer views to the previously vitalistic standpoint, and at the same time it was based on Lotze's general principles and interspersed with philosophical criticism of the concepts of force, cause, effect, law, &c.* A similar train of ideas to Lotze's is followed to-day by O. Hertwig, especially in his "Mechanismus und Biologie."† Lighter and more elegant was the polemic against vital force, and the outline of a mechanical theory which Du Bois-Reymond prefaced to his great work, "Untersuchungen uber die tierische Electricitat" (1849). It did not go nearly so deep as Lotze's essay, but perhaps for that very reason its phrases and epigrams soon became common property. We may recall how he speaks of vital force as a "general servant for everybody," of the iron atom which remains the same whether it be in the meteorite in cosmic space, in the wheel of the railway carriage, or in the blood of the thinker, and of analytic mechanics which may be applied even to the problem of personal freedom.

The most comprehensive and detailed elaboration of the mechanical theory of life is to be found in Herbert Spencer's "Principles of Biology."‡ Friedrich Albert Lange's "History of Materialism" is a brilliant plea for mechanical theories,§ which he afterwards surpassed and

* See also Lotze's interesting article "Instinct" in the same work.
† Part II. of his "Zeit- und Streit-fragen der Biologie."
‡ Second Edition, 1902.
§ In Vol. II. p. 139. 1898.

# HEREDITY

neutralised by his Kantian Criticism. Verworn, too, in his "Physiology" * gives a clear example of the way in which the mechanical theory in its most consistent form is sublimed, apparently in the idealism of Kant and Fichte, but in reality in its opposite—the Berkeleyan psychology. A similar outcome is in various ways indicated in the modern trend of things.

* "General Physiology." Translated by Lee London. 1899 P. 170

## CHAPTER IX

### CRITICISM OF MECHANICAL THEORIES

In attempting to define our attitude to the mechanical theory of life, we have first of all to make sure that we have a right to take up a definite position at all. We should have less right, or perhaps none, if this theory of life were really of a purely "biological" nature, built up entirely from the expert knowledge and data which the biologist alone possesses. But the principles, assumptions, supplementary ideas and modes of expression along all the six lines we have discussed, the style and method according to which the hypothesis is constructed, the multitude of separate presuppositions with which it works, and indeed everything that helps to build up and knit the biological details into a scientific hypothesis, are the materials of rational synthesis in general, and as such are subject to general as well as to biological criticism. What is there, for instance, in Weismann's ingenious biophor-theory that can be called specifically biological, and not borrowed from other parts of the scientific system?

One advantage, indeed, the biologist always has in this matter, apart from his special knowledge; that is, the technical instinct, the power of scenting out, so to speak, and immediately feeling the importance of the facts pertaining to his own discipline. It is this that gives every specialist the advantage over the layman in dealing with the data of his own subject. This power of instinctively appraising facts, which develops in the course of all special work, can, for instance in hypotheses in the domain of history, transform small details, which to the layman seem trivial, into weighty arguments. Similarly it may be that the success of the mechanical interpretation in regard to isolated processes may make its validity for many other allied processes certain, even though there is no precise proof of this. But we cannot regard this as a final demonstration of the applicability of the mechanical theory, since the same technical instinct in other experts leads them to reject the whole hypothesis.

But here we are met with something surprising. May it not be that while we are impelled on general grounds to contend against the mechanical interpretaton of vital phenomena, we are not so impelled on *religious* grounds? May it not be that the instinct of the religious consciousness is misleading when it impels us—as probably every one will be able to certify from his own experience —to rebel against this mechanisation of life, the mechanical solution of its mysteries? Lotze, the energetic antagonist of "vital force," the founder of the mechanical theory of vital processes, was himself a theist, and was so far from recognising any contradiction between the mechanical point of view and the Christian belief in God, that he included the former without ceremony in his theistic philosophical speculations. His view has become that of many theologians, and is often expressed in a definition of the boundaries between theology and natural science. According to the idea which was formulated by Lotze, and developed by others along his lines, the matter is quite simple. The interest which religion has in the processes of nature is at once and exclusively to be found in teleology. Are there purposes, plans, and ideas which govern and give meaning to the whole? The interest of natural science is purely in recognising inviolable causality; every phenomenon must have its compelling and sufficient reason in the system of causes preceding it. All that is and happens is absolutely determined by its causes, and nothing, no *causæ finales* for instance, can co-operate with these causes in determining the result. But, as Lotze says, and as we have repeatedly pointed out, causal explanation does not exclude a consideration from the point of view of purpose, and the mechanical interpretation does not do so either. For this is nothing more than the causal explanation itself, only carried to complete consistency and definiteness. Purposes and ideas are not efficient causes but results. Where, for instance, there is a controlled purposive occurrence, the "purpose" nowhere appears as a factor co-operating with the series of causes, for these follow according to strict law, and the "purpose" reveals itself at the close

## MECHANICAL THEORIES CRITICISED 223

of the series, as the result of a closed causal nexus, complete in itself, always provided that the initial links in the chain have been accurately estimated. The same is true of the processes of life. They are the ultimate result, strictly necessary and sufficiently accounted for in terms of mechanical sequence, of a long chain of causes whose initial links imply a definite constitution which could not be further reduced. Whether this ultimate result is merely a result or whether it is also a "purpose" is a question which, as we have seen twice already, it is wholly beyond the power of the causal mode of interpretation to answer. Given that an infinite intelligence in the world wished to realise purposes without instituting them as directly accomplished, but by letting them express themselves through a gradual "becoming," the method would be exactly what is shown in the mechanical theory of life, that is, the primitive data and starting-points would have inherent in them a peculiar constitution and a rigidly inexorable orderliness of causal sequence. And Lotze emphasises that it would also be worthier of God to achieve the greatest by means of the simplest, and to work out the realisation of His eternal purposes according to the strict inevitableness of mechanism, than to attain His ends through the complicated means, the adventitious aids, and all the irregularities implied in the incommensurable activities of a "vital force." ("God needs no minor gods.")

To Lotze himself these original data and starting-points are the primitive forms of life, which, according to his view, are directly " given," and cannot be referred back to anything else (except to " creation "). But it is obvious that his view can be enlarged and extended so as to refer the derivation of the whole animate world to the original raw materials of the cosmos (energy, matter, or whatsoever they may be), and to the orderly process by which these materials were combined in various configurations to form the chemical elements, the chemical compounds, living proteids, the first cell, and the whole series of higher forms. If this nexus has taken place, it is nothing else than the transformation of the "potential" into the "actual" through strict causality. And if this actuality proves itself to have claims, because of its own intrinsic worth, to be considered as intelligent "purpose," the whole system of means, including the starting-point, can be recognised as the means to an end, and the original wisdom and the intelligence which ordained the purpose is only glorified the more through the great simplicity, the rational comprehensibility, and the inexorable necessity of the system, which excludes all chance, and therewith all possibility of error.

This extension of Lotze's reconciliation of the mechanical causal with the teleological point of view is impressive and, as far as it goes, also quite convincing. It will never be given up, even if the point of view should change somewhat. And we have already seen that it is quite sufficient as long as we are dealing

## MECHANICAL THEORIES CRITICISED 225

only with the question of teleology. But we must ask whether religion will be satisfied with "teleology" alone, or whether this is even the first requirement that it makes in regard to natural phenomena. We have already asked the question and attempted to clear the ground for an answer. Let us try to make it more definite.

Many people will have a certain uneasiness in regard to the Lotzian ideas; they will be unable to rid themselves of a feeling that this way of looking at things is only a *pis aller* for the religious point of view, and that the fundamental requirements of religious feeling receive very inadequate satisfaction on this method. The world of life which has arisen thus is altogether too rational and transparent. It is calculable and mathematical. It satisfies well enough the need for teleology, and with that the need for a supreme, universally powerful and free intelligence; but it gives neither support nor nourishment to the essential element in religious feeling, through which alone faith becomes in the strict sense religious. Religion, even Christian religion, is, so to speak, a stratified structure, a graduated pyramid, expressing itself, at its second (and undoubtedly higher) level, in our recognition of purpose, the rationality of the world, our own spiritual and personal being and worth, but implying at its basis an inward sense of the mysterious, a joy in that which is incommensurable and unspeakable, which fills us with awe and devotion. And religion at the second

P

stage must not sweep away the essence of the stage below, but must include it, at the same time informing it with new significance. Whoever does not possess his religion in this way will agree with, and will be quite satisfied with the Lotzian standpoint. But to any one who has experience of the most characteristic element in religion, it will be obvious that there must be a vague but deep-rooted antipathy between religion and the mathematical-mechanical conception of things. Evidence of the truth of this is to be found in the instinctive perceptions and valuations which mark even the naive expressions of the religious consciousness.* For it is in full sympathy with a world which is riddled with what is inconceivable and incommensurable, in full sympathy with every evidence of the existence of such an element in the world of nature and mind, and therefore with every proof that the merely mechanical theory has its limits, that it does not suffice, and that its very insufficiency is a proof that the world is and remains in its depths mysterious. Now we have already said that the true sphere for such feeling is not the outer court

* As a remarkable instance and corroboration of this, we may refer to the ever-recurring, instinctive antipathy of deeply religious temperaments, from Augustine to Luther and Schleiermacher, to the Aristotelian mood and its conception of the world, and their sympathy with Plato's (mostly and especially in their "Platonised" expressions). The clear-cut, luminous, conception of the world which expresses everything in terms of commensurable concepts is thoroughly Aristotelian But it would be difficult to find a place in it for the peculiar element which lies at the root of all true devotional feeling, and which makes faith something more than the highest "reverence, love and trust."

## MECHANICAL THEORIES CRITICISED 227

of nature, but within the realm of the emotional life and of history, and, on the other hand, that even if the attempt to trace life back to the simpler forces of nature were successful, we should still be confronted with the riddle of the sphinx. But any one who would say frankly what he felt would at once be obliged to admit that the religious sense is very strongly stirred by the mystery of vital phenomena, and that in losing this he would lose a domain very dear to him. These sympathies and antipathies are in themselves sufficient to give an interest to the question of the insufficiency of the mechanical view of things.

For it is by no means the case that the mechanical theory, with its premisses and principles, is the interpretation that best fits the facts, and that most naturally arises out of a calm consideration of the animate world. It is an artificial scheme, and astonishing energy has been expended on the attempt to fit it to the actual world, that it may make this orderly and translucent. It certainly yields this service so far, but not without often becoming a kind of strait-jacket, and revealing itself as an artificiality. In so far as the special problems of biology are concerned, we shall afterwards follow our previous method of taking our orientation from those specialists in the subject who, in reaction from the one-sidedness of the mechanical doctrine, have founded the " neo-vitalism " of to-day. Here we are only concerned with the generalities and presuppositions of the theory.

We must dispute even the main justification of the theory, which is sought for in the old maxim of parsimony in the use of principles of explanation (*entia*, and also *principia, præter necessitatem non esse multiplicanda*), and in Kant's "regulative principle," that science must proceed as if everything could ultimately be explained in terms of mechanism. For surely our task is to try to explain things, not at any cost with the fewest possible principles, but rather with the aid of those principles which appear most correct. If nature is not fundamentally simple, then it is not scientific but unscientific to simplify it theoretically. And the proposition bracketed above has its obvious converse side, that while entities and principles must not be multiplied except when it is necessary, on the other hand their number must not be arbitrarily lessened. To proceed according to the fundamental maxims of the mechanistic view can only be wholesome for a time and, so to speak, for pædagogical reasons. To apply them seriously and permanently would be highly injurious, for, by prejudging what is discoverable in nature, it would tend to prevent the calm, objective study of things which asks for nothing more than to see them as they are. It would thus destroy the fineness of our appreciation of what there really is in nature. This is true alike of forcible attempts to reduce the processes of life to mechanical processes, and of the Darwinian doctrine of the universal dominance of utility. Both bear unmistakably the stamp of foregone conclusions, and betray

## MECHANICAL THEORIES CRITICISED 229

a desire for the simplest, rather than for the most correct principles of interpretation.

There is one point which presses itself on the notice even of outsiders, and is probably realised even more keenly by specialists. The confidence of the supporters of the mechanical theories of earlier days, from Descartes onward, that animals and the bodies of men were machines, mechanical automata, down to the mechanical theories of Lamettrie and Holbach, of *l'homme machine*, and of the *système de la nature*, was at least as great as, probably greater than, that of the supporters of the modern theories. Yet how naive and presumptuous seem the crude and wooden theories upon which the mechanical system was formerly built up, and how falsely interpreted seem the physiological and other facts which lent them support, when seen in the light of our modern physiological knowledge. Vaucanson's or Drozsch's duck-automaton or clockwork-man, with which the mechanical theorists of bygone days amused themselves, would not go far to encourage the physiologist of to-day to pursue his mechanical studies, but would rather throw a vivid light on the impossibility of comparing the living " machine " with machines in the usual sense. For things emphatically do not happen within the living organism in the same way as in the automatic duck, and the more exact the resemblance to the functions of a "real" duck became, the more did the system of means by which the end was attained become unlike vital processes. It is difficult to resist the impression that in another hundred years,—perhaps again from the standpoint of new and definitely accepted mechanical explanations,—people will regard our developmental mechanics, cellular mechanics, and other vital mechanics much in the same way as we now look on Vaucanson's duck.

Associated or even identical with this is the fact that in proportion as mechanical interpretation advances, the difficulties it has to surmount continually crop up anew. Processes which seem of the simplest kind and the most likely to be capable of purely mechanical explanation, processes such as those of assimilation, digestion, respiration, for which it was believed that exact parallels existed in the purely mechanical domain, as, for instance, in the osmotic processes of porous membranes, are seen when closely scrutinised as they occur in the living body to be extremely complex; in fact they have to be transferred "provisionally" from the mechanical to the vital rubric. To this category belong the whole modern development of the cell-theory, which replaces the previously *single* mechanism in the living body by millions of them, every one of which raises as many problems as the one had done in the days of cruder interpretation. Every individual cell, as it appears to our understanding to-day, is at least as complicated a riddle as the whole organism formerly appeared.

But further: the modern development of biology has emphasised a special problem, which was first formu-

## MECHANICAL THEORIES CRITICISED 231

lated by Leibnitz (though it is in antithesis to his fundamental Monad-theory), and which appears incapable of solution on mechanical lines. Leibnitz declared living beings to be "machines," but machines of a peculiar kind. Even the most complicated machine, in the ordinary sense, consists of a combination of smaller "machines," that is to say, of wheels, systems of levers, &c., of a simpler kind. And these sub-machines may in their turn consist of still simpler ones, and so on. But ultimately a stage is reached when the component parts are homogeneous, and cannot be analysed into simpler machines. It is otherwise with the organism. According to Leibnitz it consists of machines made up of other machines, and so on, into the infinitely little. However far we can proceed in our analysis of the parts, we shall still find that they are syntheses, made up of most ingeniously complex component parts, and this as far as our powers of seeing and distinguishing will carry us. That is to say: organisation is continued on into the infinitely little.

Leibnitz's illustration of the fish-pond is well known. He could have no better corroboration of his theory than the results of modern investigation afford. His doctrine of the continuation of organisation downwards into ever smaller expression is confirmed to a certain extent even by anatomy. By analysing structural organisation down to cells a definite point seemed to have been reached. But it now appears that at that point the problem is only beginning. One organisation is made up of other organisations—cells, protoplasm, nucleus, nucleolus, centrosomes, and so on, according to the power of the microscope; and these structures, instead of explaining the vital functions of growth, development, multiplication by division, and the rest, simply repeat them on a smaller scale, and are thus in their turn living units, the aggregation of which is illustrated better by the analogy of a social organism than by that of a mechanical structure.

In order to follow the mechanical explanation along the six lines we have previously indicated, we shall, as we have already said, entrust ourselves to the specialists who are on the opposite side. The difficulties and objections which the mechanical theory has to face have forced themselves insistently upon us even in the course of a short sketch such as has just been given, but they will be clearly realised if we approach them from the other side. But, first of all, a word as to the fundamental and, it is alleged, unassailable doctrine on which the theory as a whole is based, the " law of the conservation of energy." Tho appeal to this, at any rate in the way in which it is usually made, is apt to be so distorted that the case must first be clearly stated before we can get further with the discussion.

### The Law of the Conservation of Energy

Helmholtz's proof established mathematically what Kant had already, by direct insight, advanced as an *a priori* fundamental axiom: that in any given system the sum of energy can neither increase (impossibility of a *perpetuum mobile*) nor diminish (there is no disappearance of energy, but only transformation into another form). But even the vitalist had no need to deny this proposition. The "energy" which is required for the work of directing, setting agoing, changing and rearranging the chemico-physical processes in the body, and bringing about the effective reactions to stimuli which result in "development," "transmission," "regeneration," and so on—if indeed any energy is required—of course could not come "from within" as a spontaneous increase of the existing sum of energy—that would, indeed, be a magical becoming out of nothing!—but must naturally be thought of as coming "from without." The appeal to the law of the conservation of energy is therefore in itself irrelevant; but it conceals behind it an assertion of a totally different kind, namely, that in relation to physico-chemical sequences there can be no "without," nothing transcending them—an assertion which Helmholtz's arguments cannot and were never intended to establish. But before any definite attitude to this newly imported assertion could be taken up, it would require to be distinctly defined, and that would lead us at once into all the depths of epistemological discussion. Here, therefore, we can only say so much: If this assertion is accepted it is well to see where it carries us; namely, back to the first-described naive standpoint, which, without critical scruples, quite seriously accepts the world as it appears to it for the reality, and quite seriously speaks of an infinity lying in time behind us—and therefore come to an end—and is not in the least disturbed from its "dogmatic slumber" by this or any of the other great antinomies of our conception of the universe. And it remains, too, for this standpoint to come to terms with the fact that, in voluntary actions, of which we have the most direct knowledge, we have through our will the power of intervention in the physico-chemical nexus of our bodily energies—a fact which implies the existence of a "without," from which interpolations or influences may flow into the physico-chemical system, even if there be none in regard to the domain of "vital" phenomena. And we should require to find out through what parallelistic or abruptly idealistic system the "without" was done away with in this case. For if a transcendental basis, or reverse side, or cause of things, be admitted—even if only in the form of our materialistic popular metaphysics (the "substance" of Haeckel's "world-riddle")—then a "without," from which primarily the cosmic system with its constant sum of matter and energy is explained, is also admitted, and it is difficult to see why it should have exhausted itself in this single effort.

CRITICISMS OF THE MECHANISTIC THEORY OF LIFE

The course of the mechanistic theory of life has been surprisingly similar to that of its complement, the theory of the general evolution of the organic world.

## MECHANISTIC THEORY CRITICISED

The two great doctrines of the schools, Darwinism on the one hand, the mechanical interpretation of life on the other, are both tottering, not because of the criticism of outsiders, but of specialists within the schools themselves. And the interest which religion has in this is the same in both cases: the transcendental nature of things, the mysterious depth of appearance, which these theories denied or obscured, become again apparent. The incommensurableness and mystery of the world, which are, perhaps, even more necessary to the very life of religion than the right to regard it teleologically, reassert themselves afresh in the all-too-comprehensible and mathematically-formulated world, and re-establish themselves, notwithstanding obstinate and persistent attempts to do away with them. This is perhaps to the advantage of both natural science and religion: to the advantage of religion because it can with difficulty co-exist with the universal dominance of the mathematical way of looking at things; to the advantage of natural science because, in giving up the one-sidedness of the purely quantitative outlook, it does not give up its "foundations," its "right to exist," but only a *petitio principii* and a prejudice that compelled it to exploit nature rather than to explain it, and to prescribe its ways rather than to seek them out.

The reaction from the one-sided mechanical theories shows itself in many different ways and degrees. It may, according to the individual naturalist, affect the theory as a whole, or only certain parts of it, or only particular lines. It starts with mere criticism and with objections, which go no further than saying that "in the meantime" we are still far from having reached a physico-chemical solution of the riddle of life; it may ascend through all stages up to an absolute rejection of the theory as an idiosyncrasy of the time which impedes the progress of investigation, and as an uncritical prejudice of the schools. It may remain at the level of mere protest, and content itself with demonstrating the insufficiency of the mechanical explanation, without attempting to formulate any independent theory for the domain of the vital ; or it may construct a specifically biological theory, claiming independence amid other disciplines, and basing this claim on the autonomy of vital processes ; or it may widen out deliberately into metaphysical study and speculation. Taken at all these levels it presents such a complete section of the trend of modern ideas and problems that it would be an attractive study even apart from the special interest which attaches to it from the point of view of religious and idealistic conceptions of the universe.

Both Liebig and Johannes Muller remained vitalists, notwithstanding the discovery of the synthesis of urea and the increasing number of organic compounds which were built up artificially by purely chemical methods. It was only about the middle of the last century that the younger generation, under the leadership, in Germany, of Du Bois-Reymond in particular, went over

## VIRCHOW'S "CAUTION" 237

decidedly to the mechanistic side, and carried the doctrines of the school to ever fresh victories. But opposition was not lacking from the outset, though it was restrained and cautious.

### VIRCHOW'S "CAUTION"

Here, as also in regard to "Darwinism," which was advanced about the same time, the typical advocate of "caution" was Rudolf Virchow. His doubts and reservations found utterance very soon after the theory itself had been promulgated. In his "Cellular Pathologie," * and in an essay on "The Old Vitalism and the New," † he puts in a word for a *vis vitalis*. The old vitalism, he declared, had been false because it assumed, not a *vis*, but a *spiritus vitalis*. The substances in animate and in inanimate bodies have undoubtedly absolutely the same properties. Nevertheless, " we must at once rid ourselves of the scientific prudery of regarding the processes of life solely as the mechanical result of the molecular forces inherent in their constituent bodily parts." The essential feature of life is a derived and communicated force *additional* to the molecular forces. Whence it comes we are not told. He glided all round the problem with platitudinarian expressions, which were intended to show his own adherence as a matter of course to the new biological school, and which revealed at the same time his striking incapacity for defining a

* "Arch fur pathol. Anatomie und Physiologie," Bd. VIII. 1855.
† Vol. IX., 1856.

problem with any precision. At a "certain period in the evolution of the earth" this force arose, as the ordinary mechanical movements "swung over" into the vital. But it is thus a special form of movement, which detaches itself from the great constants of general movement, and runs its course alongside of, and in constant relation to, these. (Did ever vitalist assert more?) After thus preparing the way for a return of the veering process at a particular stage of evolution, and giving the necessary assurances against the "diametrically opposed dualistic position," Virchow employs almost all the arguments against the mechanical theory which vitalists have ever brought forward. Even the catalytic properties of ferments are above the "ordinary" physical and chemical forces. The movement of crystallisation, too, cannot be compared with the vital movement. For vital force is not immanent in matter, but is always the product of previous life.\* In the simplest processes of growth and nutrition the *vis vitalis* plays its vital *rôle*. This is true in a much greater degree of the processes of development and morphogenesis. In the phenomena of irritability life reveals its spontaneity through "responses," and so on. "Peu d'anatomie pathologique éloigne du vitalisme, beaucoup d'anatomie pathologique y ramène."

It is impossible to make much of this position. It leaves the theory with one of the opposing parties, the

\* The same is true even of crystals, "*omne crystallum e crystallo.*"

## PREYER'S POSITION

practice with the other, and the problem just where it was before.

### PREYER'S POSITION

Along with Virchow, we must name another of the older generation, the physiologist William Preyer, who combated "vitalism," "dualism," and "mechanism" with equal vehemence, and issued a manifesto, already somewhat solemn and official, against "vital force." And yet he must undoubtedly be regarded as a vitalist by mechanists and vitalists alike.* He is more definite than Virchow, for he does not content himself with general statements as to the "origin" of vital force, and of the "swinging over" of the merely mechanical energies into the domain of the vital, but holds decidedly to the proposition *omne vivum e vivo*. He therefore maintains that life has always existed in the cosmos, and entirely rejects spontaneous generation.

The fallacy, he says, of the mechanistic claims was due to the increasing number of physical explanations of isolated vital phenomena, and of imitations of the chemical products of organic metabolism. A wrong conclusion was drawn from these. "Any one who hopes to deduce from the chemical and physical properties of the fertilised egg the necessity that an animal, tormented by hunger and love must, after a

* *Cf.* "Ueber die Aufgabe der Naturwissenschaft," Jena, 1876. "Naturwissenschaftliche Tatsachen und Probleme." "Physiologie und Entwicklungslehre," 1886, in the collection of the "Allgemeiner Vereins fur Deutsche Literatur." Also in the same collection, "Aus Natur- und Menschen-leben."

certain time, arise therefrom, has a pathetic resemblance to the miserable manufacturers of homunculi." Life is one of the underivable and inexplicable fundamental functions of universal being. From all eternity life has only been produced from life.

As Preyer accepts the Kant-Laplace theory of the origin of our earth from the sun, he reaches ideas which have points of contact with the "cosmo-organic" ideas of Fechner. Life was present even when the earth was a fiery fluid sphere, and was possibly more general and more abundant then than it is now. And life as we know it may only be a smaller and isolated expression of that more general life.*

* These ideas are not fully worked out, and they are disguised in poetic form—for instance, when even the play of flames is compared to vital processes. But if they be stripped of their poetic garb, they lead to the same conclusions to which one is always led when one approaches the problem unprejudiced by naturalistic or anthropomorphic preconceptions of the relation of the infinite to the finite, or the divine to the natural. If we exclude the materialistic or semi-materialistic position which regards teleological phenomena, vital processes, and even states of sensation and consciousness as the function of a "substance" or of matter, we can quite well speak of them as general "cosmo-organic" functions of universal being, meaning that they occur of necessity wherever the proper conditions exist. According to the doctrine of potentiality and actuality, this is to say that all possible stages of the higher and highest phenomena are *semper et ubique* potentially present in universal being, and that they become actual wherever the physical processes are far enough advanced to afford the necessary conditions.

Preyer's ideas have been revived of late, especially in the romantic form, as, for instance, in Willy Pastor's "Lebensgeschichte der Erde" ("Leben und Wissen," Vol. I, Leipzig, 1903). And in certain circles, characterised by a simultaneous veneration for and combina-

## PREYER'S POSITION 241

Among the younger generation of specialists, those most often quoted as opponents of the mechanical theory are probably Bunge, Rindfleisch, Kerner von Marilaun, Neumeister and Wolff. A special group among them, not very easy to classify, may be called the Tectonists. Associated with them is Reinke's "Theory of Dominants." Driesch started from their ranks, and is a most interesting example of consistent development from a recognition of the impossibilities of the mechanistic position to an individually thought-out vitalistic theory. Hertwig, too, takes a very definite position of his own in regard to these matters. Perhaps the most original contribution in the whole field is Albrecht's "Theory of Different Modes of Regarding Things." We may close the list with the name of K. C. Schneider, who has carried these modern ideas on into metaphysical speculation. Several others might be mentioned along with and connecting these representative names.*

tion of modern natural science—Haeckel, Romanticism, Novalis and other antitheses—Fechner appears to have come to life again. The type of this group is W. Bolsche. Naturally enough, Pastor has turned his attention also to the recent views of Schroen in regard to crystallisation. The fact, *omne crystallum e crystallo*, like the corresponding fact, *omne vivum e vivo*, was long a barrier against mechanistic derivation But Schroen draws a parallel between crystallisation and organic processes, so that the alleged clearness and obviousness of the inorganic can no longer be carried over—in the old fashion—into the realm of life, but, conversely, the mystery of life must be extended downwards, and continued into the inorganic.

* Worthy of note and much cited is a somewhat indefinite essay

Q

## THE POSITION OF BUNGE AND OTHER PHYSIOLOGISTS

For a long time one of the most prominent figures in the controversy was Prof. G. Bunge, of Basle, who was one of the first modern physiologists to champion vitalism, and who has tried to show by analogies and illustrations what is necessarily implied in vital activity.* The mechanical reduction of vital phenomena to physico-chemical forces, he says, is impossible, and becomes more and more so as our knowledge deepens. He brings forward a series of convincing examples of the way in which apparent mechanical explanations have broken down. The absorption of the chyle through the walls of the intestine seemed to be a mechanically intelligible process

on "Neovitalism," by the Wurzburg pathologist, E von Rindfleisch (in " Deutsche Medizinische Wochenschrift," 1895, No. 38)

* Already given in detail in his " Lehrbuch der phys und pathol Chemie " (Second Edition, 1889), in the first chapter, "Vitalism and Mechanism." In the meantime a fifth revised and enlarged edition of Bunge's book has appeared as a " Lehrbuch der Physiologie des Menschen" (Leipzig, 1901). The relevant early essays appear here again under the title "Idealism and Mechanism." The arguments are the same. It is often supposed that it is merely a question of time, and that in the long run we must succeed in finding proofs that the whole process of life is only a complex process of movement, but the history of physiology shows that the contrary is the case All the processes which can be explained mechanically are those which are not vital phenomena at all. It is in activity that the riddle of life lies. The solution of this riddle is looked for, more decidedly than before but still somewhat vaguely. in the "idealism" of self-consciousness and its implications "*Physiologus nemo nisi psychologus.*" These views have been also stated in a separate lecture · G. Bunge, "Vitalismus und Mechanismus," (Leipzig, 1886).

## BUNGE AND OTHER PHYSIOLOGISTS 243

of osmosis and diffusion. But in reality it proves to be rather a process of selection on the part of the epithelial cells of the intestine, analogous to the selection and rejection exercised elsewhere by unicellular organisms. In the same way the epithelial cells of the mammary glands "select" the suitable substances from the blood. It is impossible to explain in a mechanical way the power which directs the innumerable different chemical and physical processes within the organism, whether they be the bewilderingly purposeful reactions in the individual life of the cell, which seem to point to psychic processes within the plasm, or the riddles of development and of inheritance in particular; for how can a spermatozoon, so small that 500 millions can lie on a cubic line, be the bearer of all the peculiarities of the father to the son?

In Lecture III. Bunge defines his attitude towards the law of the conservation of energy. In so doing he unconsciously follows the lines laid down by Descartes. All processes of movement and all functions exhibited by the living substance are the results of the accumulated potential energies, and the sums of work done and energy utilised remain the same. But the liberation and the direction of these energies is a factor by itself, which neither increases nor diminishes the sum of energies. "*Occasiones*" and "*causæ*" are brought into the field once more. The energies effect the phenomena, but they require "*occasiones*" to liberate them; thus a stone may fall to the ground by virtue of the potential energies stored in it at the time of its suspension, but it cannot fall until the thread by which it hangs has been cut. The function of the "*occasio*" itself is something quite outside of and without relation to the effect caused; it is a matter of indifference whether the thread be cut gently through with a razor or shot in two with a cannon ball.

Kassowitz* is an instructive example of how much the force of criticism has been recognised even by those occupying a convinced mechanical point of view. He subjects all the different theories which attempt to explain the chief vital phenomena in mechanical terms to a long and exhaustive examination. The theories of the organism as a thermodynamic engine, osmotic theories, theories of ferments, interpretations in terms of electro-dynamics and molecular-physics—are all examined (chap. iv.); and the failure of all these hypotheses, notwithstanding the enormous amount of ingenuity expended in their construction, is summed up in an emphatic "*Ignoramus*." "The failure is a striking one," and it is frankly admitted that, in strong contrast to the earlier mood of confident hope, there now prevails a mood of resignation in regard to the mechanical-experimental investigation of the living organism, and that even specialists of the first rank are finding that they have to reckon again seriously with vital force. This breakdown and these admissions do not exactly tend to prejudice us in favour of the

* "Allgemeine Biologie" (2 vols.), Vienna, 1899

author's own attempt to substantiate new mechanical theories.

In the comprehensive text-book of physiological chemistry by R. Neumeister, the mechanical standpoint seemed to be adhered to as the ideal. But the same writer forsakes it entirely, and disputes it energetically in his most recent work, " Betrachtungen uber das Wesen der Lebenserscheinungen "* (" Considerations as to the Nature of Vital Phenomena "). He passes over all the larger problems, such as those of development, inheritance, regeneration, and confines himself in the main to the physiological functions of protoplasm, especially to those of the absorption of food and metabolism. And he shows, by means of illustrations, in part Bunge's, in part his own, and in close sympathy with Wundt's views, that even these vital phenomena cannot possibly be explained in terms of chemical affinity, physical osmosis, and the like. In processes of selection (such as, for instance, the excretion of urea and the retention of sugar in the blood), the "aim is obvious, but the causes cannot be recognised." Psychical processes play a certain part in the functions of protoplasm in the form of qualitative and quantitative sensitiveness. All the mechanical processes in living organisms are initiated and directed by psychical processes. Physical, chemical and mechanical laws are perfectly valid, but they are not absolutely dominant. Living matter is to be defined as " a unique chemical

* Jena, 1903.

system, the molecules of which, by their peculiar reciprocal action, give rise to psychical and material processes in such a way that the processes of the one kind are always causally conditioned and started by those of the other kind." The psychical phenomena he regards as transcendental, supernatural, "mystical," yet unquestionably also subject to a strict causal nexus, although the causality must remain for ever concealed. Starting from this basis, he analyses and rejects the explanations which have been offered in terms of the analogy of ferments, enzymes, or catalytic processes. In particular, he disputes Ostwald's "Energismus" and Verworn's Biogen hypothesis.*

* *Cf* especially Verworn's example of the manufacture of sulphuric acid. See what we have previously said on the "second line" of mechanistic theory, along which Neumeister's thought mainly moves. See especially p 198. As regards the 'fifth line," the problem of the development of form in its present phase, there is an instructive short essay by Fr. Meikel (Nachrichten der K Gesellschaft der Wissenschaften Gottingen. Geschaftl Mitt. 1897, Heft 2)—" Welche Krafte wirken gestaltend auf den Korper der Menschen und Tiere?" This essay avoids, obviously intentionally, the shibboleths of controversy. The mechanical point of view and the play with mechanical analogies and models are abruptly dismissed. "If things, which were in themselves susceptible of mechanical explanations, occur in the absence of the mechanical antecedent conditions, then we must seek for other forces to enable us to understand them" And quite calmly a return is made to the old, simple conception of a "regulative" and a "formative force," inherent as a capacity *sui generis* within the "energids," the really living parts of the cell The cell-energid carries within it the "pattern" of the organisation, and the partial or perfect "capacity" ("Fertigkeit") for producing and reproducing the whole organism But these two forces ' make use of ' the physico-chemical forces as

Among the vitalists of to-day, one of the most frequently cited, perhaps, except Driesch the most frequently cited, is G. Wolff, a *Privatdozent*, formerly at Würzburg, now at Basle. He has only published short lectures and essays, and these deal not so much with the mechanical theory as with Darwinism.* But in these writings his main argument is that of his concluding chapter: the spontaneous adaptiveness of the organism, which nullifies all contingent theories to explain the purposiveness in ontogeny and phylogeny. And in his lecture, " Mechanismus und Vitalismus,"† in which he directs his attention especially to criticising Butschli's defence of mechanism, the only problem to which prominence is given is the one with which we are here concerned. In spite of their brevity, these writings have given rise to much controversy, because what is peculiar to the two standpoints is described with precision, and the problem is clearly defined. His criticism had its starting-point in, and received a special impulse from an empirical proof, due to a very happy experiment of his own, of the marvellous regenerative capacity, and the inherent purposive

tools to work out details. So to describe the state of the case is not of course a solution of the problem; it is only a figurative formulation of it. But that, at the present day, we can and must return to doing this if we are to describe things simply and as they actually occur, is precisely what is most instructive in the matter.

* "Beitrage zur Kritik der Darwinschen Lehre," which was first published in the "Biologisches Zentralblatt," 1898.

† Leipzig, 1892.

activity of the living organism. He succeeded in proving that if the lens of the eye of the newt be excised, it may be regrown. The importance of this fact is greatly increased if we trace out in detail the various impossible rival mechanical interpretations which have grown up around this interesting case. As Driesch says, " It is not a restoration starting from the wound, it is a substitution starting from a different place."

### The Views of Botanists Illustrated

It might have been expected that in the domain of plant-biology, if anywhere, the mechanistic standpoint would have been the prevailing one. For it is almost a matter of course to regard plants as devoid of sensation or "psychical" life, and as mechanical systems, chemical laboratories, and reflex mechanisms, and this way of regarding them has been made easy by the very marked uniformity and lack of spontaneity in their vital processes as compared with those of animals. But it is not the case that mechanical theories have here prevailed. The opposition to them is just as great here as elsewhere, and from the days of Wigand onwards it has been almost continuously sustained.* Very characteristic is

* Before Wigand's larger works there had appeared F. Delpino. "Applicazione della Teoria Darwinia ai Fiori ed agli Insetti Visitatori dei Fiori" (Bull. della Societa Entomologica Ital, Florence 1870). He says " Un principio intrinsico, reagente, finchè dura la vita, contro le influenze estrinseche ossia contro gli agenti chimici e fisici."

Pfeffer's "Pflanzen-Physiologie" (1897), which is written professedly from the mechanist point of view. "Vitalism," according to this authority, is to be rejected, but instead of "vital force" he offers us "given properties," and the alleged machine-like collocations of the most minute elements. In regard, for instance, to the riddle of development and morphogenesis, we must simply accept it as a "given property," that the acorn grows in an oak and nothing else. The chemical explanation of the vital functions of protoplasm is also to be rejected; as a shattered watch is no longer a watch though it remains chemically the same, so it is with protoplasm. The available chemical knowledge of the substances of which protoplasm is made up is insufficient to render the vital processes intelligible. Here, as everywhere else, we have to reckon with ultimate "properties (entities), which we neither can, nor desire to analyse further." "The human mind is no more capable of forming a conception of the ultimate cause of things than of eternity." If all the views here indicated were followed out to their logical conclusions, they would hinder rather than further the process of reduction to terms of physico-chemical sequences.

Kerner von Marilaun in his "Pflanzenleben" deliberately takes up a thorough-going vitalist position, and on this point as well as on many others he opposed the current theory of the school (Darwinism). It is true, he admits, that many of the phenomena in plants can be explained in purely mechanical terms, but they are only those which may occur also in non-living structures. The specific expressions of life cannot be explained in this way. He shows this more fully in regard to the most fundamental of all the vital processes in the plant-body—the breaking up of carbonic acid gas by the chlorophyll to obtain the carbon which is the fundamental element in all living organisms. We know the requisite conditions: the supply of raw material, and the sunlight from which the energy is derived. But how the chlorophyll makes use of these to effect the breaking up, and how it starts the subsequent syntheses of the carbon into the most complex organic compounds remains a mystery. And so on upwards through all the strictly vital phenomena.

Wiesner's* view of things is essentially similar. He gives a very impressive picture of the mystery of the chemistry of the plant, showing how small is the number of food-stuffs and raw materials in comparison to the thousands of highly complex chemical substances which the plant produces, and how much work there is involved in de-oxydising the food and in forming syntheses. He, too, refuses, as usual, to postulate " vital force." Yet to speak of " the fundamental peculiarities of the living matter inherent in the organism " and to admit that plants are " irritable," " heliotropic," " geotropic," &c., amounts to much the same thing as postulating vital

* "Elemente der Wissenschaftlichen Botanik. Biologie der Pflanzen." 1889.

VIEWS OF BOTANISTS ILLUSTRATED 251

force; that is to say, to a mere naming of the specific problem of life without explaining it. The author himself admits this when he says in another place · "If I compare organisms with inorganic systems, I find that the progress of our knowledge is continually enlarging the gulf which separates the one from the other!"

These anti-mechanical tendencies show themselves most emphatically in the work of Fr. Ludwig.* In his concluding chapter, after a discussion of the theories of Darwin, Nageli, and Weismann, he postulates, for variation, heredity, and species-formation in particular, "forces other than physico-chemical," "let us call them frankly psychical."

It is instructive to see how these "vitalistic" views crop up even in studies of detail and of the microscopically small, as for instance in E. Crato's "Beitrage zur Anatomie und Physiologie des Elementar-organismus." How the living organism contains within itself what is in its turn living, down into ever smaller detail, (amœboid movements of certain plastines, physodes,) how incomparable the living organism is with a "machine," to which its libellers are so fond of likening it, how it builds itself up, steers, and stokes itself, how it produces with "playful ease" the most marvellous and graceful forms, makes combinations and breaks them up, how analogous its whole activity is to "being able" and "willing," all this is clearly brought out.†

* "Lehrbuch der Biologie der Pflanzen." Stuttgart, 1895.
† *Cf* Cohn, "Beitrage zur Biologie der Pflanzen," vii 407  See

A very fresh and lucid presentation of the whole case is given by Borodin, Professor of Botany in St. Petersburg, in his essay," "Protoplasm and Vital Force."\* He sharply castigates the one-sidedness and impetuosity of the mechanical theory, as in Haeckel's discovery of Bathybius and of non-nucleated bacteria. The latter

especially the concluding chapter, "Einiges uber Functionen der einzelnen Zellorgane." From Zoology we may cite E. Teichmann's investigation, "Ueber die Beziehung zwischen Astrospharen und Furchen." "Experimentelle Untersuchungen am Seeigelei" ("Archiv. f. Entw. Mech." xvi. 2, 1903). This paper contains no references to "psychical phenomena," "power," or "will," and we cannot but approve of this in technical research But it is pointed out that the mechanistic interpretation of the detailed processes of development has definite limitations, and we are referred to "fundamental characters of living matter which we must take for granted."

This is even more decidedly the case in Tad. Garbowski's beautiful "Morphogenetische Studien, als Beitrag zur Methodologie zoologischer Forschung." These belong to the line of thought followed by Driesch and Wolff, who are both frequently and approvingly quoted, and they afford an excellent instance of that mood of dissatisfaction with and protest against the "dogmas" of descent, selection and phylogeny, which is observable in many quarters among the younger generation of investigators. Garbowski vigorously combats Haeckel's theories of development, especially "the fundamental biogenetic law, and the Gastræa theory." He criticises "mechanistic" interpretations of the development of the embryo, which "treat the living being morphologically, as if the matter were one of vesicles, cylinders and plates, and not of vital units": and he does not look with favour on "artificial amœbæ," which can move, creep, and do everything except live. The ideal of biology is of course always a science with laws and equations, but the key to these will not be found in mechanics Garbowski's studies may be highly recommended as giving a sharp and vivid impression of the modern antimechanistic tendencies observable even in technical research.

\* Trans. by Levinsohn. "Beilage zur Allgemeinen Zeitung," Munich, 1898 No. 166

are problematical, and the former has been proved an illusion. To penetrate farther into the processes of life is simply to become aware of an ever-deepening series of riddles. There is no such thing as "protoplasm," or "living proteid," or indeed any unified, simple "living matter" whatever. Artificial " oil-emulsion amœbæ "* bear the same relation to living ones that Vaucanson's mechanical duck bears to a real one ; that is, none at all. Our "protoplasm" is as mystical as the old " vital force," and both are only camping-grounds for our ignorance. Neither the mechanical nor the atomic theory were the results of exact investigations; they were borrowed from philosophy. We do indeed investigate the typically vital process of irritability by physical methods. But the response made by the organism to physical coercion may be called a mockery of physics. The mechanists help themselves out with crude analogies from the mechanical, conceal the problem with the name " irritability," and thus get rid of the greatest marvels. If vital force itself were to call out from its cells, " Here I am," they would probably see in it only a remarkable case of " irritability." Mechanism is no more positive knowledge than vitalism is ; it is only the dogmatic faith of the majority of present-day naturalists.

## CONSTRUCTIVE CRITICISM

Those whose protests we have hitherto been considering have not added to their criticism of the

* Bütschli, *op. cit.*, p. 200.

mechanical theory any positive contribution of their own, or at least they give nothing more than very slight hints pointing towards a psychical theory. But there are others who have sought to overcome the mechanical theory by gaining a deeper grasp of the nature of "force" in general. Their attempts have been of various kinds, but usually tend in one direction, which can perhaps be most precisely and briefly indicated through Lloyd Morgan's views, as summed up, for instance, in his essay on "Vitalism."* In the beginning of biological text-books, we usually find (he says) a chapter on the nature of "force," but it is "like grace before meat"—without influence on quality or digestion. Yet this problem must be cleared up before we can arrive at any understanding of the whole subject. In all attempts at "reducing to simpler terms," it must be borne in mind that "force" reveals its nature in ever higher stages, of which every one is new. Even cohesion cannot be reduced to terms of gravitation, nor the chemical affinities and molecular forces to something more primitive. They are already something "outside the recognised order of nature." In a still higher form force is expressed in the processes of crystallisation. At the formation of the first crystal there came into action a directing force of the same kind as the will of the sculptor at the making of the Venus of Melos. This new element, which intervenes every time, Lloyd Morgan regards, with Herbert

* "The Monist," 1899, p. 179

CONSTRUCTIVE CRITICISM 255

Spencer (" Principles of Biology "), as "due to that ultimate reality which underlies this manifestation, as it underlies all other manifestations." There can be no "understanding" in the sense of "getting behind things": even the actions of " brute matter " cannot be " understood." The play of chance not only does not explain the living; it does not even explain the not-living. But life in particular can neither be brought into the cell from without, nor be explained as simply " emerging from the co-operation of the components of the protoplasm," and it is " in its essence not to be conceived in physico-chemical terms," but represents " new modes of activity in the noumenal cause," which, just because it is noumenal, is beyond our grasp. For only phenomena are " accessible to thought."

Among the biologists who concern themselves with deeper considerations, Oscar Hertwig,* the Director of the Anatomical Institute at Berlin, has expressed ideas similar to those we have been discussing, little as this may seem to be the case at first sight. He desires to oust the ordinary mechanism, so to speak, by replacing it by a mechanism of a higher order, and in making the attempt he examines and deepens the traditional ideas of causality and " force," and defines the right and wrong of the quantitative-mathematical interpretation of nature in general, and of mechanics in particular. He

* *Cf.* " Entwicklung der Biologie in 19 Jahrhundert " (" Naturforscher Versammlung," 1900), and " Zeit- und Streit-fragen der Biologie," 1894–7, especially Part II., " Mechanik und Zoologie."

follows confessedly in Lotze's path, not so much in regard to that thinker's insistence upon the association of the causal and the teleological modes of interpretation, as in modifying the idea of causality. O. Hertwig puts forward his own theories with special reference to those of W. Roux, the founder of the new " Science of the Future "—the mechanical, and therefore only scientific theory of development, which no longer only describes, but understands and causally explains phenomena (" Archiv fur Entwicklungsmechanik "). There are two kinds of mechanism (Hertwig says): that in the higher philosophical sense, and that in the purely physical sense. The former declares that all phenomena are connected by a guiding thread of causal connection and can be causally explained. As such, its application to the domain of vital phenomena is justifiable and self-evident. But it is not justifiable if cause be simply made identical with and limited to " force," if the causal connection be only admitted in the technical sense of the transference and transformation of energy, and if, over and above, it is supposed to give an " explanation," in the sense of an insight into things themselves. Even mechanics is (as Kirchoff maintained) a " descriptive " science. Hertwig agrees with Schopenhauer and Lotze in regarding every primitive natural " force " as unique, not reducible to simpler terms, but qualitatively distinct, —a " qualitas occulta," capable not of physical but only of metaphysical explanation. And thus his conclusions imply rejection of mechanism in the cruder

CONSTRUCTIVE CRITICISM 257

sense. As such, it has only a very limited sphere of action in the realm of the living. The history of mechanical interpretations is a history of their collapse. The attempt to derive the organic from the inorganic has often been made. But no such attempts have held the field for long. We can now say with some reason that "the gulf between the two kingdoms of nature has become deeper just in proportion as our physical and chemical, our morphological and physiological knowledge of the organism has deepened." Mach's expression "mechanical mythology," is quoted, and then a fine passage on the insufficiency of the mathematical view of things in general concludes thus: "Mathematics is only a method of thought, an excellent tool of the human mind, but it is very far from being the case that all thought and knowledge moves in this one direction, and that the content of our minds can ever find exhaustive expression through it alone."

In his "Theory of Dominants," * Reinke, the botanist of Kiel, has attempted to formulate his opposition to the physico-chemical conception of life into a vitalistic theory of his own. Among biologists who confess themselves supporters of the mechanical theory, there are some who expressly reject explanations in terms of

† "Die Organismen und ihr Ursprung," published in "Nord und Sud," xviii., p. 201 seq —"Die Welt als Tat," Berlin 1899, since then in second edition.—"Einleitung in die theoretische Biologie," 1901.—And "Der Ursprung des Lebens auf der Erde," in the "Turmer-Jahrbuch," 1903.

chemical and physical principles, and emphasise, more energetically than others, that these can only give rise to vital phenomena and complex processes of movement, on the basis of a most delicately differentiated structure and architecture of the living substance in its minute details, and from the egg onwards. They have created the strict "machine theory," and they may be grouped together as the "tectonists." "A watch that has been stamped to pieces is no longer a watch." Thus the merely material and chemical is not the essential part of the living; it is the tectonic, the machinery of structure that is essential. The fundamental idea in this position is precisely that of Lotze. It is not a "mystical," vital principle, that sets up, controls, and regulates the physical and chemical processes within the developed or developing organism. They receive their direction and impulse through the fact that they are associated with a given peculiar mechanical structure. This theory certainly contains all the monstrosities of preformation in the germ, the mythologies of the infinitely small, and it suffers shipwreck in ways as diverse as the number of its sides and parts. But it has the merit of clearly disclosing the impossibilities of purely chemical explanations. Reinke's "Theory of Dominants" started from such tectonic conceptions, and so originally did Driesch's Neovitalism, of which we shall presently have to speak.

Reinke's theory has gone through several stages of

CONSTRUCTIVE CRITICISM 259

development. At first its general tenor was as follows: Every living thing is typically different from everything that is not living. What explains this difference? Certainly not the hypothesis of vital force, which is far from being clear. The idea that forces of a psychic nature are inherent in the organism is also rejected. The illustration of a watch helps us to understand. The impelling force in it is certainly not merely the ordinary force of gravity or the general elasticity of steel. The efficacy of simple forces such as these can be increased in infinite diversity by the "construction of the apparatus" in which they operate. Life is the function of a quite unique, marvellously complex, inimitable combination of machines. If these be given, the most complex processes fulfil themselves of necessity and without the intervention of special vital forces. But how can they be "given"? The sole analogy to be found is the making of real machines, artificial products as distinguished from fortuitous products. They cannot be made without the influence and activity of intelligence. To explain the incomparably more ingenious and complex vital machine as due to a fortuitous origin and collocation of its individual parts would be more absurd than it would be to think of a watch being made in this way. The dominance of a creative idea cannot but be recognised. An intelligent natural force which is conscious of its aims and calculates its means must be presupposed, if we are really to satisfy our sense of causality. It is a matter of personal conviction whether we find this force in "God" or in the "Absolute."

These views are more fully developed in the theory of dominants expounded in Reinke's later work, "Die Welt as Tat" (after what has been said the meaning of the title will be self-evident), and in his "Theoretische Biologie."* Very vigorous and convincing are the author's objections to the naturalistic theories of organic life, especially to the "self-origin" of the living, or spontaneous generation. In all vital processes we must reckon with a "physiological $x$," which cannot be eliminated, which gives to life its unique and underivable character. There are "secondary forces," "superforces," "dominants," which bring about what is peculiar in vital functions and direct their processes. "Vitalism" in the strict sense is thus here also rejected. The machine-theory is held valid. There are "dominants" even in our tools and utensils, in our hammer and spoon, and the "operation" of these cannot be explained merely physico-chemically, but through the dominants of the form, structure and composition, with which they have been invested by intelligence. The association with the views of the tectonists is so far quite apparent. But the idea of "dominants" soon broadens out. We find dominants of form-development,

* *Cf.*, the discussion by A. Drews in the "Preuss. Jahrbuch," October, 1902, p 101, a review of Reinke's "Einleitung in die theoretische Biologie."

CONSTRUCTIVE WORK OF DRIESCH 261

of evolution, and so on. What were at first only peculiarities of structure and architecture have grown almost unawares into dynamic principles of form which have nothing more to do with the mechanical theory, and which, because of their dualistic nature, result in conclusions and modes of explanation which can hardly be called very useful. The lines along which the idea has developed are intelligible enough. It started originally from that of the organism as a finished product, functioning actively, especially in its metabolism. Here the comparison with a steam engine with self-regulators and automatic whistles is admissible, and one may speak of dominants in the sense of mechanical dominants. But the idea thus started was pressed into general service. And thus arose dominants of development, of morphogenesis, even of phylogenetic evolution ("phylogenetic evolution-potential"). New dominants are added, and the theory advances farther and farther from the "machine theory," becomes ever more enigmatical, and more vitalistic.

THE CONSTRUCTIVE WORK OF DRIESCH

What in Reinke's case came about almost unperceived, Driesch did with full consciousness and intention, following the necessity laid upon him by his own gradual personal development and by his consistent, tenacious prosecution of the problem. The acuteness of his thinking, the concentration of his endeavours through long years, his comprehensive knowledge and mastery of the material, the deep logicalness and consistent evolution of his "standpoints," and his philosophical and theoretical grasp of the subject make him probably the most instructive type, indeed, we may almost say, the very incarnation of the whole disputed question. In 1891 he published his "Mathematisch - mechanische Betrachtung morphologischer Probleme der Biologie," the work in which he first touched the depths of the problem. It is directed chiefly against the merely "historical" methods in biology, used by the current schools in the form of Darwinism. Darwinism and the Theory of Descent have been so far nothing more than "galleries of ancestors," and the science ranged under their banner is only descriptive, not explanatory. Instead of setting up contingent theories we must form a "conception" of the internal necessity, inherent in the substratum itself, in accordance with which the forms of life have found expression—a necessity corresponding to that which conditions the form-development of the crystal.

Experimental investigations and discoveries, and further reflection, resulted, in 1892, in his "Entwicklungsmechanische Studien," and led him to insist on the need for what the title of his next year's work calls "Biologie als selbständige Grundwissenschaft." In this work two important points are emphasised. The first is, that biology must certainly strive after pre-

## CONSTRUCTIVE WORK OF DRIESCH

cision, but that this precision consists not in subordination to, but in co-ordination with physics. Biology must rank side by side with physics as an "independent fundamental science," and that in the form of tectonic. And the second point is, that the teleological point of view must take its place beside the causal. Only by recognising both can biology become a complete science.

In the "Analytische Theorie der organischen Entwicklung" (1894) Driesch picks up the thread where he dropped it in the book before, and spins it farther, "traversing" his previous theoretical and experimental results. In this work the author still strives to remain within the frame of the tectonic and machine theory, but the edges are already showing signs of giving way. Life, he says, is a mechanism based upon a given structure (it is however a machine which is constantly modifying and developing itself). Ontogenesis * is a strictly causal nexus, but following " a natural law the workings of which are entirely enigmatical" (with Wigand). Causality fulfils itself through " liberations," that is to say, cause and effect are not quantitatively equivalent; and all effect is, notwithstanding its causal conditioning, something absolutely new and not to be calculated from the cause, so that there can be no question

* Of all the bad Greek zoology has produced, "Ontogenesis" is probably the worst. The Becoming of the Being ! The word is used in contrast to Phylogenesis, the becoming of the race or of the species, and it denotes the development of the individual.

of mechanism in the strict sense. And the whole is directed by purpose.* The vital processes compel us to admit that it seems "as if intelligence determined quality and order." Driesch still tries to reconcile causes and purposes as different "modes of regarding things," but this device he afterwards abandons. We cannot penetrate to the nature of things either by the causal or by the teleological method. But they are—as Kant maintained—two modes of looking at things, both of which are postulates of our capacity for knowing. Each must stand by itself, and neither can have its sequence disturbed by the interpolation of pieces from the other. In the domain of the causal there can be no teleological explanation, and conversely; one might as well seek for an optical explanation of the synthesis of water; but both are true in their own place. The Madonna della Sedia, looked at microscopically, is a mass of blots, looked at macroscopically it is a picture. And it "is" both of these.

Driesch's conclusions continue to advance, led steadily onwards by his experimental studies. In the "Maschinentheorie des Lebens," † he attacks his own earlier theories with praiseworthy determination, and remorselessly pursues them to the monstrous conclusions to which they lead, and shows that they necessarily perish

* *Cf.* p. 130. Excellent observations on "purpose." If two or more chains of causes meet, we call it "chance;" if they do so constantly and in a typical manner, we call it "purpose."

† "Biolog. Centralbl.," 1896, p 363.

## CONSTRUCTIVE WORK OF DRIESCH

because of these. He had previously declared, at first emphatically, later with hesitation (we have already seen why), that every single vital process is of a physico-chemical kind, on the basis of a given "structure" of living beings. But now he considers the living organism as itself a result of vital processes—that is, of development. If this also is to be explained mechanically (as physico-chemical processes based on material structure), then the ovum must possess *in parvo* this infinitely fine structure, by virtue of which it fulfils its own physiological processes of maintenance, and also becomes the efficient cause of the subsequent development. It must bear the type of the individual and of the species, as a rudiment (or primordium) within its own structure. Every specific type must, however, according to the theory of descent, be derived through an endless process of evolution, by gradual stages, from some primitive organism. Just as in the mechanical becoming of the individual organism, so the primitive protovum must also be extraordinarily intricate and complex in its organisation if it is to give rise to all the processes of evolution and development involved in the succeeding ontogenies, phylogenies, regenerations, and so forth. This is a necessary conclusion if the machine-theory be correct, and if we refuse to admit that vital phenomena are governed by specific laws. This consequence is monstrous, and the theory of the tectonists therefore false. But if it be false, what then?

## 266   NATURALISM AND RELIGION

Driesch answers this question in the books published in subsequent years.* In these he attains his final standpoint, and makes it more and more secure. The "machine-theory," and all others like it, are now definitely abandoned. They represent the uncritical dogmatism of a materialistic mode of thought, which binds all phenomena to substance, and refuses to admit any immaterial or dynamic phenomena. The alleged initial structure is nowhere to be found. The pursuit of things into the most minute details leads to no indication of it. The chromatin, in which the most important vital processes have their basis, is very far from having this machine-like structure; it is homogeneous. The formation of the skeleton, for instance, of a Pluteus larva is due to migratory spontaneously moving cells (comparable to the leucocytes of our own body, whose migrations and activities remind one much more of a social organism than of a machine). The organism arises, not from mechanical, but from "harmoniously-equipotential systems"; that is to say, from systems every element of which has equal functional efficiency; so that each individual part bears within itself in an equal degree the potentiality of the whole—an impossibility from the mechanical point of view.

* " Die Lokalisation ( = spatial determination) morphogenetischer Vorgange, ein Beweis vitalistischen Geschehens," 1899. (In " Archiv. f. Entw.-Mechanik," viii., 1, and separately published) and " Die organischen Regulationen Vorbereitungen zu einer Theorie des Lebens," Leipzig, 1901. Also " Die ' Seele' als elementarer Natur-

## CONSTRUCTIVE WORK OF DRIESCH 267

Driesch had given an experimental basis for this theory at an earlier stage, in his experiments on the initial stages of the development of sea-urchins, starfishes, zoophytes, and the like. A Planarian worm cut into pieces developed a new worm of smaller size from each part. A mutilated Pluteus larva developed a new food-canal, and restored the whole typical form. His experiment of 1892 went farther still, for he succeeded in separating the first four segmentation-cells of the sea-urchin's egg; and from each cell obtained a developing embryo. These facts, he maintains, compel us to assume a mode of occurrence which is dynamically *sui generis*, a "prospective tendency" which is a sub-concept in the Aristotelian "Dynamis." And the essential difference between this kind of operation and a mechanical operation is, that the same typical effect is always reached, even if the whole normal causal nexus be disturbed. Even when forced into circuitous paths the embryo advances towards the same goal. Thus "vitalism," that is, the independence and autonomy of the vital processes, is proved. The effect required is attained through "action at a distance," a mode of happening which is specifically different from anything to be found in the inorganic world, and which has its *directive*, for instance, in the regeneration of lost parts,

factor," (studies on the movements of organisms), Leipzig, 1903. He gives a general review of his own evolution in the "Suddeutsche Monatshefte," January 1904, under the title "Die Selbstandigkeit der Biologie und ihre Probleme."

*not* in anything corporeal or substantial, but in the end to be attained.

In his work on "Organic Regulations," Driesch collects from the most diverse biological fields more and more astonishing proofs of the activity of the living as contrasted with physico-chemical phenomena, and of the marvellous power the organism has to "help itself" and to attain the typical form and reach the end aimed at, even under the greatest diversity in the chain of conditions. The material here brought forward is enormous, and the author's grasp of it very remarkable; and not the least of the merits of the book is, that the bewildering wealth and diversity of these phenomena, which are usually presented to us as isolated and uncoordinated instances, is here definitely systematised according to their characterisitic peculiarities, and from the point of view of the increasing distinctness of the "autonomy" of the processes. The system begins with the active regulatory functions of living matter in the chemistry of metabolism (see particularly the phenomena of immunisation), and ascends through different stages up to the regulations of regeneration. There could be no more impressive way of showing how little life and its "regulations" can be compared to the "self-regulations" of machines, or to the restoring of typical states of equilibrium and of form in the physical and chemical domain, to which the mechanists are fond of referring.

The facts thus empirically brought together are then

CONSTRUCTIVE WORK OF DRIESCH 269

linked together in a theory, and considered epistemologically. We may leave out of account all that is included in the treatment of modern idealism, immanence-philosophy, and solipsism. All this does not arise directly out of the vitalistic ideas, though the latter are fitted into an idealistic framework. Extremely vivid is the excursus on respiration and assimilation. (All processes of building up and breaking down take place within the organism under conditions notoriously different from those obtaining in the laboratory. It is radically impossible to speak of a living "substance" according to the formula $C_xH_yO_z$, which assimilates and disassimilates itself [sibi].) Excellent, too, are Driesch's remarks on materialistic elucidations of inheritance and morphogenesis. It is quite impossible to succeed with epigenetic speculations on a material basis (*cf.* Haacke). Weismann is so far right, he admits, from his materialistic premisses when he starts with preformations. But his theory, and all others of the kind, can do nothing more than make an infinitely small photograph of the difficulty. They "explain" the processes of form-development and the regeneration of animals and plants, by constructing infinitely small animals and plants, which develop their form and regenerate lost parts. And Driesch holds it to be impossible to distribute a complicated tectonic among the elements of an equipotential system. In denying the materialistic theory of development, Driesch again determinedly "traverses" his own earlier views. He does this, too, when he now rejects the reconciliation between causality and teleology as different modes of looking at things. The teleological now seems to him itself a factor playing a part in the chain of causes, and thus making it teleological. The key-word of all is to him the "entelechy" of Aristotle.

In his last work on "The Soul," Driesch follows the impossibilities of the mechanical theories from the domain of vital processes into that of behaviour and voluntary actions.

### The Views of Albrecht and Schneider.

An outlook and interpretation which Driesch* maintained for a while, but afterwards abandoned, has been developed in an original and peculiar fashion by Eugen Albrecht, Prosector and Pathologist in Munich.† It is the theory of different ways of looking at things. Albrecht indeed firmly adheres to the chemical and physical interpretation of vital processes, regards

---

\* In the "Biol Zentralbl.," June 1903, p. 427, Driesch is criticised by Moszkowski, who rejects Driesch's teleological standpoint. But even this criticism shows us how far the untenability of the mechanistic position has been recognised. It is based upon a somewhat vague dynamism, which admits that the physico-chemical and all other mechanical interpretations have been destructively criticised by Driesch, and recognises entelechy ("$\dot{\epsilon}\nu\ \dot{\epsilon}\alpha\upsilon\tau\hat{\omega}\ \tau\dot{o}\ \tau\dot{\epsilon}\lambda os\ \dot{\epsilon}\chi o\nu$") An entelechy without $\tau\dot{\epsilon}\lambda os$ !

† "Vorfragen der Biologie," 1899. "Die 'Ueberwindung des Mechanismus' in der Biologie " "Biolog. Zentralbl.," 1901, p 130

approximate completeness along these lines as the ideal of science, and maintains their essential sufficiency. But he holds that the mechanists have been mistaken and one-sided in that they have upheld this interpretation and mode of considering things as the sole and the "true" one. According to our subjective attitude to things and their changes, they appear to us in quite different series of associations, each of which forms a complete series in itself, running parallel to the others, but not intruding to fill up gaps in them. Microscopic and macroscopic study of things illustrate such separate and complete series. The classical example for the whole theory is the psycho-physical parallelism. Psychical phenomena are not "explained" when the correlated line of material changes and the phenomena of the nervous system have been traced out. Similarly with the series of " vital " phenomena, " vital " interpretation from the point of view of the "living organism," runs parallel to, but distinct from the chemical and physical analyses of vital processes. But each of these parallel ways of regarding things is "true." For the current separation of the "appearance" and "nature" of things is false, since it assumes that only one of the possible ways of regarding things, *e.g.*, the mechanical-causal mode of interpretation is essential, and that all the others deal only with associated appearance.

The idea that only one or two of these series can represent the " true nature " of the phenomenon " can only be called cheap dogma." Each series is complete in itself, and every successive phase follows directly and without a break from the antecedent one, which alone explains it. In this lies the relative justification of the ever-recurring reactions to "vitalism."

This theory of Albrecht's has all the charms and difficulties, or impossibilities, of parallelistic interpretations in general. Its validity might be discussed with reference to the particular case of psycho-physical parallelism *

To make a sound basis for itself it would require first to clear up the causality problem, and to answer, or at least definitely formulate the great question whether causing (Bewirkung) is to be replaced by mere necessary sequence—for this is where it ends. The conclusion which, with regard to biological methods and ideals, seems to make all concessions to the purely mechanical mode of interpretation, is not sufficiently obvious from the premises. If the vital series be a "real" one, we should expect that a "vitalistic" mode of interpretation, with methods and aims of its own, would be required, just as a special science of psychology is required. The assumption that each series is complete without a break, and that an all-including analysis of vital processes in terms of mechanical processes must

---

* *Cf.* Tad. Garbowski, "Morphogenetische Studien," p. 167. The illustration here employed of the arc and the "explanation of form by form" would be a good criticism of many of Albrecht's statements.

ultimately be possible, is a *petitio principii*, and breaks down before the objections raised by the vitalists. The most central problem in the whole matter, namely, the relation of the causal to the teleological, has not been touched. These two concepts would, of course, not yield "parallels," but would be different points of view, which could eventually be applied to each series.

K. Camillo Schneider,* Privatdozent in Vienna, uses the soul, the psychical in the true sense, as the explana-

* Schneider has expounded his physiological and morphological view in his "Comparative Histology." In "Vitalismus" ("Elementare Lebensfunctionen," Vienna, 1903) he sums up his vitalistic views It is a comprehensive work which goes deeper than others of its class into the detailed description and analysis of the intimate phenomena of life. Indeed it almost amounts to an independent biology. But the most essential vital problems, the development of form, regeneration, and inheritance, to which Driesch gives the fullest consideration, are all too briefly treated. In Chapters XI. and XII. the question of vitalism expands into a far-reaching discussion of the general outlook upon nature. We need not here concern ourselves with his more general views. Schneider must be regarded as a representative of the most modern tendency of "Psychism," which, stimulated by Mach, Avenarius, and the school of "immanence-philosophy," finds expression among the younger physiologists and biologists, from Schneider to Driesch, Verworn, Albrecht, and others To overthrow "materialism" and "realism," they utilise, with impetuous delight, the ancient self-evident idea that what is given to us is sensation. They confuse and identify such opposites as Kant and Berkeley, and their own position with that of "solipsism." This outlook is still vague and vacillating, and it may perhaps compel epistemology to return on its old path from the sophists to Plato, from Hume to Kant. In Schneider's case, however, the thin stream of this new sensualism is intermingled with so many intuitions and perceptions of the deeper nature of knowledge that one is now curious to know how this strange mixture of semi-materialism, idealism, solipsism, and a priorism is to make the transition from its present

tion of the vital. What had been thought secretly and individually by some of the vitalists already mentioned, but had, so to speak, cropped up only as the incidentally revealed reverse side of their negations of mechanism, Schneider attempts definitely to formulate into a theory. The chief merit of his book on "Vitalism" is to be found, in Chapters II. to X., in his thorough discussion of the chemical, physical, and mechanical theories along the special lines of each.

The list of critics might be added to, and the number of standpoints in opposition to mechanism greatly increased. This diversity of standpoint, and the individual way in which each independent thinker reacts from the mechanical theory shows that here, as also in regard to Darwin's theory of selection, we have to do with a dogmatic theory and a forced simplification of phenomena, not with an objective and calm consideration of things as they are. It is a theory where *simplex* has become *sigillum falsi*.

### How all this affects the Religious Outlook

These denials and destructive criticisms of the mechanical theory, which are now continually cropping up,

extremely labile phase to a condition of stable equilibrium. One fears lest sooner or later a reaction against the contortions of this empiricism and psychism should lead to a modern rehabilitation of mysticism or occultism. (*Cf.* p 295 ff )

In an essay on "Vitalism" in the "Preuss. Jahrbuch," Aug. 1903, p. 276, Schneider has supplemented his previous work.

THE RELIGIOUS OUTLOOK 275

lead, as must be obvious, towards a deeper conception and interpretation of reality in general, and towards a religious conception in particular. Unquestionably the most important fact in connection with them is the fresh revelation of the depth of things and of appearance, the increased recognition that our knowledge is only leading us towards mystery.

It is indeed questionable whether anything more than this can be said in regard to the problem of life, whether we ought not to content ourselves with recognising the limits of our knowledge, and reject all positive statements that go beyond these limits. For the mechanists are undoubtedly right in this, that "entelechy," "the idea of the whole," "co-operation," "guidance," "psychical factors," and the like, are only names for riddles, and do not in themselves constitute knowledge.\* The case here is somewhat similar to what we have already seen in connection with "antinomies." They, too, give us no positive insight into the true nature of things, but they at any rate prove to us that we have not yet understood what that is. And, just as they show us that our knowledge of the world as it appears to us can never be complete, so here it appears that we come upon inexplicabilities even within the domain accessible to our knowledge.

\* If the protest of natural science against these means no more than that they should be excluded as inaccessible to scientific understanding, from the domain of its investigation, but not from reality, it is perhaps fully justified in its methods.

Thus the religious conception of the world gains something here as from the antinomies, namely, a fresh proof that the world which appears to us and can be comprehended by us, proclaims its true nature and depths, but does not reveal them. Perhaps there is still another gain. For in any case the vital processes and the marvels of evolution and development are examples of the way in which physical processes are constantly subject to a peculiar guidance, which certainly cannot be explained from themselves or in terms of mechanism, organisation, and the like. All attempts to demonstrate this in detail, all "explanations" in terms of dynamic co-operation, of dominants, of ideas, or anything else, are vague, and seem to go to pieces when we try to take firm hold of them. But the fact remains none the less.

May not this be a paradigm of the processes and development of the world at large, and even of evolution in the domain of history? Here, too, all ideas of guidance, of endeavour after an aim, &c., which philosophical study of history or religious intuition seems to find, make shipwreck against the fact that every attempt to demonstrate their nature, fails. All these theories of influx, concursus, and so on, whether transcendental or immanent factors be employed, immediately become wooden, and never admit of verification in detail. But precisely the same is true of the dominance of the "idea," or of the "law of evolution," or of the "potential of development" in every developing organism. Yet incomprehensible and undemonstrable in detail as this "dominance" is, and completely as it may be concealed behind the play of physical causes, it is there, none the less.

## CHAPTER X

### AUTONOMY OF SPIRIT

THE aim of our study has been to define our attitude to naturalism, and to maintain in the teeth of naturalism the validity and freedom of the religious conception of the world. This seemed to be cramped and menaced by those " reductions to simpler terms " which we have already discussed.

But one of these reductions, the most important of all, we have not yet encountered, and it remains to be dealt with now. In comparison with this one all others are relatively unimportant, and it is easy to understand how some have regarded the problem of the relations of the naturalistic and the religious outlook as beginning at this point, and have neglected everything below it. For we have now to consider the attempt of naturalism to "reduce" spirit itself to terms of nature, either to derive it from nature, or, when that is recognised as quite too confused and impossible, to make it subject to nature and her system of laws, or to similar laws, and thus to rob it of its freedom and independence, of its essential character as above nature and free from it, and to bring it down to the level of an accompany-

## AUTONOMY OF SPIRIT

ing shadow or a mere reverse side of nature. The aggressive naturalism which we have discussed has from very early times exercised itself on this point, and has instinctively and rightly felt that herein lies the kernel of the whole problem under dispute. It has for the most part concentrated its interest and its attacks upon the "immortality of the soul." But while this was often the starting-point, the nature of soul, and spirit, and consciousness in general have been brought under discussion and subjected to attacks which sought to show how vague and questionable was the reality of spirit as contrasted with the palpable, solid and indubitable reality of the outer world. Prominence was given to the fact that the spiritual side of our nature is dependent on and conditioned by the body and bodily states, the external environment, experiences and impressions. These were often the sole, and always the chief subjects of the doctrine of the vulgar naturalism. But the same is true of the naturalism of the higher order, as we described it in Chapter II. In order to acquire definite guiding principles of investigation, it makes the attempt to find the true reality of phenomena in the mechanical, corporeal, physiological processes, and to take little or no account of the co-operation, the interpolation, the general efficiency of sensation, perception, thought, or will, and to treat them as though they were a shadow and accompaniment of reality, but not as an equivalent, much less a preponderating constituent of it. Out of these fundamental principles of investigation, and out of the opposition and doubt with which the spiritual is regarded, there is compounded the current mongrel naturalism, which, without precision in its ideas, and without any great clearness or logical consequence in its views, is thoroughly imbued with the notion that that only is truly real which we can see, hear, and touch—the solid objective world of matter and energy, and that "science" begins and ends with this. As for anything outside of or beyond this, it is at most a beautiful dream of fancy, with which it is quite safe to occupy oneself as long as one clearly understands that of course it is not true. "Nature" is the only indubitable reality, and mind is but a kind of *lusus* or *luxus naturæ*, which accompanies it at some few places, like a peculiarly coloured aura or shadow, but which must, as far as reality is concerned, yield pre-eminence to "Nature" in every respect.

The religious conception is deeply and essentially antagonistic to all such attempts to range spirit, spiritual being, and the subjective world under "nature," "matter," "energy," or whatever we may call what is opposed to mind and ranked above it in reality and value. The religious conception is made up essentially of a belief in spirit, its worth and pre-eminence. It does not even seek to compare the reality and origin of spirit with anything else whatever. For all its beliefs, the most sublime and the crudest alike, conceal within them the conviction that

## AUTONOMY OF SPIRIT

fundamentally spirit alone has truth and reality, and that everything else is derived from it. It is a somewhat pitiful mode of procedure to direct all apologetic endeavours towards the one relatively small question of "immortality," thus following exactly the lines usually adopted by the aggressive exponents of naturalism, and thus allowing opponents to dictate the form of the questions and answers. It is quite certain that all religion which is in any way complete, includes within itself a belief in the everlastingness of our spiritual, personal nature, and its independence of the becoming or passing away of external things. But, on the one hand, this particular question can only be settled in connection with the whole problem, and, on the other hand, it is only a fraction of the much farther-reaching belief in the reality of spirit and its superiority to nature. The very being of religion depends upon this. That it may be able to take itself seriously and regard itself as true; that all deep and pious feelings, of humility and devotion, may be cherished as genuine and as founded in truth; that it behoves it to find and experience the noble and divine in the world's course, in history and in individual life; that the whole world of feeling with all its deep stirrings and mysteries is of all things the most real and true, and the most significant fact of existence —all these are features apart from which it is impossible to think of religion at all. But they all depend upon the reality, independence and absolute pre-eminence of spirit. Freedom and responsibility, duty, moral control and self-development, the valuation of life and our life-work according to our life's mission and ideal aims, even according to everlasting aims, and "sub specie æterni," the idea of the good, the true and the beautiful—all things apart from which religion cannot be thought of—all these depend upon spirit and its truth. And finally "God is Spirit": religion cannot represent, or conceive, or possess its own highest good and supreme idea, except by thinking in terms of the highest analogies of what it knows in itself as spiritual being and reality. If spirit is not real and above all other realities; if it is derivable, subordinate and dependent, it is impossible to think of anything whatever to which the name of "God" can be given. And this is as true of the refined speculations of the pantheistic poetic religions, as of the idea of God in simple piety. The interest of religion as against the claims of naturalism includes all this. And it would be doing the cause of religion sorry service to extract from this whole some isolated question to which the mood of the time or traditional custom has given prominence. Our task must be to show that religion maintains its validity and freedom because of the truth and independence of spirit and its superiority to nature.

It is, of course, impossible to give an exhaustive treatment of this problem in a short study like this. The answer to this question would include the whole range of mental science with all its parts and branches.

## AUTONOMY OF THE SPIRITUAL 283

Mental science, from logic and epistemology up to and including the moral and æsthetic sciences, proves by its very existence, and by the fact that it cannot be reduced to terms of natural science, that spirit can neither be derived from nor analysed into anything else. And it is only when we have mastered all this that we can say how far and how strongly knowledge and known realities corroborate religion and its great conclusions as to spirit and spiritual existence, how they reinforce it and admit its validity and freedom. Since this is so, all isolated and particular endeavours in this direction can only be a prelude or introduction, and a more or less arbitrary selection from the relevant material of facts and ideas. And nothing more than this is aimed at in the following pages.

### NATURALISTIC ATTACKS ON THE AUTONOMY OF THE SPIRITUAL

The attacks that have been made by naturalism upon the independence and freedom of the spiritual are so familiar to every one—even from school days—through books of the type of Buchner's "Kraft und Stoff," and Haeckel's "The Riddle of the Universe," and other half or wholly materialistic popular dogmatics, that it is unnecessary to enter into any detail. Very little that is new has been added in this connection to the attack made by Plato on himself in the "Phædo" through Simmias and Kebes. It is only apparently that the modern attacks have become more serious through the deepened knowledge of natural science. At all times they have been as serious and as significant as possible, and the religious and every other idealistic conception of the universe has always suffered from them. It is plain that here, if anywhere, "faith goes against appearances," and that in the last resource we have to postulate free moral resolution, the will to believe, the desire for the ideal, for freedom, and for the eternity of the spirit, and the confidence of the spirit in itself. All this is, or at least ought to be, self-evident and generally admitted.

Let us once more take a brief survey of the reasons on the other side and arrange them in order.

That nature is everything and spirit very little seems to follow from a very simple circumstance. There are whole worlds of purely natural and corporeal existence without mind, sensation, or consciousness, which, quite untroubled by their absence, simply exist according to the everlasting laws of matter and energy. But nowhere do we find spirit or mind without a material basis. All that is psychical occurs in connection with a physical being, and with relatively few physical beings. Spirit seems wholly bound up with and dependent upon the states, development, and conditions of material being. With the body of living beings there arises what we call "soul"; with the body it grows, gains content, changes, matures, ages, and disappears. According as the body is constituted and composed, as it is influenced by heredity, race, and

## AUTONOMY OF THE SPIRITUAL 285

selection, by nutrition, mode of life, climate, and other circumstances, there are developed in a hundred different ways what we call the natural disposition or character, inclinations, virtues or vices, passions or temperaments. Even the names given to the different temperaments emphasise this dependence of what is innermost in us, the deepest tendencies of our being, on the bodily organisation and the nature of its physiological constitution. The man whose blood flows easily and freely is called sanguine, and the melancholic is the victim of his liver. According as our organs are good or bad, function freely or sluggishly, our mood rises or sinks, we are bold or cowardly, languid or impetuous, and enthusiasm is often enough only a peculiar name for a state which, physiologically expressed, might be called alcoholic poisoning. There is one soul in the sound body, another in the sickly. Fever, and the impotence of the soul against it, made Holbach a materialist. If the brain be diseased, that marvellous order of psychical processes which we call reasoning is broken; the "soul" is wholly or partly eliminated; it fades away, or becomes nothing more than a confused disconnected medley of images and desires. Even artificial interference with, and changes in the bodily organisation react upon the mind. The removal of the thyroid gland may result in idiocy. Castration not only prevents the 'breaking' of the voice in the Sistine choristers, it damps the fires of life to dulness, and makes of the impetuous Abelard a comfortable discursive father-confessor. The mind is bound up almost piece by piece with its material basis. Through the "localisation" of psychic processes in the particular parts of the brain, naturalism has enormously strengthened the impression that existed even among the ancients, that sensation and imagination are nothing more than, let us say, what the note is to a tightly stretched string. Cerebrum and cerebellum are regarded as the seats of different psychic processes. The secret of the higher processes is believed to be hidden in the grey matter of the cortex of the cerebrum. We seek and find in the various lobes and convolutions of the brain the "centres" for the different capacities, the power of sight, of smell, of moving the arms, of moving the legs, of associating ideas, of co-ordinated speech, and so on. When brain and spinal cord are injured or removed piece by piece from a pigeon or a frog, it seems as if the "soul" were eliminated piece by piece, —the capacity for spontaneous free co-ordination, for voluntary action, for the various sense-impressions, and so on from the higher to the lower. It has even been maintained that the different feelings and perceptions which are gradually acquired can be apportioned among the individual cells of the brain in which they are localised, and the thought-processes, the associations of percepts, the origin of consecutive ideas, the rapid and easy recalling of memory-images, and the process of voluntary control, of instincts, can be explained as due to the "gradual laying down of nerve-paths" between

## AUTONOMY OF THE SPIRITUAL 287

the different centres and areas of localisation in the brain. All this seems to refute utterly the old belief in the unity and personality of the soul. It is different in youth and in age, and indeed varies continually. It is the ever-varied harmony of the notes of all the strings which are represented by the fibres and ganglion-cells of the nerve-substance. It apparently can not only be completely confused and brought to disharmony, but it may be halved and divided. An almost terrifying impression was produced when Trembley in 1740 made the experiment of cutting a "hydra" in two, and showed that each of the halves became a complete animal, so that obviously each of the two halves of the soul grew into a new hydra-soul. And Trembley's hydra was only the precursor of all the cut-up worms, of the frogs, birds, and guinea-pigs that have been beheaded, or have had their brain removed, or their nerves cut, and have furnished further examples of this divisibility of "souls."

If the independence of the spiritual is thus shown to be a vain assumption, the alleged difference between the animal and the human Psyche is much more so. Not from the days of Darwinism alone, but from the very beginning, naturalism has opposed this claim to distinctiveness. But it is due to Darwinism that the fundamental similarity of the psychical in man and animals has come to be regarded as almost self-evident. The mental organisation of man, as well as his corporeal organisation, is traced back through gradual stages to animal antecedents, and in thus tracing it there are two favourite methods of procedure, which are, however, apt to be mutually destructive.

On the one hand, some naturalists regard the animal anthropomorphically, insist on its likeness to man, discovering and extolling, not without emotion, all the higher and nobler possessions of the human mind, intellectual capacities, reason, reflection, synthesis, fancy, the power of forming ideas and judgments, of drawing conclusions and learning from experience, besides will in the true sense, ethical, social and political capacities, æsthetic perceptions, and even fits of religion in elephants, apes, dogs, down even to ants and bees, and these naturalists reject old-fashioned explanations in terms of instinct, and find the highest already contained in the lowest. Those of another school are inclined to regard man theriomorphically, to insist on his likeness to animals, explaining reason in terms of perception and sensation, deriving will from impulse and desire, and ethical and æsthetic valuations from physiological antecedents and purely animal psychological processes, thus, in short, seeking to find the lowest in the highest. (We have already met with an analogous instance of a similarly fallacious double-play on parallel lines.) So it comes about that both the origin and the development of the psychical and spiritual seem to be satisfactorily cleared up and explained, and at the same time a new proof is adduced for its dependence upon the physical. For what is true of all

## AUTONOMY OF THE SPIRITUAL 289

other parts of the organisation, of the building up and perfecting of every member and every system of organs, the bony skeleton, the circulatory system, the alimentary canal, that they can be referred back to very simple beginnings, and that their evolution may be traced through all its stages—is equally true of the nervous system in general and of the brain in particular. It increases more and more in volume and in intricacy of structure, it expands the cranial cavity and diversifies its convolutions. And the more it grows, and the more complex it becomes, the more do the mental capacities increase in perfection, so that here again it seems once more apparent that the psychical is an accompaniment and result of the physical.

Popular naturalism usually stops short here, and contents itself with half-truths and inconsequences, for it naively admits that psychical processes, sensation, perception, will, have a real influence upon the physical, and, not perceiving how much the admission involves, it does not trouble itself over the fact that, for instance in the so-called voluntary movements of the body, in ordinary behaviour, the psychical, and the will, in particular, is capable of real effect, and can move hand and foot and the whole body, and thus has a real reciprocal relation with the physical. This form of popular naturalism sometimes amuses itself with assuming a psychical inwardness even in non-living matter, and admitting the co-operation of psychical motives even in regard to it.

But it is far otherwise with naturalism in the strict sense, which takes its fundamental principles and its method of investigation seriously. It is aware that such half-and-half measures interrupt the continuity of the system at the most decisive point. And therefore with the greatest determination it repeats along psychological lines the same kind of treatment that it has previously sought to apply to biological phenomena: the corporeal must form a sequence of phenomena complete in itself and not broken into from without. All processes of movement, all that looks as if it happened "through our will," through a resolve due to the intervention of a psychical motive, every flush of shame that reddens the cheek, every stroke executed by the hand, every sound-wave caused by tongue and lips, must be the result of conditions of stimulation and tension in the energy of the body itself.

This is the meaning of all those psycho-physical experiments that have been carried on with so much ingenuity and persistence (usually associated with attempts to explain vital phenomena in terms of mechanism). First, they attempt to interpret the expressions of will, feeling and need, the spontaneous activities and movements of the lowest forms of life—protists—as "pure reflexes," as processes which take place in obedience to stimuli, and thus are ultimately due to chemical and physical influences and causes without the intervention of a psychical motive; and, secondly, when this has been apparently or really achieved, the theory of irritability

## AUTONOMY OF THE SPIRITUAL 291

and reflex mechanism is pushed from below upwards, until even the most intricate and complex movements and operations of our own body, which we have wrongly distinguished as acts or behaviour from mere processes of stimulation, are finally recognised as reflexes and liberations due to stimuli. Some stimulus or other, from light or sound or something else, is, according to this theory, conducted to the nervous centre, the ganglion, the spinal cord, the cerebellum or the cerebrum. Here it produces an effect, not of a psychical nature, but some minute chemical, or physical,—or purely mechanical change, which goes through many permutations within the nervous centre itself, unites there with the stored energies, and then, thus altered, returns by the efferent nerve paths to effect a muscle-contraction in some organ, a stretching of the hand, or a movement of the whole body. The physical process is accompanied by a peculiar inward mirroring, which is the psychical penumbra or shadow of the whole business. Thus what is in reality a purely mechanical and reflex sequence appears like a psychical experience, like choice and will and psychical causality. We may be compared to Spinoza's stone; it was thrown, and it thought it was flying.

The reasons for interpreting things in this way lie in the principles of investigation. It is only in this way, we are told, that nature can be reduced to natural terms, that is, to chemistry, physics, and mechanics. Only in this way is it possible to gain a true insight into and understanding of things, and to bring them under mathematical formulæ. Thus only, too, can "the miraculous" be eliminated. For if we are obliged to admit that the will has a real influence on the corporeal, for instance upon our brain, and nerves, and arm-muscles, this would be a violation of the law of the constancy of the sum of energy. For in this case there would occur, at a certain point in the nexus of phenomena, a piece of work done, however small it might be, for which there was no equivalent of energy in the previous constitution. But this is, since the days of Helmholtz, an impossible assumption. And thus all those experiments and theories on what we have called the "second line" of mechanistic interpretation of the universe show themselves to be relevant to our present subject.

Interpretations of the psychical such as these have given rise to four peculiar "isms" of an epistemological nature, *i.e.*, related to a theory of knowledge. Not infrequently they are the historical antecedents which result in the naturalistic theory of the psychical. These are nominalism and sensualism, empiricism and a-posteriorism, which, setting themselves against epistemological rationalism, assail the dignity, the independence, and the autonomy of the thinking mind. They are so necessarily and closely associated with naturalism that their fate is intimately bound up with its fate, and they are corroborated or refuted with it. And it would be possible to conduct the whole discussion with which we

## AUTONOMY OF THE SPIRITUAL 293

are concerned purely with reference to these four "isms." The strife really begins in their camp.

The soul is a *tabula rasa*, all four maintain, a white paper on which, to begin with, nothing is inscribed. It brings with it neither innate knowledge nor commands. What it possesses in the way of percepts, concepts, opinions, convictions, principles of action, rules of conduct, are inscribed upon it through experience (empiricism). That is, not antecedent to, but subsequent to experience (a posteriori). But experience can only be gained through the senses. Only thus does reality penetrate into and stamp itself upon us. "What was not first in the senses (sensus) cannot be in the intelligence." What the senses convey to us alone builds up our mental content, from mere sensory perceptions upwards to the most abstract ideas, from the simplest psychical elements up to the most complex ideas, concepts, and conclusions, to the most varied imaginative constructions. And in the development of the mental content the "soul" itself is merely the stage upon which all that is acquired through the senses crowds, and jostles, and unites to form images, perceptions, and precepts. But it is itself purely passive, and it becomes what happens to it. Therefore it is not really spirit at all, for spirit implies spontaneity, activity, and autonomy.

Philosophy and the mental sciences have always had to carry on the strife with these four opponents. And it is in the teacup of logic and epistemology that the storm in regard to theories of the universe has arisen. It is there, and not in the domain of neurology, or zoology, that the real battle-field lies, upon which the controversy must be fought out to the end. What follows is only a sort of skirmish about the outposts.

What naturalism holds in regard to the psychical and spiritual may be, perhaps, most simply expressed by means of an illustration. Over a wide field there glide mighty shadows in constant interplay. They expand and contract, become denser or lighter, disappear for a little, and then reveal themselves again. While they are thus forming and changing, one state follows quite connectedly on another. At first one is tempted to believe that they are self-acting and self-regulating, that they move freely and pass from one state to another according to causes within themselves. But then one sees that they are thrown upon the earth from the clouds above, now in this way and now in that, that all their states and forms and changes are nothing in themselves, and neither effect anything in themselves nor react upon the occurrences and realities up above, which they only accompany, and by which they are determined without any co-operation on their own part, even in determining their own form. So it is with nature and spirit. Nature is the true effective reality; spirit is its shadow, which effects nothing either within or outside of itself, but simply happens.

## THE FUNDAMENTAL ANSWER

How can the religious conception of the world justify itself and maintain its freedom in face of such views of spirit and spiritual being? It is questionable whether it is worth while attempting to do so. Is not the essence of the validity and freedom of spirit made most certain simply through the fact that it is able to inquire into it? If we leave popular naturalism out of the question, is not the attempt made by scientific naturalism the best witness against itself? For scientific study, and the establishment of fundamental conceptions and guiding principles are only possible if mind and thought are free and active and creative. The direct experience that spirit has of itself, of its individuality and freedom, of its incomparability with all that is beneath it, is far too constant and genuine to admit of its being put into a difficulty by a doctrine which it has itself established. And this doctrine has far too much the character of a "fixed theory" to carry permanent inward conviction with it. Here again, the mistake made is in starting with scepticism and with the fewest and simplest assumptions. It is by no means the case that in order to discover the truth we must start always from a position of scepticism, instead of from calm confidence in ourselves and in our conviction that we possess in direct experience the best guarantee of truth. For we experience nothing more certainly than the content and riches of our own mind, its power of acting and creating, and all its great capacities. And it is part of the duty laid upon us by the religious conception of the universe, as well as by all other idealistic conceptions, to follow this path of self-assurance alone, that is, through self-development and self-deepening, through self-realisation and self-discipline, to use to the full in our lives all that we have in heart and mind as possibilities, tendencies, content, and capacities, and so practically to experience the reality and power of the spiritual that the mood of suspicion and distrust of it must disappear. The validity of this method is corroborated by all the critical insight into the nature of our knowledge that we have gained in the course of our study, and it might be deepened in regard to this particular case. For here, if anywhere, we must recognise the limitations of our knowledge; the impossibility of attaining to a full understanding of the true nature and depths of things applies to the inquiring mind and its hidden nature. From Descartes to Leibnitz, Kant, and Fries, down to the historian of materialism itself, F. A. Lange, it has been an axiom of the idealistic philosophy, expressed now in dogmatic, now in critical form, that the mathematical-mechanical outlook and causal interpretation of things, not excluding a naturalistic psychology, is thoroughly justifiable as a method of arranging scientifically the phenomena accessible to us and of penetrating more deeply towards an understanding of these. It is, indeed, justifiable, so long as it does not profess

# THE FUNDAMENTAL ANSWER 297

to reveal the true nature of things, but remains conscious of the free spirit, whose own work and undertaking the whole is.

Yet here again it is by no means necessary to surrender to naturalism a field which it has tried to take possession of, but is certainly unable to hold. We need not try to force naturalism to read out of empirical psychology the high conclusions as to human nature and spirit which pertain to the religious outlook, or to find in the "simplicity" of the "soul monad" a kind of physical proof of its indestructibility, or anything of that kind. We maintain that to comprehend the true inwardness of the vitality, freedom, dignity, and power of the spirit is not the business of psychology at all, but may perhaps be dealt with in ethics, if it be not admitted that with these concepts one has already entered the realm of religious experience, and that they are the very centre of religious theory. But undoubtedly we must reject in great measure the claims which naturalism makes upon our domain, and maintain that the most important starting-points for the higher view are to be found in the priority of everything spiritual over everything material, in the underivability of the spiritual and the impossibility of describing it in corporeal-mathematical terms and concepts.

### Individual Development

What lives in us, as far as we can perceive and trace it in its empirical expression, is not a finished and spiritual being that leaps, mature and complete, from some pre-existence or other into its embodied form, but is obviously something that only develops and becomes actual very gradually. Its becoming is conditioned by "stimuli," influences, impressions from without, and perfects itself in the closest dependence upon the becoming of the body, is inhibited or advanced with it, and may be entirely arrested by it, forced into abnormal developments which never attain to the level of an "ego" or "personality," but remain incomprehensible anomalies and monstrosities. In general, the psychical struggles slowly and laboriously free from purely vegetative and physiological processes, and gains control over itself and over the body. Its self-development and concentration to full unity and completeness of personality is only achieved through the deepest self-culture, through complete "simplification" as the ancients said, through great acts and experiences of inward centralisation such as that which finds religious expression in the metaphor of "regeneration." What "building up" and self-development of the psychical means remains obscure. If we think of it as a summation, an adding on of new parts and constituents, and thus try to form a concrete image of the process, we spoil it altogether. If we speak of the transition from the potential to the actual,

# INDIVIDUAL DEVELOPMENT

from the tendency to the realisation, we may not indeed spoil it, but we have done little to make the process more intelligible. So much only we can say: certain as it is that the Psyche, especially as conscious inner life, only gradually develops and becomes actual, and that in the closest dependence upon the development, maturing, and establishment of the nervous basis and the bodily organisation in general, yet the naturalistic view, *a fortiori* the materialistic, is never at any point correct. There are three things to be borne in mind. First, the origin, the "whence" of the psychical is wholly hidden from us, and, notwithstanding the theory of evolution and descent, it remains an insoluble riddle. And secondly, however closely it is associated with and tied down to the processes of bodily development, it is never at any stage of its development really a function of it in actual and exact correspondence and dependence. And finally, the further it advances in its self-realisation, the further the relation of dependence recedes into the background, and the more do the independence and autonomy of the psychical processes become prominent.

We have still to consider and amplify this in several respects, and then we may go on to still more important matters.

### UNDERIVABILITY

The first of the three points we have called attention to has, so to speak, become famous through the lectures of du Bois-Reymond, which attracted much attention, on "The Limits of Natural Knowledge," and "The Seven

Riddles of the Universe." That these thoughtful lectures made so great an impression did not mean that a great new discovery had been made, but was rather a sign of the general lack of reflection on the part of the public, for they only expressed what had always been self-evident, and what had only been forgotten through thoughtlessness, or concealed by polemical rhetoric. Consciousness, thought, even the commonest sensation of pleasure and pain, or the simplest sense-perception, cannot be compared with " matter and energy," with the movements of masses. They represent a foreign and altogether inexplicable guest in this world of matter, molecules, and elements. Even if we could follow the play of the nervous processes with which sensation, consciousness, pain, or pleasure are bound up, into their most intricate and delicate details, if we could make the brain transparent, and enlarge its cells to the size of houses, so that, with searching glance, we could count and observe all the processes, and even follow the dance of the molecules within it, we should never see "pain," "pleasure," or "thought," or anything more than bodies and their movements. A thought, such as, for instance, the perception that two and two make four, is not long or broad, above or beneath; it cannot be measured or weighed in inches or pounds like matter, tested with the manometer, thermometer, or electrometer for its potential or intensity and tension, measured by ampères or volts or horse-powers like energies and electric currents; it is something wholly different, which can be known only through inner experience, but which is much better known than anything else whatever, and which it is absolutely impossible to compare with anything but itself. Even if we admit that it can only become actual and develop as an accompaniment of processes within bodies, and only within those bodies we call " living," and that wherever bodies exist psychical phenomena occur; even if we were able, as we never shall be able, to produce living beings artificially in a retort, and even if psychical phenomena occurred in these also, we should still have made no progress towards explaining what the psychical really is. It would still only be the blazing up in these bodies of a flame which, in some inexplicable way, had fallen upon them, and associated itself with them. We do not doubt that this association, where it takes place, does so in obedience to the strictest law and the most inexorable necessity; therefore, that wherever and however the corporeal conditions are produced, sensation and consciousness will awaken. For we believe in a world governed by law. But the mystery is in no way lessened by this, and the modern theory of evolution throws no light into this utterly impenetrable darkness. In the first place, the whole idea of "explaining" in terms of "evolution" is a futile one. The process of becoming is pictured as a simple process of cumulation, a gradual increase of intensities, while the business is really one of change in quality and the introduction of what is new. In the second place, the occurrence even of the first and most primitive sensation contains the whole riddle concentrated on a single point. In the third place, the riddle meets us anew and undiminished in every developing individual. For to say that the physical inwardness, once it has arisen, is "transmitted," is not an explanation but merely an admission that the riddle exists. And the idea that the psychical is just a penumbra or shadow of reality, which comes of itself and so to speak gratis, is quite inadmissible from the point of view of strict natural science. There are no longer *luxus* and *lusus naturæ*. Reality cannot throw a "shadow." According to the principles of the conservation of matter and energy, we must be able to show whence it gets the so-called shadow, and with what it compensates for it.

### Pre-eminence of Consciousness

But we have already spent too much time over this naive mode of looking at things, which, though it professes to place things in their true light, in reality distorts them and turns them upside down. As if this world of the external and material, all these bodies and forces, were our first and most direct data, and were not really all derived from, and only discoverable by, consciousness. We have here to do with the ancient view of all philosophy and all reflection in general, although in modern days it has taken its place as a great new discovery even among naturalists themselves, by whom it is extolled and recognised as

## PRE-EMINENCE OF CONSCIOUSNESS 303

"the conquest of materialism." Such exaggerated emphasis tends to conceal the fact that this truth has been regarded as self-evident from very early times.

What is a body, extension, movement, colour, smell and taste? What do I possess of them, or know of them, except through the images, sensations and feelings which they call up in my receptive mind? No single thing wanders into me as itself, or reveals itself to me directly; only through the way in which they affect me, the peculiar changes which they work in me, do things reveal to me their existence and their special character. I have no knowledge of an apple-tree or of an apple, except through the sense perceptions they call up in me. But these sense perceptions, what are they but different peculiar states of my consciousness, peculiar determinations of my mind? I see that the tree stands there, but what is it to see? What is the perception of a colour, of light, of shade, and their changes? Surely only a peculiar change of my mind itself, a particular state of stimulus and awareness brought about in myself. And in the same way I can feel that the apple lies there. But what is the perception of resistance, of hardness, of impenetrability? Nothing more than a feeling, a change in my psychical state, which is unique and cannot be described in terms of anything but itself. Even as regards "attraction and repulsion," external existence only reveals itself to us through changes in the mind and consciousness, which we then attribute to a cause outside ourselves.

It is well enough known that this simple but incontrovertible fact has often led to the denial of the existence of anything outside of ourselves and our consciousness. But even if we leave this difficult subject alone, it is quite certain that, if the question as to the pre-eminence of consciousness and its relation to external things is to be asked at all, it should be formulated as follows, and not conversely: " How can I, starting from the directly given reality and certainty of consciousness and its states, arrive at the certainty and reality of external things, substances, forces, physics and chemistry ? "

### Creative Power of Consciousness

To this insight into the underivability and pre-eminence of consciousness over the world of external reality there must be added at this stage a recognition of its peculiar creative character. We have here to recognise that consciousness itself creates its world,—that is, the world that becomes our own through actual experience, possession, and enjoyment. We are led to this position even by the conception now current in natural science of the world as it is, not as it is mirrored in consciousness, and the theory of the "subjectivity of sensory qualities." The qualities which we perceive in things through the senses are "subjective"; philosophy has long taught that, and now natural science teaches

## CREATIVE POWER OF CONSCIOUSNESS 305

it too. That is to say, these qualities are not actually present in the things themselves; they are rather the particular responses which our consciousness makes to stimuli. Take, for instance, tone or colour. What we call tone or sound is not known to acoustics. That takes cognisance only of vibrations and the conditions of vibration in elastic bodies, which, by means of the ear and the nerves of hearing, become a stimulus of consciousness. Consciousness "responds" to this stimulus by receiving a sense-impression of hearing. But in this, obviously, there is nothing of the nature of oscillations and vibrations, but something quite different. What outside of us is nothing more than a complex process of movement according to mathematical conditions, blossoms within us to a world of sound, tone, and music. The world itself is soundless, toneless. And the same is true of light and colour; "light" and "blue" are nothing in themselves—are not properties of things themselves. They are only the infinitely rapid movements of an infinitely delicate substance, the ether. But when these meet our consciousness, they spin themselves within us into this world of light and colour, of brilliance and beauty. Thus without us there is a world of a purely mathematical nature, without quality, charm, or value. But the world we know, the world of sound, light, and colour, of all properties whatsoever, of the ugly or the beautiful, of pain and pleasure, is in the most real sense the product of consciousness itself, a creation which, incited by something outside of itself and of a totally different nature, which we can hardly call "world," evolves out of itself and causes to blossom. No part of this creation is given from without; not the blue of the heavens, for outside of us there is no colour, only vibrations of the ether; not the gold of the sun nor the red glory of the evening sky. External nature is nothing more than the stimulus, the pressure upon the mind, which liberates from its depths the peculiar reactions and responses to this stimulus, and calls them forth from its own treasure-stores. Certainly in this creating the consciousness is entirely dependent on the impressions stamped on it from outside, and to that extent upon "experience." But it is by no means a *tabula rasa*, and a merely passive mirror of the outer world, for it translates the stimulus thus received into quite a different language, and builds up from it a new reality, which is quite unlike the mathematical and qualityless reality without. And this activity on the part of consciousness begins on the very lowest stages. The simplest perception of light or colour, the first feeling of pleasure or discomfort, is a reaction of the psychical, which brings about something entirely new and unique. "The spirit is never passive."

That the psychical is not derivable from the physical, that it does not arise out of it, is not secondary to it, but pre-eminent over it, is not passive but creative; so much we have already gained to set over against naturalism. But its claims are even more affected by the fact of real psychical causality. We need not here concern ourselves with the difficult question, whether the mind can of itself act upon the body, and through it upon the external world. But in the logical consistence of naturalism there was implied not only a negative answer to this last question, but also a denial of the causality of the psychical, even within itself and its own domain. This is well illustrated in the figure of the cloud shadows. In consciousness state follows upon state, a upon b, b upon c. According to naturalism, b is not really the result of a, nor c of b, for in that case there would be independence of phenomena, and distinctness of laws in the psychical. But as all the states, a, b, and c, of the cloud shadows, depend upon states $a$, $b$, and $c$, of the clouds themselves, but do not themselves form a concatenation of causes, so all the states of the mind depend upon those of the body, in which alone there is a true chain of causes because they alone have true reality.

This is a complete distortion of the facts of the case. It would never be possible to persuade oneself or any one else that the arm, for instance, did not bend simply because we willed that it should. And it is still less possible to doubt that there are sequences of causes within the psychical, that in the world of thought and feeling, of desire and will, one thing calls up another, awakes it, impels it onwards, and influences it. Indeed, the mode of influence is peculiarly rich, subtle, and certain. Mental images and experiences arouse joy or sorrow, admiration or repulsion. One image calls up another, forces it to appear according to quite peculiar laws, or may crowd it out. Feelings call up desires, desires lead to determination. Good news actually causes joy, this is actually strengthened to willing, and the new situation gives rise to actual resolves. All this is so obvious and so unquestionable that no naturalism can possibly prevail against it. It has also long been made the subject of special investigation and carefully regulated experiment, and it is one of the chief subjects of modern psychological science. And especially as regards the different forms of "association of ideas," the particular laws of this psychical causality have been established.

It cannot be denied, however, that this psychology of association has itself in a deeper sense certain dangers from the point of view of the freedom of the mind, and it is apt to lead, not indeed to naturalistic conceptions, but to views according to which the "soul" is reduced to the level of a passive frame and stage, so to speak, for the exhibition of mental mechanics and statics. "Ideas" or thoughts, or states of feelings, are sometimes represented almost as actual little realities, which come and go in accordance with their own laws of attraction and repulsion, unite and separate again, by virtue of a kind of mental gravitation, move and crowd one another, so that one must almost say "it thinks," as one says "it rains," and not "the mind thinks" or "I

# CREATIVE POWER OF CONSCIOUSNESS 309

think." But more of this later. This psychological orderliness is in sharp antagonism to pure naturalism. It describes the laws of a sequence of causes, which have nothing to do with the physical, chemical, or mechanical, and clearly establishes the uniqueness, independence, and underivability of the psychical as contrasted with the physical.

The individuality and incommensurability of this psychical causality shows itself in another series of factors which make even the *form* of the psychical process quite distinctive, and produce phenomena which have no parallel in the material sequences of the world, indeed, conflict with all its fundamental laws. The great psychologists of to-day, Wundt in particular, and James, have frequently emphasised these factors. We can only briefly call attention to a few points, as, for instance, Wundt's theory of the creative resultants through which the psychical processes show themselves to be quite outside of the scope of the laws of equivalence which hold good in the physical. If, in the realm of the corporeal, two components of energy, a and b, come together, they unite in a common resultant c, which includes in part a new movement, in part transformation into heat, but always in such a way that c remains equal to a and b. But it is otherwise in the psychical. Here there occurs what may be called an increase (and a qualitative change) of the psychical energy. If we take the notes, c, e, and g, and call the sensation- and perception-value of the individual notes x, y, z, when they come together, the resulting sensation-value is by no means simply $x + y + z$, for a "harmony" results of which the effect is not only greater than the mere sum of $x + y + z$, but is *qualitatively* different. This is true of all domains of psychical experience. The parallels from mechanical operation cannot be applied in any case. These only supply inadequate analogies and symbols which never really represent the actual state of the case.

Let us take, for instance, a motive, $m$, that impels us towards a particular action, and another, $n$, that hinders us. If these meet in us, the result is not simply a weakening of the power of the one, and a remaining motive of the strength of $m$ minus $n$. The meeting of the two creates an entirely new and peculiar mental situation, which gives rise to conflict and choice, and the resultant victorious motive is never under any circumstances $m$-$n$, but may be a double or three-fold $m$ or $n$. Thus, in the different aspects of psychical activity, there are factors which make it impossible to compare these with other activities, remove them outside of the scope of the law of the equivalence of cause and effect, and prove that there is self-increase and growth on the part of psychical energies. And all such phenomena lead us away from the standpoint of any mere theory of association.

ACTIVITY OF CONSCIOUSNESS 311

ACTIVITY OF CONSCIOUSNESS

Naturalism takes refuge in the doctrine of association, when it does not attain anything with its first claims, and applies this theory in such a way that it seems possible from this standpoint to interpret mental processes as having an approximate resemblance to mechanically and mathematically calculable phenomena. As in physics the molecules and atoms, so here the smallest mental elements, the simplest units of feeling are sought for, and from their relations of attraction and repulsion, their groupings and movements, it is supposed that the whole mental world may be constructed up to its highest contents, will, ideals, and development of character. But even the analogy, the model which is followed, and the fact that a model is followed at all, show that this method is uncritical and not unprejudiced. What reason is there for regarding occurrences in the realm of physics as a *norm* for the psychical ? Why should one not rather start from the peculiar and very striking differences between the two, from the primary and fundamental fact, not indeed capable of explanation, but all the more worthy of attention on that account, that there is an absolute difference between physical occurrences and mental behaviour, between physical and mental causality? These most primitive and simplest mental elements which are supposed to float and have their being within the mind as in a kind of spiritual ether are not atoms at all, but deeds, actions, performances. The laws of the association of ideas are not the laws of a mental chemistry, but laws of mental behaviour; very fixed and reliable laws, but still having to do with modes of behaviour. Their separating and uniting, their

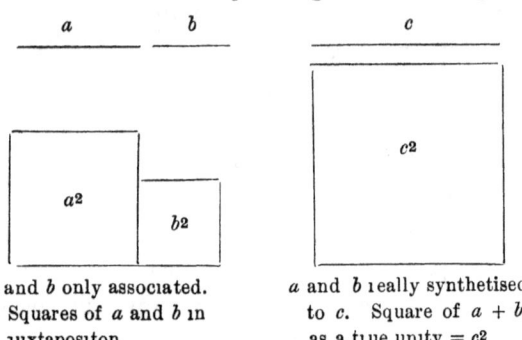

a and b only associated. Squares of a and b in juxtapositon.

a and b really synthetised to c. Square of $a + b$ as a true unity $= c^2$

relations to one another, their grouping into unities, their "syntheses," are not automatic permutations and combinations, but express the *activity* of a thinking intelligence. Not even the simplest actual synthesis comes about of itself, as psychologists have shown by a neat illustration.

Given that, through some association, the image of the line $a$ calls up that of the line $b$, and both are associatively ranged together, we have still not made the real synthesis $a + b = c$. For to think of $a$ and $b$ side by side is not the same thing as thinking of $c$, as we shall readily see if we square them. The squares of $a$ and $b$ thought of beside one another, that is, $a^2$ and $b^2$, are something quite different from the square of the really synthetised $a$ and $b$, which is $(a + b)^2 = a^2 + 2ab + b^2$, or $c^2$. This requires quite a new view, a spontaneous synthesis, which is an action and not a mere experience.

## THE EGO

It was customary in earlier psychology, as it still is in all apologetic psychology, to regard the soul as a unified, immaterial, indivisible and therefore indestructible *substance*, as a monad, which, as a unity without parts, superior to its own capacities and the changes of its states, is at all times one and the same subject. Many attempts have been made since the time of Plotinus to accumulate proofs of this substantial unity. We may leave this question untouched here, and need not even inquire whether these definitions are not themselves things of the external world employed as images and analogies and pushed too far. But there are three factors which may be established in regard to the psychical in spite of all naturalistic opposition; and those who have attempted to find proofs for the traditional idea we have noted, have usually really had these three in mind, and quite rightly so: they are, self-consciousness, the unity of consciousness, and the consciousness of the ego.

## SELF-CONSCIOUSNESS

1. Our consciousness is not merely a knowledge of many individual things, the possession of concrete and abstract, particular or general conceptions and ideas, the cherishing of sensations, feelings and the like. We

not only know, but we know that we know, and we can ponder in thought over the very fact that we are able thus to reflect in thought. Thought can turn its attention upon itself, can establish that it takes place, and how it runs its course, can reflect upon the forms in which it expresses itself, its powers, its laws, possibilities, and limits, and can ponder over the general nature of thought and the contingent individual nature of the particular thinking subject. (The very possibility and preliminary condition of moral freedom is implied in this.) How naturalism is to do justice to this fact it is not easy to see. Even if it were possible that the mental content was gained through mere experience, that comparisons, syntheses, and abstractions were formed simply according to the laws of association, and that these were sublimed and refined to general ideas, and could grow into axioms of logic and of geometry, or crystallise into necessary and axiomatic principles—none of which can happen—yet it would always be a knowledge of something. But how this something could be given to itself remains undiscoverable. The soul is a *tabula rasa* and a mere mirror, says this theory. But it would still require to show how the silver layer behind the mirror began to see itself in the mirror.

### The Unity of Consciousness

2. The same holds true of the unity of consciousness, of which we are directly convinced. It is quite inexpli-

## CONSCIOUSNESS OF THE EGO 315

cable if consciousness is a function of the extended and divisible physical substratum which is built up of nerve-cells and nerve-fibres. And yet this unity is the fundamental condition of our whole inner life.

Even the facts of association demonstrate it. Two images could not come together, the one could not call up the other, if they were not possessed in the same consciousness, and could unite in it. It is the preliminary condition of every higher mode of thought, of every relating of things, of every comparison and abstraction. No judgment can be formed, no conclusion drawn without this. How could a predicate become associated with its subject, or a principal clause with its subordinate clause, if they were in separate consciousnesses, and how could the conclusion be drawn from them?

### CONSCIOUSNESS OF THE EGO

3. This unified self-consciousness is consciousness of the ego. It is only by means of an artificial abstraction that we can leave out of account in the consideration of processes of thought the peculiar factor of personal relationship that absolutely attaches to every thought within us. There are no thoughts in general that play their part of themselves alone. "It" never "thinks" in me. On the contrary, all sensation, thought, and will has in every human being a peculiar central relationship to which we refer when we say "my idea," "my sensation." What the "I" is cannot be defined. It is that through which the relation of all

experiences and actions is referred to a point, and through which the treasuring of them for good or ill, the appreciation, the valuation of them is accomplished. And it plays its part even in the case of cold and indifferent items of knowledge. For instance, that twice two are four is not simply a perception, it is *my* perception. Of the ego itself nothing more can be said than that it is the thought of me as the subject of all experience, willing, and action, and if we try to take hold of it nothing more than this formula remains. Yet the fact that the ego is the subject of all this, gives conduct, will, and experience that peculiar character which distinguishes them from mere action and reaction. For it is directly certain that all the psychical contents are not only co-existences in one consciousness but that they are possessed by it.

Thus in summing up we have to say, that it is through the ego that all psychical activities and experiences are centred and related, that the ego is itself the point of relation, that it is the reason of the unity of consciousness and of the possibility of self-consciousness, and that in all this it is the most certain reality, without which the simplest psychical life would be impossible. At the same time, it is difficult to state what the "ego" is in itself, apart from the effects in which it reveals itself.

## CHAPTER XI

### FREEDOM OF SPIRIT

THE consciousness of the ego leads us naturally to the consciousness of freedom. Freedom of the mind is no simple idea; it embraces various contents which bear the relation of stages to one another, and each higher stage presupposes the one below it. Freedom is, first of all, the word which expresses that we are really agents, not mere points of transit for phenomena foreign to ourselves, but starting-points of phenomena peculiar to us, actual causes, beings who are able to initiate activity, to control things and set them in motion. Here the whole question of freedom becomes simply the question of the reality and causality of the will. Is the will something really factual, or is it only the strange illusion to which Spinoza, for instance, referred in his illustration of the flying stone? It would be purely an illusion of that kind if materialism were the true interpretation of things, and the psychical were nothing more than an accompaniment of other "true" realities, and even if the doctrine of psychical atoms we have already mentioned were correct.

This idea of freedom speedily rises to a higher plane.

Freedom is always freedom from something, in this case from a compulsion coming from outside, and from things and circumstances foreign to us. In maintaining freedom of the mind it is asserted that it can preserve its own nature and laws in face of external compulsion or laws, and in face of the merely psychological compulsion of the " lower courses of thought," even from the " half-natural " laws of the association of ideas. Thus " freedom " is pre-eminently freedom of thought. And in speaking thus we are presupposing that the mind has a nature of its own, distinguished even from the purely psychological nature, and has a code of laws of its own, lying beyond the scope of all natural laws, which psychical motives and physical conditions may prevent it following, but which they can never suspend or pull down to their own level.

" Der Mensch ist frei, und war' er in Ketten geboren."

Here at last we arrive at what is so often exclusively, but erroneously, included under the name of freedom, or " freedom of the will," that is practical freedom, the freedom to recognise moral laws and ideals, and to form moral judgments against all psychological compulsion, and to will to allow ourselves to be determined by these. From this question of moral freedom we might finally pass to that with which it is usual over-hastily to begin : the problem of so-called freedom of choice, of the " equilibrium " of the will, a problem in which are centred all the purely theoretical interests of the doctrine of the will in general, and ethical

## FREEDOM OF SPIRIT

interests in particular. The whole domain is so enormous that we cannot even attempt to sketch it here. The general bearing of the whole can be made clearest at the second stage, but we cannot entirely pass over the first.

In this inquiry into the problem of the will it is not necessary to discuss whether we are able by it to bring about external effects, movements, and changes in our bodies. We may postpone this question once more. The most important part of the problem lies in the domain of the psychical. To move an arm or a leg is a relatively unimportant function of the will as compared with the deliberate adoption of a rule of conduct, with inward self-discipline, self-culture, and the development of character.

That we " will," and what it is to will, cannot really be demonstrated at all, or defended against attacks. It simply *is* so. It is a fundamental psychical fact which can only be proved by being experienced. If there were anywhere a will-less being, I could not prove to him that there is such a thing as will, because I could never make clear to him what will is. And the theories opposed to freedom of the will cannot be refuted in any way except by simply saying that they are false. They do not describe what really takes place in us. We do not find within ourselves either the cloud-shadows or the play of psychical minima already referred to, with their crowding up of images, bringing some into prominence and displacing them again while we remain passive—we find ourselves *willing*. These theories should at least be able to explain whence came this marvellous hallucination, this appearance of will in us, which must have its cause, and they should also be able to say whence came the idea of the will. Spinoza's example of the stone, which seemed to itself to fly when it was simply thrown, does not meet the facts of the case. If the thrown stone had self-consciousness, it would certainly not say, "I am flying," but would merely wonder, "What has happened to me suddenly?"

We cannot demonstrate what will is, we can only make it clear to ourselves by performing an act of will and observing ourselves in the doing of it. Let us compare, for instance, a psychical state which we call "attention" with another which we call "distraction." In this last there is a stage where the will rests. There is actually an uninhibited activity of "the lower course of thought," a disconnected "dreaming," a confused automatic movement of thoughts and feelings according to purely associative laws. Then suddenly we pull ourselves together, rouse ourselves out of this state of distraction. Something new comes into the course of our thoughts. It is the will. Now there is control and definite guidance of our thoughts and rejection of subsidiary association—ideas that thrust themselves upon us. Particular thoughts can be selected, particular feelings or mental contents kept in focus as long as we desire. In thus selecting and guiding ideas, in

FREEDOM OF SPIRIT 321

keeping them in mind or letting them go, we see the will in action.

This brings us to freedom of thought. This lies in the fact, not merely that we can think, but that we can and desire to think rightly, and that we are able to measure our thoughts by the standard of "true" or "false." Naturalism is proud of the fact that it desires nothing more than to search after truth. To this it is ready to sacrifice all expressions of feeling or sentiment, and all prejudices. The truth, the whole truth, and nothing but the truth is its ideal, even if all pet ideas have to give way before it. It usually saddles itself with the idea of the good and the beautiful along with this "idea of truth," but is resolved, since it must soon see for itself that it is able to secure only a very doubtful basis for these, to sacrifice them to truth if need be. This is worthy of honour,* but it implies a curious self-deception. For if naturalism be in the right, thought is not free, and if thought be not free there can be no such thing as truth, for there can be no establishing of what truth is.

Let us attempt to make this plain in the following manner: According to the naturalistic-psychological theory, the play of our thoughts, our impressions of things and properties, their combination in judgments, or in "perceptions," are dependent on physiological

* Though somewhat inconsequent, since at any rate the enthusiasm for truth could not result from a naturalistic, but only from some kind of idealistic basis.

processes of the brain, and therefore upon natural laws, or, according to some, on peculiar attractions and repulsions among the impressions themselves, regulated by the laws of association. If that and that only were the case, I should be able to say that such a conception was present in my mind, or that this or that thought had arisen in me, and I might perhaps be able to trace the connection which made it necessary that it should arise at that particular time. But every thought would be equally right. Or rather there could be no question of right or wrong in the matter at all. I could not forbid any thought to be there, could not compel it to make way for another, perhaps exactly its opposite. Yet I do this continually. I never merely observe what thoughts are in my own mind or in another's. For I have a constant ideal, a plumb-line according to which I measure, or can measure, every train of thought. And I can compel others to apply this same plumb-line to their thoughts. This plumb-line is logic. It is the unique law of the mind itself which concerns itself about no law of nature or of association whatsoever. And however mighty a flood of conceptions and associations may at times pour through me in consequence of various confused physiological states of excitement affecting the brain, or in consequence of the fantastic dance of the associations of ideas, the ego is always able in free thought to intervene in its own psychical experiences, and to test which combinations of ideas have been logically thought out and are therefore right, and which are wrong. It often enough refrains from exercising this control, leaving the lower courses of thought free play. Hence the mistakes in our thinking, the errors in judgment, the thousand inconsistencies and self-deceptions. But the mind can do otherwise, can defend itself from interruptions and extraneous influences by making use of its freedom and of its power to follow its own laws and no others. It is thus possible for us to have not only psychical experiences but knowledge; only in this way can truth be reached, and error rejected. Thus science can follow a sure course. Thus alone, for instance, could the great edifice of geometry and arithmetic have been built up in its indestructible certainty. The progress from axiom to theorem and to all that follows is due to free thought, obeying the laws of inference and demonstration, and entirely unconcerned about the laws of association or the natural laws of the nervous agitations, the electric currents, and other plays of energy which may go on in the brain at the same time. What have the laws of the syllogism to do with the temporary states of tension in the brain, which, if they had free course, would probably follow lines very different from those of Euclid, and if they chanced once in a way to follow the right lines from among the millions of possibilities, would certainly soon turn to different ones, and could never examine them to see whether they were right or not. Thus it is not any highly aspiring emotional desire or any premature prejudice, but the solid old science of logic that first and most determinedly shuts the door in face of the claims of naturalism. If we combine this with what has already been said on page 154, we shall see how dangerous it would be for naturalism to be proved right in the dispute; for then it would be wholly wrong.

For, as it is only through the free, thinking mind that true and false can be distinguished and brought into relation with things, so only through it can we have an ideal of truth to be recognised and striven after, and that spontaneous, pertinacious, searching, following, and discovering which constitutes science as a whole and in detail. And in so far as naturalism itself claims to be nothing more than an attempt towards this goal, it is itself only possible on the basis of something which it denies.

Freedom of thought is also the most obvious example of that freedom of the spirit in morally " willing," which it is the business of ethical science to teach and defend. As in the one case thought shows itself superior to the physiologically or psychologically conditioned sequence of its concepts, so the free spirit, in the uniqueness of its moral laws, reveals itself as lord over all the motives, the lower feelings of pleasure and pain that have their play within us. As in the one case it is free to measure according to the criteria of true or false, and thus is able to intervene in the sequence of its own conceptions, correcting and confirming, so in the other it is able to estimate by the criteria of good or bad. As in the one case it carries within it its own fundamental laws as logic, so in the other the moral ideals and fundamental judgments which arise out of its own being. And in both cases it is free from nature and natural law, and capable of subordinating nature to its own rules, in so far as it " wills," and of becoming subordinate to nature—in erroneous thinking and non-moral acting—in so far as it does not will

FEELING, INDIVIDUALITY, GENIUS, AND MYSTICISM

The four things here mentioned are very closely associated with one another, especially the second and third, as is easily perceived, but the second is rooted in the first. And in the second and third there is already to be discovered a factor which goes beyond the sphere of the purely rational, and is no longer accessible to our comprehension, but carries us over into the sphere of the fourth. This is really true even of the phenomena of moral consciousness and moral " freedom. " In this quality, and in the ethical ideal of "personality," there is implied something that is inaccessible to a purely rational consideration, and is directly related to mystery and divination. (What is "personality"? We all feel it. We respect it from the depths of our soul wherever we meet it. We bow down before it unconditionally. But what it is no philosophy has ever yet been able definitely to state. In seeking to comprehend it intuition and feeling must always play the largest part.)

#### Feeling

It is in the four attributes here emphasised that the true nature of mind in its underivability and superiority to all nature first becomes clear. All that we have so far considered under the name of mind is only preliminary and leads up to this. All reality of external things is of little account compared with that of the mind. It does not occur to any one in practice to regard anything in the whole world as more real and genuine than his own love and hate, fear and hope, his pain, from the simplest discomfort due to a wound to the pangs of conscience and the gnawings of remorse—his pleasure, from the merest comfort to the highest raptures of delight. This world of feeling is for us the meaning of all existence. The more we plunge ourselves into it, the deeper are the intricacies and mysteries it reveals. At every point underivable and unintelligible in terms of physiological processes, it reveals itself from stage to stage as more deeply and wholly unique in its relations, interactions, and processes, and grows farther and farther beyond the laboured and insufficient schemes and formulæ under which science desires to range all psychical phenomena.

#### Individuality

It is especially in "feeling" that what we call individuality has its roots. The individual really means the "indivisible," and in the strict sense of the word need mean nothing more than the ego, and the unity

INDIVIDUALITY 327

of consciousness of which we have already spoken. But through a change in the meaning of the word we have come to mean much more than that by it. This individuality forces itself most distinctly upon our attention in regard to prominent and distinguished persons. It is the particular determination of their psychical nature that marks them out so distinctly, and it often rather escapes analysis and characterisation than is attained by it. "Individuum est ineffabile." It can only be grasped intuitively and by experience. And people of a non-reflective mood are usually more successful in understanding it than those who reflect and analyse. It requires "fine feeling," which knows exactly how it stands towards the person in question, which yet can seldom give any definite account of his characteristics. Individuality usually meets us most obviously in exceptional men, and we are apt to contrast these with ordinary men. But on closer examination we see that this difference is only one of degree. "Individuality" in a less marked manner belongs to them all, and where it exists it is a distinctly original thing, which cannot be derived from its antecedents. No psyche is simply derivable from other psyches. What a child receives from its parents by "heredity" are factors which, taken together, amount to more than the mere sum of them. The synthesis of these is at once the creation of something new and peculiar, and what has been handed down is merely the building material. This can be felt in an intensified and striking degree in regard to "pronounced individuality," but careful study will disclose the fact that there are no men quite alike. This kind of "creative synthesis," that is, the underivability of the individual, was the element of truth in the mythologies of "creationism" held by the Church fathers, or in the theory of the "pre-existence of the soul" maintained by Plato and others.

And from this point of view we must safeguard what has already been said in regard to the culture and gradual development of our psychical inner nature. It is true that the "soul" does not spring up ready-made in the developing body, lying dormant in it, and only requiring to waken up gradually. It really becomes. But the becoming is a self-realisation. It is not true that it is put together and built up bit by bit by experience, so that a different being might develop if the experiences were different. It is undoubtedly dependent upon experience, impressions, and circumstances, and without these its development would be impossible. But these impressions act as a stimulus, developing only what is previously inherent. They do not themselves create anything. A characteristic pre-determination restricts the development to comparatively narrow limits. And this is identical with the individuality itself. A man may turn out very different according to circumstances, education, influences. But he would nevertheless recognise "himself" under any circumstances. He will never become anything of which

# GENIUS, MYSTICISM

he had not the possibility within him from the very beginning, any more than the rose will become a violet if it is nurtured with a different kind of manure.

## Genius

We cannot venture to say much about genius and the mystery of it. In it and its creative power something of the spirit, the nature of the spirit, seems to look up at us, as we might think of it in itself and apart from the limits of existence in time and space. It is usually most obvious and most accessible to us in the domain of art. But it has its place too in the realm of science. And it is most of all genius, and therefore most inaccessible to us ordinary mortals, in the domain of religion.

## Mysticism

Even " pronounced individuality " " has an element of mysticism " in it—of the non-rational, which we feel the more distinctly the more decidedly we reject all attempts to make it rational again through crude or subtle mythologies. This is much more true of genius, artistic insight, and inspiration. But these are much too delicate to be exposed to the buffeting of controversy, much more so the dark and mysterious boundary region in the life of the human spirit which we know under the name of mysticism in the true sense, without inverted commas. It is not a subject that is adapted for systematic treatment. Where it has been subjected to it, everything becomes crude and repulsive, a mere caricature of pure mysticism like the recrudescent occultism of to-day. Therefore it is enough simply to call the attention of the sympathetic reader to it and then to pass it by. In face of the witness borne to it by all that is finest and deepest in history, especially in the history of religion, naturalism is powerless.

### Mind and Spirit. The Human and the Animal Soul

What is the relation between the human and the animal mind? This has always been a vital question in the conflict between naturalism and the religious outlook. And as in the whole problem of the psychical so here the interest on both sides has been mainly concentrated on the question of "mortality" or "immortality." Man is immortal because he has a soul. Animals " have no souls." " Animals also have souls, differing only in degree but not in substantial nature from the soul of man: as they are mortal, man must be so too." "Animals have minds: the merely psychical passes away with the body. But man has spirit in addition. It is imperishable." These and many other assertions were made on one side or the other. And both sides made precisely the same mistake: they made the belief in the immortality of our true nature dependent upon a proof that the soul has a physical "substantial nature," which is to be regarded as an indestructible substance, a kind of spiritual atom. And on the other hand they over-

## MIND AND SPIRIT

looked the gist of the whole matter, the true starting-point, which cannot be overlooked if the religious outlook is not to be brought into discredit. It is undoubtedly a fundamental postulate, and one which the religious outlook cannot give up, that the human spirit is more than all creatures, and is in quite a different order from stars, plants, and animals. But absolutely the first necessity from the point of view of the religious outlook is to establish the incomparable value of the human spirit; the question of its "substantial nature" is in itself a matter of entire indifference. The religious outlook observes that man can will good and can pray, and no other creature can do this. And it sees that this makes the difference between two worlds. Whether the bodily and mental physics in both these worlds is the same or different, is to it a matter rather of curiosity than of importance

What occurs or does not occur within the animal mind is, as a matter of fact, wholly hidden from us. We have no way of determining this except by analogy with ourselves, and therefore our idea of it is necessarily anthropomorphic. And apologists are undoubtedly right when they maintain that this is far too much the case. To reach a more unprejudiced attitude towards the customary anthropomorphisation of animals, it is profitable to study Wundt's lectures on "The Human and the Animal Mind" (see especially Lecture XX.). Perhaps it is true that, notwithstanding all the much-praised cleverness, intelligence and teachableness of elephants, dogs, and chimpanzees, they are incapable of forming "general ideas," "rules," and "laws," of forming judgments in the strict sense, and constructive syllogisms, that they have only associations of ideas, and expectations of similar experience, but no thinking in conceptual terms, and cannot perceive anything general or necessary, that they recognise *a posteriori* but not *a priori*, as Leibnitz supposed, and that they form only perceptual inferences, not judgments from experience. But it is not easy to see that this contributes anything of importance to our problem. It does not even help us in regard to the interesting question of a physical guarantee for the indestructibility of the soul. For even if the psychical acts of animals were fewer and less important than they are admitted to be, they have certainly sensations, images, feelings, pleasure, pain, and desire. All these are of a psychical nature, immaterial, and underivable from the material. And it is difficult to see, for instance, why the forming of judgments should be regarded as more durable and indestructible than sensation and desire. The difference lies higher than this,—not in the fact that man has a few "capacities" more than the animal, but in the difference in principle, that the psychical in man can be developed to spirit, and that this is impossible anywhere else. The very example that naturalism loves to cite in its own favour makes its error clear. It asks whether the difference, let us say, between a Fuegian and one of the higher mammals such as an ape, is not much less than

## MIND AND SPIRIT

that between a Fuegian and a European. This sounds obvious, if we measure simply by habits, morals, and possibly also the content of feeling and imagination in a "savage" as we find him. And yet it is obviously false. I can *train* a young ape or an elephant, can teach it to open wine-bottles and perform tricks. But I can *educate* the child of the savage, can develop in him a mental life equal in fineness, depth, and energy, frequently more than equal, to that of the average European, as the mission to the Eskimos and to the Fuegians proves, and as Darwin frankly admitted. Psychical capacity is nothing more than raw material. It is in the possibility of raising this to the level of spirit, of using the raw material to its purpose, that the absolute difference, the impassable gulf between man and animals lies.

Even in animals there is a primitive thinking, rising above the level of blind instinct. But it can neither be schooled, nor is it capable of developing even the crudest beginnings of science. Even the animal has a sensory satisfaction in colour, form and tone (not nearly so much, however, as the theory of sexual selection requires us to suppose). But art, even the most rudimentary self-expression of the spirit upon this basis, is wholly sealed to it. Even the animal possesses strong altruistic instincts, impulses towards companionship, pairing, and caring for its young, and some have seen in this the beginnings of morality. But morality is a matter of the spirit, which begins with the idea of duty and rises to the recognition of an ideal of life. Nowhere else do we see so directly and emphatically the incomparability of the natural-psychical and the spiritual as in the idea of duty and an ideal of life, although the contrast is equally great at all points of the spiritual life.

Finally and highest of all, we have the capacity of the human spirit to rise to religion and the greatest heights of feeling. In science and art, in morality and religion, the spirit possesses itself. And as such it is a unique and strange guest in this world, absolutely incomparable with anything beneath or around it. It may, perhaps, be true that the psychical difference between the ape and man is smaller than that between the ape and unicellular organisms (though we really can know nothing about that). But nowhere in the animal world does the psychical overstep the limits of purely natural existence, of striving after and being prompted by the directly and purely natural ends of a vegetative and animal instinctive life, physical pleasure, self-preservation, and the maintenance of the species

And there is more than this. However different the psychical equipment may be at different animal stages, it has one thing in common in them all, it is absolutely limited to what is given it by nature. An animal species may last for a million years. But it has no history. It is and remains the same history-less natural product. In this respect the animal is not a step in advance of the stone or the crystal. The only thing it can achieve is to express more or less perfectly the character of the

## MIND AND SPIRIT

species. This is the utmost height of its capacity. But for man this is only the starting-point, and the really human begins just there. What is implicit in him as *homo sapiens*, a member of a zoological order, is nothing more than the natural basis upon which, in human and individual history, he may build up an entirely unique and new creation, an upper story: the world and life of the spirit.

It is also erroneous to regard the gradual development of the psychical capacities at the different levels of animal evolution as the development of and preparation for the human spirit. It is not the spirit, but the raw material of it, that is thus being prepared and developed. It is as if, in the history of colour manufacture, an "evolution" of colour were taking place. The quality of the colour gradually becomes better and better. Each generation learns to make it purer and more brilliant. But the painting which is painted with the most brilliant colour cannot be regarded as a link in the evolutionary sequence, and is certainly not the crown and culmination of the pigment; the latter is only the gradual perfecting of a necessary preliminary condition.

It is only of secondary interest to point out the immense leaps in the evolution of colour and colour-technique, and especially the vast difference between the last stage and the one before it, or, to drop the metaphor, the enormous psychological differences between the animal and the human mind.

There is no doubt that an apologetic which interests itself in such matters would find abundant opportunity for work, and could find a powerful argument against a too hasty naturalism in the differences between animal and human psychical capacities, which have been recognised much more sanely and clearly through recent investigation than they usually were in earlier times. But the question has no special interest for us here.

## Personality

In as far as man is endowed with a capacity for spiritual life and spiritual possession, he is likewise destined for personality. This includes and designates everything that expresses the peculiar dignity of human nature. Personality is a word which gives us an inward thrill. It expresses what is most individual in us, what is set before us, our highest task and the inmost tendency of our being. What is personality? Certainly something which is only a rudiment in us at birth, and is not then realised, and at the same time an ideal which we feel more or less indistinctly, but without being able to outline it clearly. To exhaust the idea as far as possible is the task of ethical science. But one thing at any rate we can affirm about it with certainty: it is absolutely bounded off from the whole world and all existence as a self-contained and independent world in itself. The more we become persons, the more clearly, definitely, and indissolubly we raise ourselves with our spiritual life and spiritual possessions out of all the currents of natural phenomena, the more do we cease to be mere modes of a general existence and happening that flows about us, and in which we would otherwise float with vaguely defined outlines. A microcosm forms itself in contradistinction to the macrocosm, and a unity, a monad, arises, in regard to which there is now warrant for inquiring into its duration and immortality as compared with the stream of general becoming and passing away. For what does it matter to religion whether, in addition to physical indivisible atoms, there are spiritual ones which, by reason of their simplicity, are indestructible ? But that the unities which we call personalities are superior to all the manifoldness and diversity of the world, that they are not fleeting fortuitous formations among the many which evolution is always giving rise to and breaking down again, but that they are the aim and meaning of all existence, and that as such they are above the common lot of all that has only a transient meaning and a temporal worth—to inquire into all this and to affirm it is religion itself.

### Parallelism

The independence and underivability of the psychical, the incomparability of its uniformities with those of mechanical or physico-chemical laws, has proved itself so clear and incontrovertible, notwithstanding all the distortions of naturalism, that it is now regarded as a self-evident fact, not only among philosophers and epistemologists, and technical psychologists, but for the last decade even among all thinking men, and "materialism" is now an obsolete position. It was too crude and too contrary to all experience to define the relation between physical and mental, as if the latter were a mere secretion of the former, although a very subtle one, or a mere epi-phenomenon of it, in such a way that all reality and effectiveness was on the side of the physical.

In place of this, another theory has become widespread, which claims to define the relation of the two series of phenomena better and more adequately: the theory of psychophysical parallelism. It is not new. There are occasional indications of it even in Aristotle's psychology. It was suggested by Descartes in his automaton theory, by the occasionalists in their parable of the two watches running in exact agreement; it was developed by Spinoza and Leibnitz, and refined by the idealistic philosophers, by Schopenhauer, Fechner, and the modern psychologists. The form in which it is most prevalent now is that given to it by Spinoza, and he is usually referred to in connection with it. Its general tenor is as follows: The physical cannot be referred back to the psychical, nor the psychical to the physical. Both orders of phenomena run side by side as parallels that never separate. Both represent a concatenation of causes complete in itself, that is never broken, or interrupted, or completed. And in both there is real causality. Thought

## PARALLELISM

really causes thoughts and feelings. Movement really causes movements. But the one series is always strictly correlated with the other, and corresponds with it. And thus all existence is double, and man is an obvious illustration of this. To every thought, feeling, or exercise of will there corresponds some excitement, movement or change in the body. I will: my arm moves. Subtle nervous processes run their course in my brain, and I think. That I will has its sufficient reasons, its causes lie entirely in the preceding state of my mind, in motives of feeling, in ideas which again have their efficient causes in a previous psychical condition, and so on. And that my arm moves has its efficient cause in the stored-up energies of the muscle-substance, in the stimulus and impulse conveyed by the motor nerve from the brain. And these conditions have their purely physiological causes and reasons again in preceding purely physiological states and processes. (It goes without saying that a mechanical theory of life is the necessary presupposition of this parallelistic theory.) But both sets of processes correspond exactly one to another, and the first is only the inner aspect of the second, and the second the outer aspect of the first. Thus it is quite true that my arm moves when I will. But in reality it is quite as true to say that when my arm moves I will. But we must not substitute "because" for "when." This theory must maintain, and does maintain, that even the most abstract and subtle ideas, the deepest processes of consciousness, have some corresponding bodily processes, either in the brain or in the nervous substance generally, and, on the other hand, that no physical process is without this psychical inwardness. The result is that this inwardness and soul are attributed also to the purely material world, the world of "dead" matter. In this way it is believed that everything gets its due; the thorough mechanical explicability of bodily phenomena, and the law of the conservation of energy and of matter, and, on the other hand, very decisively also, the independence and uniqueness of law which can no longer be denied to the psychical. And from this latter standpoint sharp protests are raised against all materialistic distortions. The only thing denied is the old idea of the "influxus physicus," the idea, that is, that mind can operate beyond itself and take effect on the physical world, and conversely the physical world upon it. This again is regarded as a breach of the law of the conservation of energy. For if the bodily affects consciousness, then at a given moment a certain amount of energy must be transformed into something that is not energy. And if consciousness affects the bodily, a process of movement must suddenly occur, for which no previous equivalent of energy can be shown.

This standpoint is most impressively set forth in Paulsen's widely read "Introduction to Philosophy." The same ideas form the central feature in the work of Fechner, which is having such a marked renaissance to-day.

It seems as though all higher estimates of spirit, even the religious estimate, could quite well rest upon this basis. For full scope is here given to the idea that mind and the mental sciences have their own particular field. God, as the absolute all-consciousness and self-consciousness, comprehending within Himself all individual consciousness, is thought of as the eternal correlate of this universe in space. And the theory has room also for a belief in immortality. Of all imaginative attempts to make the idea of immortality clear and possible, undoubtedly that of Fechner is the grandest and most effective. And it, too, is based entirely upon the idea of parallelism. (Yet as a matter of fact it could be shown that neither mortality nor immortality really fit into the scheme of this conception.)

Though its main features are very similar as set forth by its various champions, this theory differs according to the way in which this astonishing and mysterious co-ordination, this parallelism itself, is explained. How is it that "thought" and "extension" can correspond to one another?

The answer may be either naively dogmatic, that this is one of the great riddles of the universe, and that we must simply take it for granted. Others declare with Spinoza that the two series of phenomena are only the two sides of one and the same fundamental being and happening, which may be designated as *natura sive deus*, and that what is inwardly unified expresses itself outwardly in these two forms of being. But because both sides, thought and extension, are only expressions of one and the same fundamental substance, they correspond exactly to one another. The best illustration of this is Fechner's simile of the curved line. It is concave on one side, convex on the other, and thus entirely different on the two sides. But at every point the concavity corresponds exactly to the convexity. And this is possible because the two are the inner and the outer aspects of the same line.

Others, again, go back to the fundamental ideas of critical idealism, and declare the whole extended world accessible to the senses and the mechanical-physical nexus of cause and phenomena, to be simply the form of appearance in which the fundamentally spiritual existence presents itself to our senses. Body, movement, physiological processes, are all nothing more than the will, to speak with Fichte and Schopenhauer, or the idea, or the spirit itself, which appears thus to sensory beings. Other theories, some of them new, are also put forward.

## No Parallelism

For a long time it seemed as if the theory of parallelism was to gain general acceptance. One might write a whole history of the gradually increasing criticisms of, and reactions from the academic theories which had become almost canonical. But we may here confine ourselves to the most general of the objections to the parallelistic theory. They apply to the general

NO PARALLELISM 343

idea of parallelism itself, and affect the different standpoints of the parallelists in different degrees. The theory in no way corresponds to what we find in ourselves from direct experience. It is only with the greatest difficulty that we can convince ourselves that our arm moves only when and not because we will. The consciousness of being, through the will, the actual cause of our own bodily movements is so energetic and direct and certain, that it maintains its sway in spite of all objections, and confuses the argument even of the parallelists themselves. Usually after they have laid the foundations of a purely parallelistic theory, they abandon it again as quickly as possible, and revert to the expressions and images of ordinary thought. Indeed we have no clearer and more certain example of causality in general than in our own capacity for controlling changes in our own bodies. Further, a very fatal addition and burdensome accessory of the parallelistic theory is involved in the two corollaries it has above and beneath it. On the one hand there is the necessity for attributing soul to everything. These mythologies of atom-souls, molecule-souls, this hatred and love which are the inner aspects even of the simple facts of attraction and repulsion among the elements, fit better into the nature-philosophy of Empedocles and Anaxagoras than into ours. The main support, indeed the sole support, of this position is that this world of the infinitely little cannot be brought under control as far as its "soul" is concerned. Thus we can impute "a soul" to it without danger. On the other hand, there is a difficulty which made itself felt even in regard to Spinoza's system. All bodily processes must have psychical processes corresponding to them, said Spinoza. Conversely, all ideas in their turn must have bodily processes. To the system including all bodily processes corresponds the sum-total of psychical processes. This sum-total we call the soul. And in its entirety it is the *idea corporis*. If "soul" were really nothing more than this, the theory of parallelism might be right. But it is more than this. It rises above itself, and becomes also the *idea ideæ*; it is self-consciousness and the consciousness of the ego; it makes its own thought and the laws of it, its feelings and their intensity—its experiences in short—a subject of thought. How does this fit in with parallelism? Wundt himself, the most notable modern champion of parallelism, admits and defines these limits of the parallelistic theory on both sides.

Furthermore, the theory of parallelism, notwithstanding its opposition to materialism, must presuppose that localisation of psychical processes of which we have already spoken, and to which all naturalism appeals with so much emphasis. Because of the fact that particular psychical functions seem to be limited to a particular and definable area of the brain-cortex, or to a spot which could be isolated on a particular convolution, it seemed as if naturalism could prove that "soul" was obviously a function of this particular

## NO PARALLELISM

organ or part of an organ. According to the theory of parallelism this does not follow. It would assert. " What in one aspect appears to be a psychical process, appears in another aspect to be a definite physiological process of the brain." Yet it is clear that in order to gain support for the doctrine of mutual correspondence, parallelism has also the same interest in such localisation. For this is the only method by which it can empirically control its theory. But this whole idea of localisation does not hold good to anything like the extent to which the members of the naturalistic school are wont to assert that it does. In regard to this point, too, there has been considerable disillusioning in recent years. Perhaps all that can be said is, that localisation of psychical processes is a fact analogous to the fact that sight is associated with the optic nerves and hearing with the auditory nerves. Progressive investigation leads more and more clearly to the recognition of a fact which makes localisation comparatively unimportant, namely, the vicarious functioning of different parts of the brain. In many cases where this or that " centre " is injured, and rendered incapable of function, or even extirpated, the corresponding part of the mind is by no means destroyed along with it. At first the miud may suffer from " the effect of shock " as the phrase runs, but gradually it may recover and the same function may be transferred to another part of the brain, and there be fulfilled sometimes less perfectly, sometimes quite as perfectly as before. We had to deal with this fact of vicarious function in discussing the general theory of life. It is one of the greatest difficulties in the way of the mechanistic and materialistic theories. But it must give some trouble to the parallelists too.

We need not speak of the wonderful duplication of all existence which parallelism must establish, though it is difficult to evade the question how a *natura sive deus* could have come, so superfluously, to say the same thing twice over. Superfluously, for since both are alike self-contained and independent of one another, one can have no need of the other.

One objection, however, may be urged against both parallelism and materialism, which makes them both impossible, and that is, automatism. Both parallelism and materialism maintain that the sequence of physical processes is complete in itself and can be explained in terms of itself. *All* physical processes! Not only the movements of the stars, the changes in inanimate matter, the origin and evolution of the forms of life, but also what we call actions, for instance the movements of our arms and our legs, and the complicated processes affecting the breathing organs and tongue, which we call "speech." Every plant, every animal, every human being must be as it is and where it is, must move and act, must perform its functions, which we explain as due to love or hate, to fear or hope, even if there were no such thing as sensation, will, idea, neither love nor hate, fear nor hope. More than this, all that

## NO PARALLELISM 347

we call history, building towns and destroying them, carrying on war and concluding peace, uniting into states and holding national assemblies, going to school and exercising mouth and tongue, argument, making books and forming letters, writing Iliads, Bibles, and treatises on the soul or on free will, holding psychological congresses and talking about parallelism;—all this must have been done even if there had been no consciousness, no psychical activity in any brain! This is the necessary consequence to which the theories of parallelism and materialism lead. If it does not follow, then there was from the outset no meaning in establishing them. But the monstrosity of their corollary is fatal to them. It is idle to set up theories in which it is impossible to believe.

There is another consideration that affects parallelism alone. Since the theory credits each of the two series with a closed and sufficient causal sequence, each of which excludes the other, it does away with causality altogether. That the one line runs parallel with the other excludes the idea that a unique system of laws prevails, determining the character and course of each line. One of the two lines must certainly be dependent, and one must lead. Otherwise there can be no distinctness of laws in either. Let us recall our illustration of the cloud shadows once more; the changing forms of the shadows correspond point for point with those of the clouds only because they are entirely dependent upon them. We may illustrate it in this way: a parallel may be drawn to an ellipse, it also forms a closed curved line. But it is by no means again an ellipse, but is an entirely dependent figure without any formula or law of its own. Parallelism must make one of its lines the leading one, which is guided and directed by an actual causal connection within itself. The other line may then run parallel with this, but its course must certainly be determined by the other. And as the line of corporeal processes, with its inviolable nexus of sequences, is not easily broken, parallelism, after many hard words against materialism, frequently returns to that again or becomes inconsistent. But if one says that the two aspects of phenomena are only the forms of one fundamental phenomenon, that means taking away actual causality from both alike, and leaving only a temporal sequence. For then the actually real is the hidden something that throws the cloud-shadows to right and left. But in the sequence of shadows there is no causal connection, only a series of states succeeding one another in time, and this points to a causal connection elsewhere.

It is easy enough to find examples to prove that the mental in us influences the bodily. But the most convincing, deepest and most trustworthy of these are not the voluntary actions which are expressed in bodily movements, nor even the passions and emotions, the joy which makes our blood circulate more quickly, and the shame which brings a flush to our foreheads, the suggestions which work through the mind towards the reviving, vitalising or healing of the body, but the cold and simple course of logical thought itself. Through logical thinking we have the power to corrrect the course of our conceptions, to inhibit, modify, or logically direct the natural course, as it would have been had it been brought about by our preceding physiological and psychical states, if they were dominant and uncontrolled. But if so, then we must also have the power, especially if it be widely true that physiological states correspond to psychical states, to influence, inhibit, modify the nerve-processes in our brain, or to liberate entirely new ones, namely, those that correspond to the corrected conceptions.

The law of the conservation of energy is here applied in as distorted a sense as we detected before in regard to the general theory of life. And what we said there holds good here also. That something which is in itself not energetic should determine processes and directions of energy is undoubtedly an absolute riddle. But to recognise this is less difficult than to accept the impossibilities which mechanism and automatism offer us here, even more pronouncedly than in regard to the theory of life. Perhaps one of the familiar antinomies of Kant shows us the way, not, indeed, to find the solution of the riddle, but to recognise, so to speak, its geometrical position and associations. We have already seen that inquiry into the causal conditions of processes lands us in contradictions of thought, which show us that we can never really penetrate into the actual state of the matter.

Perhaps we have here to do only with the obverse side of the problem dealt with there. There the chain of conditions could not be finished because it led on to infinity, where, however, it was required that it should be complete. Here again the chain is incomplete. In the previous case a solution is found through the naive proceeding of simply breaking the empirical connection of conditions and postulating beginnings in time. In this case, the admission of an *influxus physicus* transforms consciousness almost unnoticed into a mechanically operative causality. The proper attitude in both cases is a critical one. We must admit that we cannot penetrate into the true state of the case, because the world is deeper than our knowledge, we must reject parallelism as being, like the *influxus physicus*, an unsatisfactory cutting of the critical knot, and we must frankly recognise the incontrovertible fact, never indeed seriously called in question, of the controlling power of the mind, even over the material.

## The Supremacy of Mind

From the standpoint we have now reached we can look back once more on those troublesome naturalistic insinuations as to the dependence of the mind upon the body, which we have already considered. It is evident to us all that our mental development and the fate of our inner life are closely bound up with the states and changes of the body. And it did not need the attacks and insinuations of naturalism to point this

## THE SUPREMACY OF MIND 351

out. But the reasons brought forward by naturalism are not convincing, and all the weighty facts it adduces could be balanced by facts equally weighty on the other side. We have already shown that the apparently dangerous doctrine of localisation is far from being seriously prejudicial. But if the dependence of the mind upon the body be great, that of the body upon the mind is greater still. Even Kant wrote tersely and drily about "the power of our mind through mere will to be master over our morbid feelings." And every one who has a will knows how much strict self-discipline and firm willing can achieve even with a frail and wretched body, and handicapped by exhaustion and weakness. Joy heals, care wastes away, and both may kill. The influence which "blood" and "bile" or any other predisposition may have upon temperament and character can be obviated or modified through education, or transformed and guided into new channels through strong psychical impressions and experiences, most of all by great experiences in the domain of morals and religion. No one doubts the reality of those great internal revolutions of which religion is well aware, which arise purely from the mind, and are able to rid us of all natural bonds and burdens. This mysterious region of the influence of the mind in modifying bodily states or producing new ones is in these days being more and more opened up. That grief can turn the hair grey and disgust bring out eruptions on the skin has long been known. But new and often marvellous facts are being continually added to our knowledge through curious experiments with suggestion, hypnosis, and auto-suggestion. And we are no longer far from believing that through exaltations, forced states of mind associated with auto-suggestion, many phenomena, such as "stigmata," for instance, which have hitherto been over hastily relegated to the domain of pious legend, may possibly have a "scientific" background.

## "The Unconscious"

But one has a repugnance to descending into this strange region. And religion, with its clear and lofty mood, can never have either taste for or relationship with considerations which so easily take an "occult" turn. Nor is its mysticism concerned with physiologies. But it is instructive and noteworthy that the old idealistic faith, "It is the mind that builds up the body for itself," is becoming stronger again in all kinds of philosophies and physiologies of "the unconscious," as a reaction from the onesidedness of the mechanistic theories, and that it draws its chief support from the dependence of nervous and other bodily processes upon the psychical, which is being continually brought into greater and greater prominence. The moderate and luminous views of the younger Fichte, who probably also first introduced the now current term "the unconscious," must be at least briefly mentioned. According to him, the impulse towards the development of form which is inherent in everything living, and which

## IS THERE AGEING OF THE MIND 353

builds up the organism from the germ to the complete whole, by forcing the chemical and physical processes into particular paths, is identical with the psychical itself. In instincts, the unconscious purposive actions of the lower animals in particular, he sees only a special mode of this at first unconscious psychical nature, which, building up organ after organ, makes use in doing so of all the physical laws and energies, and is at first wholly immersed in purely physiological processes. It is only after the body has been developed, and presents a relatively independent system capable of performing the necessary functions of daily life, that it rises beyond itself and gradually unfolds to conscious psychical life in increasing self-realisation. Edward von Hartmann has attempted to apply this principle of the unconscious as a principle of all cosmic existence. And wherever, among the younger generation of biologists, one has broken away from the fascinations of the mechanistic theory, he has usually turned to " psychical " co-operating factors.

### Is there Ageing of the Mind?

Naturalism is also only apparently right in asserting that the mind ages with the body. To learn the answer which all idealism gives to this comfortless theory, it is well to read Schleiermacher's " Monologues," and especially the chapter " Youth and Age." The arguments put forward by naturalism, the blunting of the senses, the failing of the memory, are well known. But here again there are luminous facts on the other side which are much more true. It is no wonder that a mind ages if it has never taken life seriously, never consolidated itself to individual and definite being through education and self-culture, through a deepening of morality, and has gained for itself no content of lasting worth. How could he do otherwise than become poor, dull and lifeless, as the excitability of his organ diminishes and its susceptibility to external impressions disappears? But did Goethe become old? Did not Schleiermacher, frail and ailing as he was by nature, prove the truth of what he wrote in his youth, that there is no ageing of the mind?

The whole problem, in its highest aspects, is a question of will and faith. If I know mind and the nature of mind, and believe in it, I believe with Schleiermacher in eternal youth If I do not believe in it, then I have given away the best of all means for warding off old age. For the mind can only hold itself erect while trusting in itself. And this is the best argument in the whole business.

But even against the concrete special facts and the observable processes of diminution of psychical powers, and of the disappearance of the whole mental content, we could range other concrete and observable facts, which present the whole problem in quite a different light from that in which naturalism attempts to show it. They indicate that the matter is rather one of the rusting of the instrument to which the mind is bound

## IS THERE AGEING OF THE MIND 355

than an actual decay of the mind itself, and that it is a withdrawing of the mind within itself, comparable rather to sleep than to decay. The remarkable power of calling up forgotten memories in hypnosis, the suddenly re-awakening memory a few minutes before death, in which sometimes the whole past life is unrolled with surprising clearness and detail, the flaming up anew of a rusty mind in moments of great excitement, the great clearing up of the mind before its departure, and many other facts of the same nature, are rather to be regarded as signs that in reality the mind never loses anything of what it has once experienced or possessed. It has only become buried under the surface. It has been withdrawn from the stage, but is stored up in safe treasure-chambers. And the whole stage may suddenly become filled with it again.

The simile of an instrument and the master who plays upon it, which is often used of the relation between body and mind, is in many respects a very imperfect one; for the master does not develop with and in his instrument. But in regard to the most oppressive arguments of naturalism, the influence of disease, of old age, of mental disturbances due to brain changes, the comparison serves our turn well enough, for undoubtedly the master is dependent upon his instrument; upon an organ which is going more and more out of tune, rusting, losing its pipes, his harmonies will become poorer, more imperfect. And if we think of the association between the two as further obstructed, the master becoming deaf, the stops confused, the relation between the notes and pipes altered, then what may still live within him in perfect and unclouded purity, and in undiminished richness, may present itself outwardly as confused and unintelligible, may even find only disconnected expression, and finally cease altogether; so that no conclusion would be possible except that the master himself had become different or poorer. The melancholy field of mental diseases perhaps yields proofs against naturalism to an even greater degree than for it. It is by no means the case that all mental diseases are invariably diseases of the brain, for even more frequently they are real sicknesses of the mind, which yield not to physical but to psychical remedies. And the fact that the mind can be ill, is a sad but emphatic proof that it goes its own way.

## Immortality

It is in a faith in a Beyond, and in the immortality of our true being, that what lies finely distributed through all religion sums itself up and comes to full blossoming: the certainty that world and existence are insufficient, and the strong desire to break through into the true being, of which at the best we have here only a foretaste and intuition. The doctrine of immortality stands by itself as a matter of great solemnity and deep rapture. If it is to be talked about, both speaker and hearers ought to be in an exalted mood. It is the conviction which, of all religious convictions,

# IMMORTALITY

can be least striven for consciously; it must well forth from devotional personal experience of the spirit and its dignity, and thus can maintain itself without, and indeed against much reasoning. To educate and cultivate it in us requires a discipline of meditation, of concentration, and of spiritual self-culture from within outwards. If we understood better what it meant to "live in the spirit," to develop the receptivity, fineness, and depth of our inner life, to listen to and cultivate what belongs to the spirit, to inform it with the worth and content of religion and morality, and to integrate it in the unity and completeness of a true personality, we should attain to the certainty that personal spirit is the fundamental value and meaning of all the confused play of evolution, and is to be estimated on quite a different scale from all other being which is driven hither and thither in the stream of Becoming and Passing away, having no meaning or value because of which it must endure. And it would be well also if we understood better how to listen with keener senses to our intuitions, to the direct self-consciousness of the spirit in regard to itself, which sleeps in every mind, but which few remark and fewer still interpret. Here, where the gaze of self-examination reaches its horizon, and can only guess at what lies beyond, but can no longer interpret it, lie the true motives and reasons for our conviction of immortality. An apologetic cannot do more than clear away obstacles, nor need it do much more than has hitherto been done. It reminds us, as we have already seen, that the world which we know and study, and which includes ourselves, does not show its true nature to us; hidden depths lie behind appearances. And it gathers together and sums up all the great reasons for the independence and underivability of the spiritual as contrasted with the corporeal. The spiritual has revealed itself to us as a reality in itself, which cannot be explained in terms of the corporeal, and which has dominion over it. Its beginning and its end are wholly unfathomable. There is no practical meaning in discussing its "origin" or its "passing away," as we do with regard to the corporeal. Under certain corporeal conditions it is there, it simply appears. But it does not arise out of them. And as it is not nothing, but an actual and effective reality, it can neither have come out of nothing nor disappear into nothing again. It appears out of the absolutely transcendental, associates itself with corporeal processes, determines these and is determined by them, and in its own time passes back from this world of appearance to the transcendental again. It is like a great unknown sea, that pours its waters into the configuration of the shore and withdraws them again. But neither the flowing in nor the ebbing again is of nothing or in nothing. Whether and how it retains the content, form, and structure that it assumes in other spheres of animate and conscious nature, when it retires into the transcendental again; or whether it dissolves and breaks up into the universal we do not know; nor do we attribute everlastingness to those individual forms of consciousness which we call animal souls. But of the self-conscious, personal spirit religion knows that it is everlasting. It knows this from its own sources. In its insight into the underivability and autonomy of the spiritual it finds warrant and freedom to maintain this knowledge as something apart from or even in contrast to the general outlook on the world.

## CHAPTER XII

### THE WORLD AND GOD

THE world and nature are marvellous in their being, but they are not "divine"! The formula "*natura sive deus*" is a monstrous misuse of the word "*deus*," if we are to use the words in the sense which history has given to them. God is the Absolute Being, perfect, wholly independent, resting in Himself, and necessary; nature is entirely contingent and dependent, and at every point of it we are impelled to ask "Why?" God is the immeasurable fulness of Being, nature is indeed diverse in the manifoldness of her productions, but she is nevertheless limited, and her possibilities are restricted within narrow limits. God is the unrestrained, and everlasting omnipotence itself, and the perfect wisdom; nature is indeed mighty enough in the attainment of her ends, but how often is she obstructed, how often does she fail to reach them, and how seldom does she do so perfectly and without mistakes? She shows wisdom, indeed, cunning in her products, subtlety and daintiness, taste and beauty, all these often in an overwhelming degree, yet just as often she brings forth what

## THE WORLD AND GOD

is meaningless, contradictory and mutually hurtful, traverses her own lines, and bewilders us by the brutality, the thoughtlessness, and purposelessness, the crookedness, incompleteness, and distortedness of her operations. And what is true of the world of external nature is true in a far greater degree of the world of history. Nature is not a god, but a demigod, says Aristotle. And on this, Pantheism with its creed, "*natura sive deus*," makes shipwreck. The words of this *credo* are either a mere tautology, and "*deus*" is misused as a new name for nature; or they are false. It is not possible to transfer to nature and the world all the great ideas and feelings which the religious mind cherishes under the name of "God."

On the other hand, nature is really, as Aristotle said, δαιμονία, that is, strange, mysterious, and marvellous, indicating God, and pointing, all naturalism and superficial consideration notwithstanding, as we have seen, to something outside of and beyond itself. Religion demands no more than this. It does not insist upon finding a solution for all the riddles of theoretical world-lore. It is not distressed because the course of nature often seems to our eyes confused, and to our judgment contradictory and unintelligible at a hundred places and in a hundred respects. On the contrary, that this is the case is to religion in another aspect a strong stimulus and corroboration. "The world is an odd fellow; may God soon make an end of it," said Luther, and thus gave a crude but truly religious parallel to the words of Aristotle, ἡ γὰρ φύσις δαιμονία 'αλλ' οὐ θεία, (Aristot. "De Divin. in Somn.," c. ii.). It is part of the very essence of religion, as we have seen, to read in the pages of nature, insufficiency, illusion, and perplexities, and to be made thereby impatient and desirous of penetrating to the true nature of things. Religion does not claim to be directly deducible out of a consideration of nature; it demands only the right and freedom to interpret the world in its own way. And for this it is sufficient that this world affords those hints and suggestions for its convictions that we have seen it does afford. To form clear ideas in regard to the actual relations of the infinite to the finite, and of God to the world, and of what religion calls creation, preservation, and eternal providence, self-revelation in the world and in history, is hardly the task of religion at all, but rather pertains to our general speculative instinct, which can only satisfy itself with the help of imagination. Attempts of this kind have often been made. They are by no means valueless, for even if no real knowledge can be gained by this method, we may perhaps get an analogue of it which will help us to understand existence and phenomena, and to define our position, as well as to give at least provisional answers to many pressing questions (such, for instance, as the problem of theodicy).

If we study the world unprejudiced by the naturalistic interpretation, or having shaken ourselves free from it, we are most powerfully impressed by one fundamental

THE WORLD AND GOD 363

phenomenon in all existence: it is the fact of evolution. It challenges attention and interpretation, and analogies quickly reveal themselves which give something of the same trend to all such interpretations. From stage to stage existence advances onwards, from the world of large masses subject only to the laws of mechanics, to the delicately complex play of the forces of development in growth and other vital processes. The nature of the forces is revealed in ever higher expression, and at the same time in ever more closely connected series of stages. Even between the inorganic and the organic there is an intermediate stage—crystal formation— which is no longer entirely of the one, yet not of the other. And in the organic world evolution reveals itself most clearly of all; from the crudest and simplest it presses onwards to the most delicate and complex. In the corporeal as in the psychical, in the whole as in each of its parts, there are ever higher stages, sometimes far apart, sometimes close together. However we picture to ourselves the way in which evolution accomplishes itself in time, we can scarcely describe it without using such expressions as "nature advances upwards step by step," "it presses and strives upwards and unfolds itself stage by stage."

And it is with us as it was with Plato; we inform the world with a soul, with a desire and endeavour which continually expresses itself in higher and higher forms. And it is with us also as with Fichte; we speak of the will which, unconscious of itself, pours itself forth in unconscious and lifeless nature, and then on this foundation strives forward, expressing its activity in ever higher developments, breaking forth in life, sensation, and desire, and finally coming to itself in conscious existence and will. The whole world seems to us a being which wills to become, presses restlessly forward, and passes from the potential to the actual, realising itself. And the height of its self-realisation is conscious, willing life.

This outlook is lofty and significant, it supplies a guiding clue by which the facts of life and nature can be arranged. The religious outlook, too, when it wishes to indulge in speculation, can make use of this guiding thread. It will then say: God established the world as "a will to existence, to consciousness, to spirit," He established it, not as complete, but as becoming. He does not build it as a house, but plants it, like a flower, in the seed, that it may grow, that it may struggle upwards stage by stage to fuller existence, aspiring with toil and endeavour towards the height where, in the image of the Creator, as a free and reasonable spirit capable of personality, it may realise the aim of its being. Thus the world is *of* God, that is, its rudiments came from God, and it is *to* God, in the purpose of likeness to God. And it is imbued with the breath of Godhead which moves in it and impels it onwards, with the logos of the everlasting Zeus of whom Cleanthes sings, with the spirit of Jehovah whom Isaiah and the Psalmist praise, and

THE WORLD AND GOD 365

whom the poet of the Creation figuratively paints; the divine breath is in everything that lives, from grass to flower, from animal to man. But it is implanted as becoming. And in regard to this, religion can say of the whole world what it says of man. For man, too, is not given as a finished product, either as regards the genus or the individual, but as a rudiment, with his destiny to work out, in historical becoming, by realising what is inherent in him. We call this freedom. And an adumbration of such freedom, which is the aim of self-realisation, would help us to penetrate deeply into the nature of things. Many riddles and apparent contradictions could be fitted in with this view of things : the unity of the world, and yet the gradations; the relationship of all living creatures, the unity of all psychical life, and yet the uniqueness of the rational spirit; causal concatenation, yet guidance by means of the highest ideas and purposes; the tentativeness, illogicalness, and ineffectiveness of nature, unconsciously pressing forward along uncertain paths, yet the directness and purposefulness of the main lines of evolution in general. This God-awakened will to be lies at the roots of the mysteries of development in all living creatures, of the unconscious purposiveness of instinctive action, of the gradually ascending development of psychical life and its organ. Operating in crystals and plants purely as a formative impulse and "entelechy," it awakes in the bodies of animals more and more as "soul." Then it awakes fully in man, and in him, in an entirely new phase of real free development, it builds itself up to spirit. It resembles a stream whose waves flow casually and transiently in animal consciousness, and are soon withdrawn again, to break forth anew at another place, in the personal spirit, where they attain to permanent indissoluble form, since they have now at last attained to self-realisation, and fulfilled the purpose of all cosmic existence, the reflecting of the eternal personality in the creature. But it is only in human history that what was prepared for in natural evolution is completed.

The riddle of theodicy thus becomes easier, for what surrounds us in nature and history has not come direct from the hand of eternal wisdom, but is in the first place the product of the developing, striving world, which only gradually and after many mistakes and failures works out what is inherent in it as eternal idea and aim. We see and blame its mistakes, for instance in our own human structure. We see the deficiencies in the historical course of things. But when we find fault we do not see that evolution and self-realisation and freedom are more worthy of praise than ready-made existence incapable of independent action.

This principle of development, wherever it is regarded as "world-soul" or as "will" or as the "unconscious," is frequently, through pantheism and the doctrine of immanence, made equivalent with the object of religion, with God. This is an impossible undertaking. We cannot worship what only reaches its full development

THE WORLD AND GOD 367

in ourselves. But that we *can* worship, and that it is only in the feeling of complete dependence that the full depth of what is developing within us to conscious life reveals itself, proves better than anything else that God is above all "World-will." It was more than allegory when Plato in Timæus set the "eternal father and creator of the world" above all soul and psyche. And it was religion that broke through when Fichte in his little book, "Anweisung zum seeligen Leben," set being before becoming, and God above the creatures struggling towards self-realisation. Religion knows in advance that this is so. And calm reflection confirms it. All that we have already learnt of the dependence, conditionedness, and contingent nature of the world is equally true of a world "evolving itself" out of its potentiality, of a will to existence, and of an unconscious realising itself. No flower can grow and develop without being first implicit in the seed. Nothing can attain to "actuality," to realisation, that was not potentially implied in the beginning. But who originated the seed of the world-flower? Who enclosed within it the "tendencies," the "rudiments" which realise themselves in evolution? Invariably "the actual is before the potential" and Being before Becoming. A world could only become if it were called to become by an everlasting Being. God planting the world-flower that it might radiate forth in its blossoms His own image and likeness, is an allegory which may well symbolise for religion the relation between God and the world. And thus it is possible to draw the outline of a religious outlook on the world, into which the results of world-lore could well be fitted. This frame was constructed by Plato on the basis of a religious study of things, and after Plato it was first definitely outlined in Fichte's too much forgotten but unforgettable books "Bestimmung des Menschen" and "Anweisung zum seeligen Leben," and it is thus a new creation of the great German idealism and its mighty faith. And it is not easy to see why it should be abandoned, why we should give it up in favour of an irreligious, semi-naturalistic outlook on the world.

One thing, however, must be kept constantly in mind : even such an interpretation of the world as this is poetry, not knowledge. There is a poetry of the will to live, of the unconscious, which is struggling towards existence, but there is no philosophy. There are only analogies and hints of what goes on at the foundations of the world. In particular, the unconscious creative impulse in all living organisms, this "will" towards form, its relationship with instinct and the relationship of instinct to conscious psyche, afford us a step-ladder of illustrations, and an illustration of the step-ladder of the "will towards existence," which invite us to overstep the bounds of our knowledge, and indulge in our imagination. We can say nothing of pre-conscious consciousness and will, we can at best only make guesses about them. We cannot think definitely of a general world-will, which wills and aspires in individual beings; we cannot picture to ourselves the emergence of the individual "souls" of animals and man from a universal psyche. Imagination plays a larger part here than clear thinking. And for our present purpose it must be clearly borne in mind that religion does not require any speculative construction of theories of the world. But "you shall know that it is your imagination which creates the world for you."\* And if a speculative construction be desired, it will always be most easily attained along these lines, and will in this way come nearest to our modern knowledge of nature. We must remember, too, that the objections which may be urged against this form of speculation are equally applicable against any other. For the origin of the individual psyche, the graduated series of its forms, the development of one after the other, and of that of the child from that of its parents, are riddles which cannot be solved by any speculative thinking. Monadology, theories of the pre-existence of the soul, creationism, or the current traducianism—which to-day, with its partly or wholly materialistic basis, is just as naive as the older—all reveal equal darkness. But the speculation we have hinted at, if it gives no explanation, at least supplies a framework for many questions which attract us, and do so even from the point of view of religion: for instance the collective, diffuse, and almost divisible nature of consciousness in the lower stages, its increasing and ever more strict centralisation, the natural

\* Schleiermacher, "Reden uber die Religion," ii.

relationship of the psychical in man to the psychical in general, and yet its incommensurability and superiority to all the world.

But let us once more turn from all the poetical and imaginative illustrations of the relation of God to the world, which can at best be only provisional, and only applicable at certain points, to the more general aspect of the problem. Religion itself consists in this: believing and experiencing that in time the Eternal, in the finite the Infinite, in the world God is working, revealing Himself, and that in Him lies the reason and cause of all being. For this it has names like creation, providence, self-revelation of God in the world, and it lives by the mysteries which are indicated under these names. The mysteries themselves it recognises in vague or naïve forms of conception long before it attempts any definite formulation. If dogmatics begin with the latter, some form or other of the stiff and wooden doctrines of *concursus*, of *influxus ordinarius* and *extraordinarius* usually develops with many other subtleties, which are nothing more than attempts to formulate the divine influence in finite terms, and to think of it as a force along with other forces. Two series of causes are usually distinguished; the system of causes and effects within the world, according to which everything natural takes place, the "*causæ secundariæ*"; and in addition to these the divine causality co-operating and influencing the others, ordering them with gentle and delicate pressure, and guiding them towards their true

THE WORLD AND GOD 371

end, and which may also reveal itself as "*extraordinaria*" in miracles and signs. This double operation is regarded as giving rise to all phenomena, and in it consists guidance, dispensation, providence, and natural revelation.

This kind of conception is extremely primitive, and is unfavourable to religion itself, for in it mystery is done away with and arranged according to rubric, and everything has become quite "simple." Moreover, this doctrine has a necessary tendency to turn into the dreaded "Deism." According to the deistic view, God made the world in the beginning, and set the system of natural causes in motion, in such a way that no farther assistance was given, and everything went on of itself. This theory is incredibly profane, and strikes God out of the world, and nature, and history at a single stroke, substituting for Him the course of a well-arranged system of clockwork. But the former theory is a very unsatisfactory and doubtful makeshift as compared with that of deism, for it is impossible to see why, if God arranged these *causæ secundariæ*, He should have made them so weak and ineffective that they need all these ingenious *concursus, influxus, determinationes, gubernationes*, and the like. Both theories are crude fabrications of the dogmatists, and they have nothing left in them of the piety they were intended to protect, nor do they become any better in this respect, however many attempts are made to define them. Religion possesses, without the aid of any stilted and artificial theories, all the things we have named above, and especially and most directly the last of them, namely, the experience of the revelation and communication of the Divine in the great developments and movements of spiritual and religious history. And it finds its corroboration and justification and freedom not by way of dogmatics but of criticism. It is impossible to distinguish artificially two sets of causes, and to give to the world what is alleged to be of the world, and to God what is alleged to be of God. But it is permissible to point to the insufficiency of our causal study in general, and to the limits of our knowledge. Even when we have established it as a fact that all phenomena are linked together in a chain of causes we are still far from having discovered how things actually come to pass. Every qualitative effect and change is entirely hidden from us as far as the cause of its coming about and its real and inner nature are concerned. Every effect which in kind or quantity goes beyond its cause (and we cannot make anything of the domain of living forms, of the psychical and of history without these), shows us that we are still only at the surface. Indeed, even mechanical action, often alleged to be entirely intelligible, such as the transference or transformation of energy, is, as we have seen, a complete riddle. In addition, all causality runs its course in time, and therefore partakes of all the defects and limitations of our views of time. And finally we are guided by the Kantian antinomy regarding the conditions of what is

THE WORLD AND GOD 373

'given.' It destroys the charm of the "purely causal" point of view by showing that this in itself cannot be made complete and is therefore contradictory. Moreover, in the phenomena of life, and in the fact that consciousness and will control our corporeal processes, and yet can hardly be thought of as a cause "co-operating" with other causes, we found an analogy, if a weak and obscure one, of the relation that a divine teleology and governing of the world may bear to mundane phenomena. Thus mystery remains in all its strength and is not replaced by the surrogate of a too simple and shallow dogmatic theory. In confessing mystery and resting content with it we are justified by reflection on the nature and antinomy of our knowledge.

All this is true also of what religion means by creation. In the feeling of complete humility, in its experience of absolute dependence and conditionedness, the creature becomes conscious of itself as a creature, and experiences with full clearness what it means to be a "creature" and "created." The dogmatic theory is here again only a surrogate of mystery. And again critical self-reflection proves a better guide than any theory of creation, which is quite in its place as a means of expression in religious discourse and poetry, but is quite insufficient as true knowledge. That we must but cannot think of this world either as beginning or as not-beginning is the analogue in knowledge of what religion experiences in mystery; and that this contingent and conditioned world is founded in everlasting, necessary, true Being, is the analogue of what religion possesses and knows through devout feeling, more directly and clearly than by any thinking, of the relations of God to the world.

www.ingramcontent.com/pod-product-compliance
Lightning Source LLC
Chambersburg PA
CBHW071225230426
43668CB00011B/1308